Philippians

Good News Commentaries

MARK, by Larry W. Hurtado

JOHN, by J. Ramsey Michaels

HEBREWS, by Donald A. Hagner

PHILIPPIANS, by F. F. Bruce

I and II THESSALONIANS, by Earl F. Palmer

JAMES, by Peter H. Davids

Philippians

F. F. Bruce

A GOOD NEWS COMMENTARY

New Testament Editor

W. Ward Gasque

1817

HARPER & ROW, PUBLISHERS, SAN FRANCISCO

Cambridge, Hagerstown, New York, Philadelphia
London, Mexico City, São Paulo, Sydney

To Douglas and Betty Buckley

FIRST EDITION

Designed by Design Office Bruce Kortebein

Library of Congress Cataloging in Publication Data

Bruce, F. F. (Frederick Fyvie), 1910–
   PHILIPPIANS.
   (A Good News Commentary)
   Bibliography: p.
   Includes index.
   1. Bible. N.T. Philippians—Commentaries.
I. Bible N.T. Philippians. Today's English. 1983.
II. Title. III. Series
BS2705.3.B78 1983   227'.6077   82-48919
ISBN 0-06-061138-3

83 84 85 86 87 10 9 8 7 6 5 4 3 2 1

About the Series

This is the first major series to use the popular Good News Bible, which has sold in the millions. Each volume is informed by solid scholarship and the most up-to-date research, yet each is biblically faithful and readily understandable to the general reader. Features include:

Introductory material highlighting authorship, dating, background information, and thematic emphases—plus a map

Full text of each Good News Bible book, with running commentary

Special end notes giving references for key words and concepts and providing suggestions for further reading

Full indexes for Scripture and Subjects/Persons/Places

Series Editor W. Ward Gasque is Vice-Principal and Professor of New Testament at Regent College in Vancouver. A former editor-at-large for *Christianity Today*, he is the author of numerous articles and books and has edited *In God's Community: Studies in the Church and Its Ministry, Handbook of Biblical Prophecy, Apostolic History and the Gospel,* and *Scripture, Tradition, and Interpretation.* Dr. Gasque's major involvement is in the provision of theological resources and education for the laity.

Contents

Foreword: The Good News Bible Commentary Series   ix

Introduction   xiii

1. Prescript *(Phil. 1:1–2)*   1
2. Introductory Thanksgiving *(Phil. 1:3–6)*   6
3. Interlude *(Phil. 1:7–8)*   10
4. Intercessory Prayer *(Phil. 1:9–11)*   12
5. Paul's Present Situation *(Phil. 1:12–14)*   16
6. Various Motives for Gospel Witness *(Phil. 1:15–17)*   19
7. Life or Death? *(Phil. 1:18–26)*   23
8. Steadfastness amid Suffering *(Phil. 1:27–30)*   32
9. Call for Mutual Consideration *(Phil. 2:1–5)*   37
10. The Christ Hymn *(Phil. 2:6–11)*   44
11. Encouragement to Fidelity *(Phil. 2:12–13)*   56
12. Paul's Hope of the Philippians *(Phil. 2:14–16)*   59
13. Paul's Libation on the Philippians' Sacrifice *(Phil. 2:17–18)*   63
14. Timothy's Forthcoming Visit *(Phil. 2:19–24)*   66
15. Commendation of Epaphroditus *(Phil. 2:25–30)*   70
16. First Conclusion: Call to Rejoice *(Phil. 3:1)*   76
17. Warning Against "Workers of Iniquity" *(Phil. 3:2–3)*   78
18. Paul's Former Code of Values *(Phil. 3:4–6)*   82
19. Paul's Present Code of Values *(Phil. 3:7–11)*   87
20. Paul's Ambition *(Phil. 3:12–14)*   95
21. Spiritual Maturity *(Phil. 3:15–16)*   99
22. Imitation of Paul *(Phil. 3:17)*   102

23. Warning Against Enemies   *(Phil. 3:18–19)*   104

24. Heavenly Citizenship and Hope   *(Phil. 3:20–21)*   108

25. Exhortation to Stand Firm   *(Phil. 4:1)*   112

26. Fresh Plea for Unity   *(Phil. 4:2–3)*   113

27. Repeated Call to Rejoice   *(Phil. 4:4)*   116

28. Encouragement to Faith   *(Phil. 4:5–7)*   117

29. Second Conclusion: Food for Thought   *(Phil. 4:8–9)*   120

30. Paul's Sufficiency   *(Phil. 4:10–13)*   123

31. Appreciation of Earlier Gifts   *(Phil. 4:14–17)*   127

32. Acknowledgment of Present Gift   *(Phil. 4:18–20)*   130

33. Final Greetings   *(Phil. 4:21–22)*   132

34. Grace-Benediction   *(Phil. 4:23)*   135

Postscript   136

List of Abbreviations   138

For Further Reading   141

Subject Index   149

Scripture Index   153

Foreword

The Good News Bible Commentary Series

Although it does not appear on the standard best-seller lists, the Bible continues to outsell all other books. And in spite of growing secularism in the West, there are no signs that interest in its message is abating. Quite to the contrary, more and more men and women are turning to its pages for insight and guidance in the midst of the ever-increasing complexity of modern life.

This renewed interest in Scripture is found outside of, as well as in, the church. It is found among people in Asia and Africa as well as in Europe and North America; indeed, as one moves outside of the traditionally Christian countries, interest in the Bible seems to quicken. Believers associated with the traditional Catholic and Protestant churches manifest the same eagerness for the word that is found in the newer evangelical churches and fellowships.

Millions of individuals read the Bible daily for inspiration. Many of these lay Bible students join with others in small study groups in homes, office buildings, factories, and churches to discuss a passage of Scripture on a weekly basis. This small-group movement is one that seems certain to grow even more in the future, since leadership of nearly all churches is encouraging these groups, and they certainly seem to be filling a significant gap in people's lives. In addition, there is renewed concern for biblical preaching throughout the church. Congregations where systematic Bible teaching ranks high on the agenda seem to have no difficulty filling their pews, and "secular" men and women who have no particular interest in joining a church are often quite willing to join a nonthreatening, informal Bible discussion group in their neighborhood or place of work.

We wish to encourage and, indeed, strengthen this worldwide movement of lay Bible study by offering this new commentary series. Although we hope that pastors and teachers will find these volumes helpful in both understanding and communicating the Word of God, we do not write primarily for them. Our aim is, rather, to provide for the benefit of the ordinary Bible reader reliable guides to the books of the Bible, representing the best of contemporary scholarship presented in a form that does not require formal theological education to understand.

The conviction of editors and authors alike is that the Bible belongs to the people and not merely to the academy. The message of the Bible is too important to be locked up in erudite and esoteric essays and monographs written for the eyes of theological specialists. Although exact scholarship has its place in the service of Christ, those who share in the teaching office of the church have a responsibility to make the results of their research accessible to the Christian community at large. Thus, the Bible scholars who join in the presentation of this series write with these broader concerns in view.

A wide range of modern translations is available to the contemporary Bible student. We have chosen to use the Good News Bible (Today's English Version) as the basis of our series for three reasons. First, it has become the most widely used translation, both geographically and ecclesiastically. It is read wherever English is spoken and is immensely popular with people who speak English as a second language and among people who were not brought up in the church. In addition, it is endorsed by nearly every denominational group.

Second, the Good News Bible seeks to do what we are seeking to do in our comments, namely, translate the teaching of the Bible into terms that can be understood by the person who has not had a strong Christian background or formal theological education. Though its idiomatic and sometimes paraphrastic style has occasionally frustrated the scholar who is concerned with a minute examination of the original Greek and Hebrew words, there can be no question but that this translation makes the Scripture more accessible to the ordinary reader than any other English translation currently available.

Third, we wish to encourage group study of the Bible, particularly by people who have not yet become a part of the church but who are interested in investigating for themselves the claims of Christ. We believe that the Good News Bible is by far the best translation for group discussion. It is both accurate and fresh, free from jargon, and, above all, contemporary. No longer does the Bible seem like an ancient book, belonging more to the museum than to the modern metropolis. Rather, it is as comprehensible and up-to-date as the daily newspaper.

We have decided to print the full text of the Good News Bible—and we are grateful for the kind permission of the United Bible Societies to do this—in our commentary series. This takes up valuable space, but we believe that it will prove to be very convenient for those who make use of the commentary, since it will enable them to read it straight through like an ordinary book as well as use it for reference.

Each volume will contain an introductory chapter detailing the background of the book and its author, important themes, and other helpful information. Then, each section of the book will be expounded as a whole, accompanied by a series of notes on items in the text that need further clarification or more detailed explanation. Appended to the end of each volume will be a bibliographical guide for further study.

Our new series is offered with the prayer that it may be an instrument of authentic renewal and advancement in the worldwide Christian community and a means of commending the faith of the people who lived in biblical times and of those who seek to live by the Bible today.

W. WARD GASQUE

ITALIA

Rome
Aricia
Puteoli •Neapolis
Pompeii

MACEDONIA
Philippi

Thessalonica
Beroea
GREECE
Delphi
Corinth
Athens
Sparta

Lesbos
Samos
Miletus
Cos
Halicarnassus
Tralles
Ephesus
Sardis
Philadelphia
Pergamum
Adramyttium

Delos
Paros
Melos

CRETE
Gortyna

Rhodes

PONTUS
Heraclea
Sinope

GALATIA
Ancyra

PHRYGIA CAPPADOCIA
Iconium
Antioch
Apamea
Laodicea

PAMPHYLIA
Perge Side
Derbe Tarsus
Seleucia

COMMAGENE

MESOPOTAMIA
Tigris River

Euphrates River

SYRIA
Antioch
•Apamea
Damascus
Palmyra

Pumbeditha
Nehardea
Babylon

ARABIA
Jerusalem
JUDEA

Aradus
Tripolis
Berytus
Sidon
Tyre
Ptolemais
Salamis

CYPRUS
Paphos

Mediterranean Sea

CYRENAICA

Alexandria
Pelusium
Bubastis
Leontopolis
Athribis
Memphis
Arsinoe Heracleopolis
Philadelphia
Tebtynis
Oxyrhynchus

E G Y P T
Nile R

• City
with
Jewish
community

miles
50   100
0   50 100 150 km

Used with permission of Macmillan Publishing Company from *The Macmillan
Bible Atlas*, Revised Edition, by Yohanan Aharoni and Michael Avi-Yonah.
Copyright © 1964, 1966, 1968, 1977 by Carta Ltd.

Introduction

Background to the Letter

Philippi

The city of Philippi bears the name of Philip II, king of Macedonia, who founded it in 356 B.C. There had previously been on the site a Thracian village known by its Greek name Krenides ("springs"). The place was taken over in 361 B.C. by settlers from the island of Thasos led by an Athenian exile named Callistratus. The main attractiveness of the place lay in its proximity to the gold mines of Mount Pangaeus, which Philip made sure of controlling by means of his new foundation. It was also strategically important because it commanded the land route to the Hellespont (Dardanelles) and Bosporus, and so across into Asia.

Luke describes it as "a city of the first district of Macedonia"[1]—that is, the first of four districts into which Macedonia was divided by the Romans in 167 B.C.—and adds that it was a Roman colony (Acts 16:12). It was first made a colony by the Roman leaders Antony and Octavian in 42 B.C. after their victory at Philippi over Brutus and Cassius, the assassins of Julius Caesar; the victors settled a number of their veteran soldiers there. Twelve years later Octavian, having in turn defeated Antony at the battle of Actium, settled several of Antony's disbanded troops there, together with families from Italy whom he dispossessed in order to make room for his own veterans, and renamed the colony after himself: Colonia Iulia Philippensis. Three years later, when Octavian assumed the style of Augustus, the name of the colony was amplified: Colonia Iulia Augusta Philippensis.[2]

The citizens of a Roman colony were themselves Roman citizens; the constitution of a Roman colony was modeled on that of the mother city, Rome, with two collegiate magistrates at the head of it. In most colonies these collegiate magistrates were officially known as the *duo uiri* (or *duumuiri iuri dicundo*, "the two men for administering justice"). In some colonies, however, they preferred to be known by the more distinguished title of praetor; of the chief magistrates of Capua, in Italy, for example, Cicero remarked that, "while they are called *duo uiri* in the other colonies, these men wished to be called praetors."[3] This appears to have been true also of the chief magistrates of Philippi: Luke refers to them by a Greek term (*stratēgoi*) that served as the equivalent of the title "praetors" (Acts 16:22, 35, 36, 38). Like the chief magistrates of Rome, those of Roman colonies were attended by lictors bearing the *fasces*, or bundles of rods, that were their badges of office. The lictors in attendance on the Philippian praetors appear in Luke's narrative under their Greek designation *rhabdouchoi*, literally, "rod-bearers" (Acts 16:35, 38).

Macedonia

Macedonia, the territory to which Philippi belonged, was an ancient kingdom in the Balkan peninsula, bounded on the south by Thessaly and on the east and northeast by Thrace. When the Persians invaded Europe at the beginning of the fifth century B.C., the kings of Macedonia collaborated with them and so were able to preserve a limited independence for themselves.[4] Even so, the Macedonian king Alexander I gave secret aid to the Greek states farther south that were attacked by Xerxes in 480 B.C.[5] He and his successors patronized Greek culture; Alexander himself, as crown prince of Macedonia, was allowed to compete in the Olympic games (open to none but Greeks) because his family claimed to be of Argive descent.[6] By the fourth century B.C. Macedonia was, for most practical purposes, part of the Greek world. Philip II of Macedonia (359–336 B.C.), by diplomacy and military conquest, made himself master of the city-states of Greece. After his assassination his son Alexander III (Alexander the Great) inherited his Greco-Macedonian dominion and made it the base for his conquest of western Asia (as far east as the Indus valley) and Egypt. But with the division of Alexander's empire soon after his death in 323 B.C., Macedonia became a separate kingdom once more.

The kingdom of Macedonia clashed with the Romans when Philip V (221–179 B.C.) made a treaty with their enemy Hannibal during the Second Punic War.[7] The Romans were able to stir up sufficient trouble for Philip on the eastern side of the Adriatic to keep him occupied, and his treaty with Hannibal remained ineffective. When the Second Punic War was at an end and Hannibal was dead, the Romans found a pretext for declaring war on Philip. The war ended in 197 B.C. with Philip's defeat at Cynoscephalae in central Thessaly.[8] He was obliged henceforth to confine his rule to Macedonia and not intervene in the affairs of the Greek city-states farther south.

Philip's son Perseus in his turn excited Rome's suspicions; these were further fomented by his enemy the king of Pergamum, an ally of Rome. The ensuing Third Macedonian War (as it is called by Roman historians) ended in 168 B.C. with a Roman victory at Pydna, a city in the coastal plain of southern Macedonia.[9] The Romans then abolished the royal dynasty of Macedonia and divided the kingdom into four republics.[10] But in 149 B.C., an adventurer named Andriscus, claiming to be a son of Perseus, reunited Macedonia under his rule for a short time.[11] When the Romans put Andriscus down in 148 B.C., they decided that the only course to take with Macedonia was to annex it as a province.[12] The four republics set up twenty years before remained as geographical districts but retained little political significance.

To consolidate their hold on the new province, the Romans built a great military road, the Egnatian Way, from Apollonia and Dyrrhachium on the Adriatic to Thessalonica; it was in due course extended eastward to Philippi and its port Neapolis (modern Kavalla), and later still to Byzantium.[13]

Macedonia thus became a base for the further expansion of Roman power. It was made a senatorial province by the emperor Augustus in 27 B.C. His successor Tiberius had it transferred to his own control as an imperial province in A.D. 15, but Claudius handed it back to the senate in A.D. 44.[14] The proconsul (as the governor of a senatorial province was called) had his seat of administration at Thessalonica.

The Coming of the Gospel

Christianity reached Macedonia less than twenty years after the death of Christ. One of the earliest New Testament documents—the first letter to the Thessalonians—was sent from Corinth, probably in the fall of A.D. 50, to the young church of Thessalonica.[15] The letter, which is sent in the names of Paul, Silvanus, and Timothy, indicates that the church of Thessalonica came into existence through a visit that those three men had paid to the city not long before. Their visit to Thessalonica had been preceded by a visit to Philippi, where they were "mistreated and insulted" (1 Thess. 2:2).

The outline of the movements of Paul and his companions that can be gathered from 1 Thessalonians agrees so well with the more detailed record of Acts 16:6–18:5 that the Acts record, which comes from a later date, can be confidently accepted as providing a historical framework within which the more incidental data of the Pauline correspondence can be read with greater understanding.

When Paul set out with his colleague Silvanus (called Silas in Acts) after the Council of Jerusalem to traverse Asia Minor from the Cilician Gates westward, Macedonia did not figure in their travel plans. So far as can be ascertained from the narrative of Acts, they were heading for Ephesus. But they were prevented from continuing their journey in that direction and found themselves obliged (accompanied now by Timothy, who had joined them at Lystra) to turn northwest from Iconium or Pisidian Antioch until they reached the Aegean Sea at the port of Troas (Alexandria Troas). Here the first of the "we" passages of Acts begins: the narrative continues in the first person plural (which most probably indicates unobtrusively that the narrator himself was present at the events so recorded):

"That night Paul had a vision in which he saw a Macedonian standing and begging him, 'Come over to Macedonia and help us!' As soon as Paul had this vision, we got ready to leave for Macedonia, because we decided that God had called us to preach the Good News to the people there" (Acts 16:9, 10).

The missionary party, now increased to four (it appears) by the addition of the narrator (whom we take to be Luke), crossed by sea from Troas to Neapolis and traveled from there about ten miles along the Egnatian Way to Philippi.

Paul's usual practice when visiting a Gentile city was to make for the local synagogue in order to find an audience among the Jews and God-fearing Gentiles who attended it. In Philippi, it seems, there was not a large enough Jewish community to form a regular synagogue congregation (for which the quorum was ten men).[16] But there was an informal meeting place outside the city, by the river Gangites, where some women assembled on the Sabbath day to recite the appointed prayers. These women may have comprised both Jews and God-fearers (Gentiles who adhered to the Jewish form of worship without becoming full proselytes); their leader was Lydia, a native of Thyatira in Asia Minor, who traded in the purple dye manufactured from the juice of the madder root for which her home country had long been famed. (Homer describes how "a Maceonian or Carian woman stains ivory with purple dye.")[17] Lydia and some of her companions formed the nucleus of the church of Philippi. The women of Macedonia had long been famed for their initiative and influence, and that noble tradition was well maintained by the women in the Macedonian churches.[18]

Lydia put her house at the disposal of the missionaries, and it was evidently the meeting place of the church that quickly came into being in Philippi.

The missionaries, however, ran into trouble when Paul exorcised from a slave girl "an evil spirit that enabled her to predict the future"

(Acts 16:16). The spirit is technically called a pythonic spirit; that is to say, it was a pale reflection of the spirit that empowered the Pythian prophetess at Delphi to speak as the mouthpiece of Apollo. As a result of the exorcism the girl was no longer able to tell fortunes. (There is a literary parallel in Menander's *Theophoroumenē* (*The Divinely Inspired Woman*), a play in which a slave girl loses her cymbals and tambourine and, with them, the gift of prophecy that depends on them.[19] The Philippian owners of the slave girl were annoyed at the loss of the regular income her fortune-telling brought them; Paul, they thought, was guilty of wanton interference with their property rights. He and Silvanus (the two full Jews in the missionary quartet) were therefore dragged before the magistrates in the forum, and a charge was laid against them: "These men are Jews, and they are causing trouble in our city. They are teaching customs that are against our law; we are Roman citizens, and we cannot accept these customs or practice them" (Acts 16:20, 21). The bystanders joined in the attack, and the magistrates, deciding that these two unwelcome foreigners needed to be taught a sharp lesson, ordered them to be beaten with the lictors' rods and locked up overnight.

When the lictors arrived at the jail next morning to expel the two men from Philippi, they were presented with a protest that they had to take back to the magistrates. Paul and Silvanus were Roman citizens and should not have been subjected to such treatment as they had received. The magistrates had listened to the charge laid against them without troubling to investigate it or inviting the two accused men to give their account of the matter.[20] If Paul and Silvanus asserted their Roman citizenship in the forum, no heed was paid to them in the general excitement. But now they asserted it in quieter circumstances. The magistrates had to pay attention now and apologize for having beaten Roman citizens without a regular trial and conviction. They could not summarily expel Roman citizens from a Roman city, but they did earnestly beg them to leave: they felt unequal to the responsibility of protecting them from public resentment. By setting the legal record straight Paul and Silvanus made sure that their Philippian converts would not incur the odium of being associated with criminals.

The best-known episode of Luke's narrative of the evangelization of Philippi tells of the earthquake that struck at midnight while Paul and Silvanus were "praying and singing hymns to God" in the darkness of the inner prison, and of the jailer's alarm, attempted suicide, and conversion (Acts 16:25–34). This episode, which is detachable from its context, has literary affinities of its own. In the first-century Greek work called *Testa-*

ment of Joseph (one of the collected *Testaments of the Twelve Patriarchs*), Joseph tells how his Egyptian master "flogged me and sent me into Pharaoh's jail. When then I was in fetters, the Egyptian woman heard me in the house of darkness singing hymns to the Lord and glorifying my God, rejoicing with cheerful voice."[21] There is no question of direct literary dependence one way or the other, but both documents draw on a common stylistic convention. The general idea appears a little later in the Stoic writer Epictetus: "Then we shall be emulators of Socrates, when we can write paeans in prison."[22]

As for the effects of the earthquake at midnight, Origen in the mid–third century, if not the pagan Celsus some fifty years earlier, suggested a parallel between Luke's account and the description in the *Bacchae* of Euripides of the escape of the bacchanals and Dionysus from Pentheus's prison: "the bonds were loosed from their feet of their own accord, and the keys undid the doors without mortal hand."[23] The literary affinities of the episode cannot fail to be recognized, but they do not undermine the historicity of the event.

The Church of Philippi

Paul and Silvanus had to leave Philippi; the magistrates' polite request was no more to be ignored than the lictors' forceful eviction would have been. But they left behind them a young church, comprising ardently committed converts whose affection for their apostle was shown by gifts that they sent him on more than one occasion, beginning within a few weeks of his departure (see Phil. 4:15, 16). Timothy accompanied his two senior colleagues; Luke perhaps stayed on in Philippi. It is noteworthy that the first of the "we" passages of Acts comes to an end in Philippi (Acts 16:17) and the second one begins in Philippi (Acts 20:5). If Luke was in Philippi continuously during the intervening seven or eight years, the Philippian Christians may well have come to regard him as one of themselves: it is even possible that they appointed him to represent them among the delegates from various churches contributing to the Jerusalem relief fund who accompanied Paul to Judaea in A.D. 57. No member of the Philippian church is mentioned in the list of Paul's travel companions in Acts 20:4 (but the list is probably not complete); those who are listed, says Luke, "went ahead and waited for us in Troas" while "we" (that is, Paul, with the narrator and possibly one or two others) "sailed from Philippi after the Festival of Unleavened Bread" (Acts 20:5, 6). They would have embarked actually at Neapolis, the port of Philippi. In A.D. 57 the Festival of Unleavened Bread fell during the week of April 7–14.

The church of Philippi, then, was the last of Paul's churches west of the Aegean with which he had personal contact before his last, fateful visit to Jerusalem. It continued to communicate with him as it had done from its foundation, and his letter to the Philippians gives the reader some idea of the pleasure this church gave him every time he thought of it and of his appreciation of its members' unfailing kindness and affection.

That the Philippian church preserved the same character half a century later appears in its care for Ignatius, bishop of Antioch, when he was on his way to Rome under military guard to be exposed to the beasts in the arena. Like Paul before him, Ignatius sailed from Troas to Neapolis and continued his journey by land along the Egnatian Way.[24] Details of Ignatius's stopover in Philippi are lacking, but the Philippian Christians were sufficiently interested in him to write to Polycarp, bishop of Smyrna, asking him to send them copies of any of Ignatius's letters that might be available to him.[25] Polycarp's reply to their request has survived. At the beginning of his letter he expresses his joy that they "have followed the example of true love and have helped on their way, as opportunity offered, those who were bound in chains." Such chains, he says, are an ornament for saints; they are "the diadems of those who have been truly chosen by God and our Lord" (among these he is thinking pre-eminently of Ignatius). Then he adds, "I rejoice also that your firmly rooted faith, renowned since early days, endures to the present and produces fruit for our Lord Jesus Christ."[26] The tree that Paul and his associates had planted continued to bear witness to the quality of their workmanship.

Character, Occasion, and Purpose of the Letter

Argument

The letter is sent to the Christian community of Philippi by Paul, who joins Timothy's name with his own in the opening salutation.

After the salutation and the assurance of his profound thanksgiving and prayer for his friends at Philippi, Paul tells them how his present situation, despite the restrictions of imprisonment, has promoted the spread of the gospel among the officials in whose care he is and has encouraged many of the local Christians to be more uninhibited in witnessing to their faith. Even if some of them are impelled by motives that are not at all friendly to Paul, the fact remains that Christ is being proclaimed, and this makes Paul rejoice. He does not know what the outcome of his imprisonment will be, but his resolve is that, whether it is ended by release or by execution, the glory of Christ will be promoted.

He then makes an appeal for harmony among the members of the Philippian church: he deprecates petty jealousies and antipathies and reminds them of Christ's self-forgetfulness in becoming a servant to others and enduring death by crucifixion. After further words of encouragement, in which Paul's sense of personal involvement in the spiritual well-being of his converts is made very clear, he tells them that he will soon send Timothy to see them and bring back news of them. Right now, he says, he is sending back Epaphroditus, one of themselves, who had recently come to discharge a service to him on their behalf and had incurred serious illness in doing so.

Then, with "In conclusion, my brothers . . . " (3:1), he gives the impression that he is bringing the letter to an end, when suddenly he puts the readers on their guard against subversive intruders and (partly by way of countering the influence of such people) sets out, with reference to his own experience, the essence of Christian faith and life.

Further words of admonition (4:1-9) are followed by thanks for a gift that Epaphroditus has brought to him from Philippi (4:10-20). The letter closes with a final doxology, greetings, and benediction.

Authorship

That Philippians is a genuine letter of Paul has been generally accepted.

The first serious challenge to its authenticity was made in the 1840s by F. C. Baur of Tübingen.[27] Baur quoted the verdict of an older scholar, W. M. L. de Wette,[28] to the effect that its genuineness was "above all question" and took leave to suggest a number of points that might weigh against this verdict.

One of these points was the alleged employment of certain Gnostic ideas and expressions with which the writer's mind was evidently filled and which appear especially in the christological passage, Philippians 2:6-11.[29] Another was the repetitious character of the document. It was marked, Baur thought, "by a want of any profound and masterly connexion of ideas, and by a certain poverty of thought."[30] He added that there could be found "no motive or occasion for it, no distinct indication of any purpose, or of any leading idea."[31] The polemic outburst of Philippians 3:2–19 was regarded as a "weak and lifeless" imitation of 2 Corinthians 11:13–15.[32] The reference in Philippians 4:15, 16 to repeated gifts received from Philippi was felt to be at variance with Paul's affirmation in 1 Corinthians 9:15–18 and elsewhere that he chose not to be supported by his converts but to earn his living by his own work. It was based, Baur thought, on 2 Corinthians 11:9, where Paul does mention one exception to his regular policy—an occasion in Corinth when his needs were met by friends from Macedonia.[33]

Finally Baur, who took Rome to be the place of imprisonment from which Philippians was supposed to be written, argued that its picture of the progress of the gospel in Rome at the time indicated lacks corroboration. The clue to this picture, and to the mention of "God's people who belong to the Emperor's palace" (4:22), was provided (he thought) by the reference to one Clement in Philippians 4:3. This Clement, according to Baur, was intended to be identified with Titus Flavius Clemens, related by marriage to the emperor Domitian, at whose initiative he was put to death in A.D. 95. He was allegedly introduced into the letter by the postapostolic author who was acquainted with the growing Clementine legend. In this legend Clement was one of Peter's converts; by bringing him into contact with Paul the author of Philippians made his contribution to the posthumous reconciliation of the two apostles who (as Baur believed) were opponents in their lifetime.[34]

Some of Baur's arguments were matters of opinion and feeling, some were bound up with a particular reading of the evidence, but the argument about Clement was simply wrong. The Clement of Philippians 4:3 is a Philippian Christian, otherwise unknown to us but not in any way associated with Rome. None of Baur's arguments about Philippians has commended itself to later generations of Pauline scholarship.

More recently a question mark has been set against the Pauline authorship of the letter on the basis of a statistical analysis of the language.[35] This argument also has failed to win general acceptance; the document is too short to provide cogent evidence of this kind.

Occasion

It is evident that Philippians was written while Paul was in prison and awaiting a judgment that would affect his liberty and perhaps his life.[36] Three times in the first chapter he mentions his imprisonment and integrates it into the course of his apostolic ministry: he claims to be stationed where he is "for the work of defending the gospel" (Phil. 1:16). Through his imprisonment, indeed, the gospel was being promoted in quarters to which it might not otherwise have found access.

But where was this imprisonment? Paul does not say explicitly. His Philippian friends did not need to be told. They knew where he was: they had lately sent Epaphroditus, one of their number, to visit him (2:25). The traditional answer to the question has been Rome;[37] but in more recent times both Ephesus and Caesarea have been suggested.

The claims of Ephesus have been defended by A. Deissmann, G. S. Duncan, and others.[38] It is quite probable that Paul was imprisoned at least once during his residence in Ephesus (A.D. 52–55), but the imprisonment that he was undergoing when he sent this letter to Philippi can scarcely have been an Ephesian imprisonment. When he says that "the whole palace guard and all the others here know that I am in prison because I am a servant of Christ" (1:13), the Greek word translated "palace guard" is *praitōrion*, a borrowing from Latin *praetorium*. His use of a loanword suggests that it bears its technical sense. The word denotes the headquarters of a praetor, more particularly the commanding officer's headquarters in a military camp. In the city of Rome under the empire it meant the praetorian guard, the emperor's personal bodyguard. Farther afield it was used for the headquarters of a provincial governor, but of the governor of an imperial province, who had military units under his command. There is no known instance in imperial times of its use for the headquarters of a proconsul, the governor of a senatorial province such as Asia was at this time.

Appeal has been made to inscriptional evidence for the presence of a *praetorianus* (member of the praetorian guard) in the vicinity of Ephesus, but this evidence is irrelevant for the matter under discussion. The *praetorianus* mentioned in three Latin inscriptions was a *former* member of the praetorian guard who later discharged police duties as a *stationarius* on a Roman road in the province of Asia.[39]

If Ephesus is ruled out as the place from which the letter was sent, Caesarea comes up for consideration. Its claims have been ably defended by a number of scholars, most notably Ernst Lohmeyer.[40] In favor of Caesarea is the express statement of Acts 23:35 that Paul was kept under guard there "in Herod's *praetorium*" (GNB paraphrases "in the governor's headquarters"). This was an official building set up by Herod the Great on the artificial acropolis that he had constructed for his new city of Caesarea between 22 and 12 B.C.; it appears to have served now as headquarters for the Roman procurator of Judaea. Since the procurator had auxiliary cohorts under his command, his headquarters could properly be designated the *praetorium*.[41]

In the closing years of his Aegean ministry Paul organized a collection in the churches of his Gentile mission field for the relief of the poverty of the Jerusalem church. At Whitsuntide, A.D. 57, he came to Jerusalem with representatives of those churches, who were to hand over their churches' contributions to the leaders of the church of Jerusalem. Not many days after his arrival he was attacked by a hostile crowd in the temple precincts and rescued by members of the Roman garrison in the Antonia fortress, which overlooked the outer court of the temple. The commanding officer of the garrison took him into custody and sent him to the procurator Felix at Caesarea.

Paul remained in Caesarea for two years (A.D. 57–59), waiting for Felix to promulgate a judicial decision on his case (Acts 24:26, 27). Felix, in fact, never got around to pronouncing a formal verdict on Paul: Luke puts this procrastination down to his hope of receiving a bribe from Paul or his friends. Felix knew that Paul had come to Judaea with a substantial sum for disbursement in Jerusalem (Acts 24:17) and surmised that he might have access to further funds. But Paul had every reason to suppose that Felix's verdict, when it was given, would be favorable and that he would be discharged. This, it could be argued, would provide a suitable background for his optimism: "I know that I will . . . stay on with you all, to add to your progress and joy in the faith" (Phil. 1:25).

But Caesarea was a political backwater. If it was there that Paul was imprisoned when he wrote to the Philippians, certainly everybody in Herod's *praetorium* would know that he was there and why he was there, but would there be anything very remarkable about that? There were Christians in Caesarea, but were they sufficiently numerous or diversified to take sides with or against Paul in the manner described in Philippians 1:15–18? Even if they were stimulated by his enforced residence in that city to preach the gospel with renewed enthusiasm, Caesarea offers too restricted a setting to account for the joyful enthusiasm that Paul expresses in telling how his imprisonment has worked out for the advance of the gospel.

Rome, however, would present a very different picture.

Felix was recalled from Judaea in A.D. 59, without having discharged Paul. He was succeeded as procurator by Festus. When Festus began to reopen Paul's case, Paul soon realized that he might be exposed to mortal danger through action Festus, in his inexperience, seemed likely to take. He availed himself therefore of a Roman citizen's privilege and "appealed to Caesar"—that is to say, he appealed to have his case transferred from the provincial governor's court to the direct jurisdiction of the emperor in Rome. To Rome, then, Paul was sent, and he arrived there early in A.D. 60. He spent the next two years under house arrest waiting for his case to be heard. When his case came up, he would probably have to answer more charges than one. The charge pressed against him when he was arrested in Jerusalem was one of violating the sanctity of the temple, but that could be easily rebutted. Mention is made, however, of a charge of disturbing the Roman peace throughout the provinces of the empire (Acts 24:5). This was a serious charge, and although Paul could give a powerful reply to it, there was no means of knowing how it would be handled before the imperial tribunal.

While Paul waited for his case to be heard before Nero, it would have been supremely exhilarating for him to see how the gospel was spreading in Rome through his presence there, in custody though he was. In favor of a Roman provenance for the letter, moreover, is the reference to the "saints . . . of Caesar's household" (GNB: "God's people . . . who belong to the Emperor's palace") who, along with other Christians, send their greetings to the Philippian church (Phil. 4:22). True, the imperial civil service was staffed by members of Caesar's household—largely his freedmen—and these were to be found throughout the provinces. But they were concentrated mainly in Rome, and only in Rome would they be sufficiently numerous to include a significant body of Christians.[42]

If it be concluded that this letter was sent from Rome, it becomes necessary to relate Paul's declared expectation and intention to visit Philippi shortly (Phil. 1:25–27; 2:24) to his earlier plan, disclosed in Romans 15:24, 29, of going on from Rome to Spain. When he sent his letter to the Romans at the beginning of A.D. 57, he was in course of bidding farewell to the Aegean world. To the same effect is Luke's report of Paul's words to the elders of the Ephesian church when he met them briefly at Miletus on his last journey to Jerusalem: "I know that none of you will ever see me again" (Acts 20:25). If Philippians is to be dated during his Roman imprisonment, or even during his Caesarean imprisonment, he must have changed his plans substantially.

Paul's travel plans were never inflexible: they were always subject to his awareness of divine guidance. Indeed, his readiness to change them could at times prove disconcerting to his friends and give his opponents ground for charging him with vacillation (cf. 2 Cor. 1:15–2:1). When he told the Roman Christians of his plan to spend a short time with them on his way to Spain, he foresaw the possibility of trouble arising during his imminent visit to Jerusalem, but he did not foresee his arrest there, his subsequent two years' captivity in Caesarea, his being sent under armed guard to Rome, and his further two years' house arrest there while he awaited the summons to appear before Caesar. This unforeseen and unforeseeable sequence of events might well have moved him to reconsider his travel plans. News kept on reaching him from his friends in the Aegean world that made him decide they needed a further visit from him as soon as he was free to pay one. A similar expectation is expressed in his letter to Philemon of Colossae (also probably to be dated during his Roman imprisonment): "get a room ready for me, because I hope that God will answer the prayers of all of you and give me back to you" (Philem. 22).

If a Roman dating of Philippians is probable on other grounds, Paul's expressed hope of revisiting Philippi is not a decisive argument against such a dating.

The number of journeys back and forth between Philippi and Paul's place of imprisonment that the letter implies has been thought to favor an Ephesian rather than a Roman provenance.[43] The journey in either direction between Rome and Philippi required about forty days;[44] one could sail from Philippi to Ephesus in a week to ten days.[45]

At the time the letter was written

a. news of Paul's imprisonment was taken to Philippi;

b. Epaphroditus traveled from Philippi to hand over a gift to Paul (4:18);

c. news reached Philippi of Epaphroditus's illness (2:26);

d. news reached Epaphroditus of the Philippians' anxiety at the report of his illness (2:26);

e. Epaphroditus was about to set out for Philippi, carrying Paul's letter (2:25, 28);

f. Timothy was to follow him shortly, as soon as Paul's prospects became clearer (2:19–23);

g. Paul himself hoped to visit Philippi, in the event of his release (2:24).

Four of these journeys had been completed; the last three were to be undertaken in the near future. But the first four have been set out in a manner that implies that Epaphroditus fell ill after he arrived at the place where Paul was: as is suggested below in the comment on 2:26, this is not necessarily so; he may have fallen ill on the way to Paul. This would reduce the time required for the successive journeys. In any case, as C. H. Dodd puts it, "wherever Paul may have been at the time, circumstances compelled frequent intercommunication with Philippi, and if Ephesus was near, the Roman imprisonment was long."[46] Paul spent two years in Rome before his case came up for hearing; when this letter was written, a decision about him was imminent. There was plenty of time for all the journeys to have taken place.

It has been argued that Paul's expression of thanks to the Philippians because "after so long a time" they had shown their care for him again (4:10) "cannot be construed except as a rebuke, and a sarcastic rebuke at that,"[47] if the letter was not sent until the period of his Roman imprisonment. This also has been urged as an argument in favor of an Ephesian provenance. As will be shown in the commentary on that passage, however, Paul and the Philippians both knew that the long intermission in their sending him gifts was due to his own financial policy, not to any negligence on their part.[48] Others indeed have maintained that the expression of thanks in 4:10–20 constitutes a separate short letter, earlier than the main letter into which it has been editorially inserted.

This raises the question whether or not the letter as it has been handed down to us is a composite document.

Unitary or Composite?

It is more especially in recent times that questions have been seriously raised about the literary unity of the letter.[49] Polycarp, indeed, writing to the Philippian Christians in the earlier part of the second century, reminds them how Paul not only taught them "the word of truth" when he was present with them "but also when he was absent wrote letters to you" (*To the Philippians* 3:2). But it would be risky to infer from this that he knew parts of the canonical letter as separate documents: if he is not using a generalizing plural, he may have in mind other letters than the one that has survived.

Many commentators (perhaps most) still maintain the unity of the document, but several regard it as composite. Günther Bornkamm has described it as a "Pauline letter-collection."[50] There are in particular two sections that are thought to be insertions into the main letter: (*a*) the note of thanks in 4:10–20 and (*b*) the section beginning at 3:2 and continuing into chapter 4.

Note of Thanks (4:10–20). The note of thanks in 4:10–20 is linked with the main body of the letter by the reference to Epaphroditus (4:18; cf. 2:25–30). It is one and the same mission of Epaphroditus that is mentioned in both places. But those who infer from 2:25–30 that Epaphroditus spent a considerable time with Paul after he delivered the Philippians' gift to him, and fell ill during that time, conclude that Paul must have sent his note of thanks quite soon after he received the gift and not waited until Epaphroditus was able to return home. Hence the note of thanks must have been sent earlier than the main letter.[51]

But if (as is more probable) Epaphroditus fell ill on his way to Paul, and Paul sent him back to Philippi earlier than had been planned, to relieve his Philippian friends' anxiety about him, then it was most convenient that Epaphroditus should carry Paul's note of thanks to Philippi—either along with, or as part of, a larger letter (see comments on 2:26–28). (If it was sent along with the larger letter, it was subsequently attached to it.)

Warning Against Troublemakers (3:2 ff.). Three noteworthy features of this section are (a) its coming after "In conclusion" (3:1), (b) its difference in tone from the rest of the letter, and (c) its resemblance to the last four chapters of 2 Corinthians.

The phrase "In conclusion" in 3:1 (caught up again in 4:8) might be thought to prepare the reader for the end of the letter, but not much can be built on this by itself, since in informal letters (not to speak of sermons) words suggesting that the end of the composition is approaching may come quite a long way before the actual end.

But the sudden severity of the warning in this section and the resemblance in tone and subject to 2 Corinthians 10–13 call for some explanation. There are differences, indeed: whereas in 2 Corinthians 10–13 the "false apostles" have already been at work in Corinth, it is not implied in Philippians 3:2 ff. that the troublemakers are already active in Philippi—still less that there was any disposition in the Philippian church to give them a sympathetic hearing.

In Corinth the intruders claimed better credentials and higher achievements than Paul, and he felt obliged, "talking like a fool" (2 Cor. 11:21), to argue that, if such credentials and achievements as they put forward were really necessary and important, then he could produce a more impressive record than any of them. He takes a similar line in Philippians 3:4–16, remarking that, if it were fitting to have confidence in natural endowments and accomplishments, he would have no lack of ground for such confidence. But those things he had formerly valued he now wrote off as worthless—and then he launches into an eloquent statement of the things he really values: the personal knowledge of Christ, the sharing of his sufferings, the hope of resurrection with him, and the ambition to apprehend the high purpose for which he was once apprehended by Christ.

C. H. Dodd, who accepted Philippians as a unitary document and dated it during Paul's Roman imprisonment, could quote Philippians 3:13–16 as showing "most clearly what experience had made of this naturally proud, self-assertive and impatient man," as providing evidence for his thesis that about the time of Paul's "trouble . . . in the province of Asia" (2 Cor. 1:8) he underwent a "second conversion" which resulted in a marked change of temper.[52] But it is difficult to recognize this "change of temper" in Paul's treatment of the troublemakers in the very context of 3:13–16—in his castigation of the "dogs" of 3:2 or his denunciation of the libertines of 3:18, 19. True, he says that he writes these denunciatory words "with tears," whereas in 2 Corinthians 10–13 he may have written more in anger than in sorrow, but there is not much to choose between his language here and his language there. If there is any substance in Dodd's thesis of a "second conversion" (and there is some), then it must be said with T. W. Manson that Philippians 3:2 ff. "is more easily understood before the second conversion than after it."[53]

It is unlikely that anything can be inferred from a change in perspective that has been detected between Paul's expectation in 3:20, 21 of sharing the bodily "change" that surviving believers will undergo at the advent of Christ and his expectation in 1:23 of being "with Christ" at death; the possibility of execution as the outcome of his impending trial sufficiently accounts for his outlook in 1:23, whereas in 3:20, 21 he is voicing (perhaps in a credal form) the hope of Christians in general.

Apart from that, if it were possible to overcome such a breach of "bibliographical probability"[54] as the division of Philippians into two originally separate letters, much could be said in favor of dating 3:2 ff. in the same general period as 2 Corinthians 10–13, while dating the letter as a whole to the later stages of Paul's Roman imprisonment. Although the unsympathetic persons of 1:15–18 are not identical with the people mentioned so severely in 3:2, 18, 19 (and, indeed, do not appear to have adulterated the gospel), yet the mildness with which Paul refers to them marks a notable contrast with his fierce invective against the others and suggests that a period of mellowing has intervened. Paul has learned to see cause for thanksgiving in a situation that at one time might have made him explode with indignation.

If we suppose that another letter, or part of another letter, begins at 3:2, how far does it go? Certainly as far as 4:1, with its plea to the Philippians to "stand firm in . . . the Lord,"[55] but perhaps as far as 4:3,[56] and possibly even as far as 4:9.[57] If it does go on to 4:9, we should have a satisfactory ending to a letter, the last paragraph beginning "In conclusion, my brothers" (4:8) and ending with a benediction: "the God who gives us peace will be with you." The main letter would then announce its conclusion with "In conclusion, my brothers, be joyful in . . . the Lord" (3:1), followed by the note of thanks (4:10–20) and the final greetings and benediction (4:21–23). But arguments for treating Philippians as a composite work are at best tentative. The judgment of W. G. Kümmel must command respect: "There is . . . no sufficient reason to doubt the original unity of the transmitted Philippians."[58]

Purpose

The purpose of the letter can be inferred only from a consideration of its contents.

Epaphroditus was going back to Philippi at Paul's insistence, and Paul took the opportunity to give him a letter for the Philippian Christians, thanking them for the gift that Epaphroditus had brought from them and for their general and constant partnership in his ministry, and incidentally explaining why he was sending Epaphroditus back so promptly.

At the same time he took the opportunity to let them know his present situation, to prepare them for Timothy's prospective visit, which might be followed (he hoped) by a personal visit from Paul himself. He warned them against a variety of persons who were going around among the churches subverting Christian faith and morals. But his principal purpose was evidently to encourage a spirit of unity among them. What militated chiefly against this was a natural tendency to self-assertiveness, which Paul deprecated with all the earnestness of which he was capable. The example of Christ should inspire his followers to put the interests of others before their own and to be marked by a spirit of spontaneous self-forgetfulness and self-sacrifice. If they learned this lesson, they would not only fill Paul's cup of joy to overflowing, they too would be liberated from internal tensions and would be able, with Paul, to rejoice in the Lord.

Note: A list of the abbreviations used in the commentary is found at the end of the book (see pp. 138-40). See also For Further Reading (pp. 141-148); full bibliographical references for works referred to in short-form notes within the commentary are supplied there.

Notes

1. This rendering (GNB) is probably original, although it is not found in the Greek manuscripts; it is preserved in some manuscripts of the Latin Vulgate and in medieval Provençal and German versions based on the Latin; see E. Haenchen, *The Acts of the Apostles*, p. 474.

2. For the full name see the Latin inscription from Philippi reproduced by M. N. Tod in *Annual of the British School at Athens* 23 (1918–19), p. 95, no. 21.

3. Cicero, *On the Agrarian Law* 2.93.

4. Herodotus, *History* 5.17 f.

5. Ibid. 7.173; 9.45.

6. Ibid. 5.22; 8.137.

7. Polybius, *History* 7.9.

8. Ibid. 18.22–28.

9. Ibid. 31.29.

10. Livy, *History* 45.29.5 ff.; cf. J. A. O. Larsen, *Greek Federal States*.

11. Diodorus, *History* 32.9b, 15; Florus, *Epitome* 1.30.

12. Florus, *Epitome* 1.32.3; cf. M. G. Morgan, "Metellus Macedonicus and the Province Macedonia," *Historia* 18 (1969), pp. 422–46.

13. Strabo, *Geography* 7.7.4. See, for a good popular account, F. O'Sullivan, *The Egnatian Way*.

14. From A.D. 15 to 44 Macedonia was combined with Achaia to the south and Moesia farther north to form one imperial province (Tacitus, *Annals* 1.76.4; 1.80.1). An imperial province, unlike a senatorial province, required the presence of military units and was governed by a legate directly appointed by the emperor. See also F. Papazoglu, "Quelques aspects de l'histoire de la province Macédoine," in *Aufstieg und Niedergang der römischen Welt*, ed. H. Temporini and W. Haase, 2.7.1 (Berlin and New York: de Gruyter, 1979), pp. 302–69.

15. Cf. F. F. Bruce, *1 & 2 Thessalonians*.

16. The technical term for this quorum of ten men is *minyān*.

17. Homer, *Iliad* 4.141 f.

18. Cf. W. W. Tarn and G. T. Griffith, *Hellenistic Civilisation*, pp. 98 f.; W. D. Thomas, "The Place of Women in the Church at Philippi," *ExpT* 83 (1971–72), pp. 117–20. See comment on 4:3 below.

19. Cf. T. B. L. Webster, *An Introduction to Menander* (Manchester: Manchester University Press, 1974), p. 191.

20. Behind the Greek phrase translated "not found guilty of any crime" (Acts 16:37) W. M. Ramsay discerned the Roman legal term *re incognita*, "without investigating the case" (*St. Paul the Traveller and the Roman Citizen*, pp. 224 f.).

21. *Testament of Joseph* 8:4 f. See W. K. L. Clarke, "St. Luke and the Pseudepigrapha," *JTS* 15 (1914), p. 599; "The Use of the Septuagint in Acts," *BC* 1.2 (London: Macmillan, 1922), pp. 77 f.

22. Epictetus, *Dissertations* 2.6.26.

23. Euripides, *Bacchae* 447 f., cf. 586 ff.; see Origen, *Against Celsus* 2.34. On a recurring pattern followed in accounts of escapes from prison (cf. also Acts 5:19–23; 12:6–11) see R. Reitzenstein, *Die hellenistischen Wundererzählungen* (Leipzig: Teubner, 1906), pp. 120–122.

24. Ignatius, *To Polycarp* 8:1.

25. Polycarp, *To the Philippians* 13:2.

26. Ibid. 1:1, 2.

27. F. C. Baur, *Paul: His Life and Works*, vol. 2, pp. 45–79.

28. W. M. L. de Wette, *Lehrbuch der historisch-kritischen Einleitung in die kanonischen Bücher des Neuen Testaments*, p. 268.

29. Baur, vol. 2, pp. 46–53.

30. Ibid., p. 53.

31. Ibid., p. 53.

32. Ibid., p. 55.

33. Ibid., pp. 56–58. See comment on 4:16.

34. Ibid., pp. 58–64. The historical Flavius Clemens is mentioned by Dio Cassius, *Hist.* 67.14; Suetonius, *Domitian* 15.1. The full flowering of the Clement legend, which involves a confusion of Flavius Clemens with the apostolic father Clement of Rome, appears in the fourth-century *Clementine Recognitions* and *Clementine Homilies.*

35. Cf. A. Q. Morton, "The Authorship of Greek Prose," *JRStatSoc* series A 127 (1965), pp. 169–233; "The Authorship of the Pauline Corpus," in *The New Testament in Historical and Contemporary Perspective: Essays in Memory of G. H. C. Macgregor*, ed. W. Barclay and H. Anderson, pp. 209–35; *The Integrity of the Pauline Epistles* (Manchester: Manchester Statistical Society, 1965); M. Levison, A. Q. Morton, and W. C. Wake, "On Certain Statistical Features of the Pauline Epistles," *Philosophical Journal* 3 (1966), pp. 129–48.

36. This was contested by T. W. Manson, who suggested that the imprisonment mentioned in Phil. 1:7, 13 f., 17, was Paul's imprisonment in Philippi (Acts 16:23–39) or a brief period in custody in Corinth pending his appearance before Gallio (Acts 18:12–17); he dated Philippians during Paul's Ephesian ministry and judged that the imprisonment was a recent one, not one actually being endured at the time of writing (*Studies in the Gospels and Epistles*, pp. 149–67).

37. Cf. the "Marcionite" prologue: "The Philippians are Macedonians. These, having received the word of truth, remained steadfast in the faith. The apostle commends them, writing to them from prison in Rome."

38. Cf. A. Deissmann, "Zur ephesinischen Gefangenschaft des Apostels Paulus," in *Anatolian Studies Presented to Sir W. M. Ramsay*, ed. W. H. Buckler and W. M. Calder, pp. 121–27; P. Feine, *Die Abfassung des Philipperbriefes in Ephesus*; W. Michaelis, *Die Gefangenschaft des Paulus in Ephesus; Der Brief des Paulus an die Philipper*, J. H. Michael, *The Epistle of Paul to the Philippians*; G. S. Duncan, *St. Paul's Ephesian Ministry*; "A New Setting for Paul's Epistle to the Philippians," *ExpT* 43 (1931–32), pp. 7–11; "Were Paul's Imprisonment Epistles Written from Ephesus? *ExpT* 67 (1955–56), pp. 163–66;

"Paul's Ministry in Asia—The Last Phase," *NTS* 3 (1956–57), pp. 211–18.

39. *CIL* III. 6085, 7135, 7136.

40. E. Lohmeyer, *Der Brief an die Philipper*, pp. 3 f., 38–49; also L. Johnson, "The Pauline Letters from Caesarea," *ExpT* 68 (1956–57), pp. 24–26; J. J. Gunther, *Paul: Messenger and Exile*, pp. 98–107; J. A. T Robinson, *Redating the New Testament*, pp. 60 f., 77–79.

41. Pilate's occasional headquarters in Jerusalem are referred to as the *praetorium* in Mark 15:16; John 18:28, 33; 19:8.

42. B. Reicke ("Caesarea, Rome and the Captivity Epistles," in W. W. Gasque and R. P. Martin, ed., *Apostolic History and the Gospel*, pp. 277–86), who argues for the Caesarean provenance of the other captivity epistles but for the Roman provenance of Philippians, thinks that "it was impossible for the readers to misunderstand the reference to Rome and Nero's clients" in this greeting; he compares the mention in six Roman inscriptions (*CIJ* 284, 301, 338, 368, 416, 496) of the synagogue of the *Augustenses*, "the imperial freedmen" (p. 285). Compare comment and additional note ad loc.

43. See Duncan, *St. Paul's Ephesian Ministry*, pp. 80, 81.

44. See W. M. Ramsay, "Roads and Travel (in NT)," in *HDB* 5, pp. 375–402 (especially p. 385).

45. See the itinerary in Acts 20:6–16.

46. C. H. Dodd, "The Mind of Paul: II," in *New Testament Studies*, p. 97.

47. Manson, *Gospels and Epistles*, p. 157.

48. Compare Dodd, *New Testament Studies*, pp. 97, 98.

49. They were raised sporadically at an earlier date: one of the first scholars to point to the problems posed by the accepted unity of the letter was S. Le Moyne, *Varia Sacra* (Leiden: Daniel à Gaesbeeck, 1685), vol. 2, pp. 332–43.

50. G. Bornkamm, "Der Philipperbrief als paulinische Briefsammlung" in W. C. van Unnik, ed., *Neotestamentica et Patristica*, pp. 192–202. See also F. W. Beare, *A Commentary on the Epistle to the Philippians*, pp. 4, 149–57; B. D. Rahtjen, "The Three Letters of Paul to the Philippians," *NTS* 6 (1959–60), pp. 167–73; W. Schmithals, *Paul and the Gnostics*, pp. 67–81.

51. See Beare, *Philippians*, p. 150. Rahtjen, "The Three Letters," p. 170, argues that Epaphroditus had already been sent back to Philippi when Paul wrote 2:25–30—that Paul says not "I am all the more eager, then, to send him to you" (2:28) but "I sent him therefore the more eagerly" (the tense of *epempsa* [send] indicating an event in past time.)

52. Dodd, *New Testament Studies*, pp. 80–82.

53. Manson, *Gospels and Epistles*, pp. 163, 164.

54. With this mild but scholarly expression of reproach F. G. Kenyon was accustomed to put down some literary-critical hypotheses (as in *The Bible and Modern Scholarship* [London: John Murray, 1948], p. 37). But that such a breach did occasionally happen is shown by the (practically certain) insertion of the later "Constitution of Draco" into the Aristotelian *Constitution of Athens*, of which Kenyon produced the first printed edition in 1891.

55. So Beare, *Philippians*, pp. 24, 25.

56. So Bornkamm, "Der Philipperbrief als paulinische Briefsammlung," p. 195; also (earlier) J. E. Symes, "Five Epistles to the Philippians," *The Interpreter*, 10 (1913–14), pp. 167–70.

57. So Rahtjen, "The Three Letters," pp. 171, 172. He, however, regards 3:2–4:9 as a *later* letter, which "follows the classical pattern of the Testament of a dying father to his children."

58. W. G. Kümmel, *Introduction to the New Testament*, p. 237. The unity of the letter is defended also by B. S. Mackay, "Further Thoughts on Philippians," *NTS* 7 (1960–61), pp. 161–70; V. P. Furnish, "The Plan and Purpose of Philippians iii," *NTS* 10 (1963–64), pp. 80–88; T. E. Pollard, "The Integrity of Philippians," *NTS* 13 (1966–67), pp. 57–66; R. Jewett, "The Epistolary Thanksgiving and the Integrity of Philippians," *NovT* 12 (1970), pp. 40–53.

---

* The "Marcionite" prologues to Paul's letters are prologues included in many Latin manuscripts that, because of their contents, have been thought to stem from Marcion (ca. A.D. 144) or his followers.

Prescript

From Paul and Timothy, servants of Christ Jesus—
  To all God's people in Philippi who are in union with Christ Jesus, including the church leaders and helpers: ²May God our Father and the Lord Jesus Christ give you grace and peace.

The prescript, or introductory salutation, of an ancient letter regularly contained three elements: (*a*) the name of the sender or senders; (*b*) the name of the recipient or recipients, and (*c*) a word of greeting or good wishes. Examples abound from letters of the New Testament period, in Greek and in Latin, both literary and nonliterary; earlier examples are the extracts from the official correspondence of the Persian court quoted in the book of Ezra; compare Ezra 7:12, "From Emperor Artaxerxes to the priest Ezra, scholar in the Law of the God of Heaven [: greeting]." This pattern is followed here, as in all the NT letters: Paul and Timothy are named as the senders and "all God's people in Philippi" as the recipients, and the word of good wishes is "grace and peace."

1:1 / **Paul** is the sole author of the letter, even if Timothy's name is conjoined with his in the prescript. Immediately after the prescript he says, "I thank my God" (not, as in Col. 1:3, in a letter where Timothy's name similarly appears along with Paul's in the prescript, "we . . . give thanks to God"). Later in this letter Timothy is referred to by name in the third person (2:19).

Timothy is associated with Paul in the prescript as a gesture of friendship. He was with Paul at the time of writing and may even have taken down the letter at Paul's dictation. He was well known to the Philippian Christians, having been a member of the missionary team that first brought the gospel to their city (his presence is implied, though not expressly asserted, in the narrative of Acts 16:11–40).

Timothy was a native of Lystra in Lycaonia, the son of a mixed marriage, since his mother was Jewish and his father Greek. He was brought up in the Jewish faith but was not circumcised in infancy. During Barnabas and Paul's first visit to his home town (Acts 14:8–20) he was converted to Christianity. When Paul passed that way again a year or two later he was impressed by Timothy's spiritual development, which was attested to by senior Christians in Lystra and Iconium. He decided to enlist Timothy as a junior associate in his apostolic ministry but circumcised him first to regularize his anomalous religious status: as the son of a Jewish mother he was no Gentile Christian but a Jew in everything but circumcision. Both Paul and he knew that his circumcision made no difference to his status in the sight of God, but it was intended to remove what would have been an absolute barrier to any relations on Paul's part with synagogue authorities (Acts 16:1–3). Timothy willingly joined Paul and served him devotedly as his aide-de-camp—how devotedly can be gathered from Paul's appreciative words in 2:20–22.

Paul and Timothy are described as **servants** (lit., "slaves") **of Christ Jesus**. In Romans 1:1 Paul introduces himself as "a servant [lit., 'slave'] of Christ Jesus and an apostle chosen and called by God." In addressing the Philippians Paul had no need to stress his apostolic authority as he did in addressing the churches of Galatia and Corinth: there was no disinclination to recognize his authority in Philippi, as there was in those other churches.

It has been argued that the term "servants" here does not bear the common sense of "slaves" because the Greek word (*doulos*) is used in LXX (the Greek version of the Old Testament) of someone whom God uses for a special ministry or through whom he speaks, like Moses (Neh. 10:29), Joshua (Josh. 24:29), David (Ps. 89:20 [LXX: 88:21]), Jonah (2 Kings [LXX: 4 Kingdoms] 14:25), each of whom is called "the servant (Gk. *doulos*) of the LORD." The readers of Paul's letters, however, would more readily have taken him to mean that he was the "slave" of Christ in the humble sense that the word normally had among them. No doubt Paul did esteem it a high honor to be the servant of Christ, but he implied by his choice of the word meaning "slave" that he was totally at the disposal of his Master. Yet for that very reason his words and actions carried his Master's authority, and in his bondservice to that Master he realized perfect freedom.

The recipients of the letter are called **God's people**—literally, "saints" or "holy people" (those whom God has set apart for himself)—a very common designation for Christians in Paul's letters (cf. Rom. 1:7; 1 Cor. 1:2; 2 Cor. 1:1; Eph. 1:1; Col. 1:2). The designation (Gk. *hagios*) goes back to OT times: when God made a covenant with the Israelites after delivering them from Egypt, he called them "a people dedicated to me alone" (Exod. 19:6) and charged them, "you must be holy, because I am holy" (Lev. 11:45). This charge is carried over into the NT and laid upon the people of the new covenant. The Christian usage may also have been influenced in some degree by Daniel's description of the elect remnant of the end time as "the people of the Supreme God," literally, "the saints of the Most High" (Dan. 7:18, 22, 27). It is Daniel's description that Paul probably has in mind when he says that "God's people [lit., 'the saints'] will judge the world" (1 Cor. 6:2).

He writes, then, **to all God's people in Philippi**–that is, to the whole church in that city. His earlier letters are explicitly addressed to churches in various places (cf. Gal. 1:2; 1 Thess. 1:1; 2 Thess. 1:1; 1 Cor. 1:2; 2 Cor. 1:1); he varies his wording in his later letters to churches (cf. Rom. 1:7; Col. 1:2; Eph. 1:1). He describes them as being **in union with Christ Jesus**. This is the GNB amplification of Paul's expression, which is literally rendered "in Christ Jesus" and indicates that those who believe in Christ are united to him: the new corporate life into which they have entered is their share in his resurrection life. The idea is much the same as that which Paul elsewhere expresses by speaking of believers as members of the body of Christ (cf. 1 Cor. 12:12 f., 27; Rom. 12:4 f.).

Among those to whom the letter is sent special mention is made of **the church leaders and helpers**. The Greek words so translated came later to have the official sense of "bishops" and "deacons" (these English words are in fact derived from the two Greek words). Paul and his colleagues encouraged the development of qualities of leadership in the churches that they planted. Where the rank and file were slow in giving proper recognition to those members who displayed such qualities, they were urged to do so; the potential leaders might indeed be mentioned by name (as in 1 Cor. 16:15–18). There was no one official designation for church leaders in the Pauline churches. In Thessalonica they are called "those who work among you, who guide and instruct you in the Christian life" (1 Thess. 5:12). It may have been the Philippian Christians themselves who referred to their church leaders as *episkopoi*, "those who exercise oversight" (the same term is applied to the elders of the Ephesian church in Acts 20:28 to express their responsibility as spiritual shepherds). The **helpers** (Gk. *diakonoi*) would be those who performed any service in the church. In the Pastoral Letters their duties are more formalized (cf. 1 Tim. 3:8–13).

The reason for the special mention of **the church leaders and helpers** is uncertain. Many expositors, from Chrysostom on, have suggested that they were specially responsible for sending Epaphroditus with a gift to Paul. F. W. Beare thinks it probable that Paul wished to bring Epaphroditus's services to the attention of the leaders. E. Best envisages the possibility that Paul had received a letter statedly sent *from* "the saints in Christ Jesus who are at Philippi, with the bishops and deacons," and took up this form of words in his reply, rather pointedly refraining from giving himself any title but "slave of Christ Jesus."

When, about fifty years later, Polycarp wrote to the Philippian church, it was still administered by a plurality of leaders, to whom he refers as "elders" (*To the Philippians* 6:1; 11:1).

1:2 / At this stage in the prescript of a Greek letter the writer would normally wish the recipients "joy"; in a Latin letter he would wish them "good health." Paul inherited the Hebrew (and general Semitic) usage that wished the recipients "peace" (Heb. *shalom*), but he regularly amplifies this to "grace and peace." This may have been a form of words current in benedictions in synagogue or church. In a Jewish apocalyptic work from later in the first century, a letter purporting to have been sent by Baruch to the tribes of Israel deported by the Assyrians is superscribed "Mercy and peace" (2 Baruch 78:2). Peace is the sum total of all blessings, temporal and spiritual, and grace is the source from which they come.

The **grace and peace** that Paul invokes on his correspondents is almost always derived from **God our Father and the Lord Jesus Christ**. The close coupling of Christ with God in such expressions bears witness to the place Christ occupies in Paul's thought. As the risen and exalted one he has been invested by God with the designation "Lord"—"the name that is greater than any other name" (2:9)—and wears a heavenly humanity (1 Cor. 15:45–49). God and Christ are entirely at one in the procuring and bestowal of salvation. The unconditioned good will to human beings that has been manifested in the saving work accomplished on the cross is indiscriminately called "the grace of God" (e.g., Rom. 5:15) and "the grace of the Lord Jesus Christ" (e.g., Phil. 4:23). Similarly, the state of life into which that saving work brings believers—peace with God and peace with one another—is indiscriminately called "the peace of God" (4:7) and "the peace of Christ" (Col. 3:15).

Additional Notes

1:1 / On Paul's circumcision of Timothy see M. Hengel, *Acts and the History of Earliest Christianity*, p. 64.

4

On the phrase **servants of Christ Jesus** see K. H. Rengstorf, *TDNT,* vol 2, pp. 261–80, s.v. *doulos,* etc. (especially 276, 277). G. Sass, "Zur Bedeutung von *doulos* bei Paulus," *ZNW* 40 (1941), pp. 24–32, concludes that for Paul this is a title of honor.

On the expression **God's people . . . who are in union with Christ Jesus** (cf. 4:21) see O. E. Evans, *Saints in Christ Jesus: A Study of the Christian Life in the New Testament.* See also the chapter "The Corporate Christ" in C. F. D. Moule, *The Origin of Christology,* pp. 47–96.

In the Pastoral Letters the terms *episkopos* and *presbyteros* are still used interchangeably, and there were apparently several officers so designated in one church (cf. 1 Tim. 3:2; 5:17; Titus 1:5, 7); their qualifications are set out in detail. The next occurrence in extant Christian literature of *episkopoi* and *diakonoi* coupled together as here is in *Didache* 15:1. Elsewhere in the Pauline letters the people here called *episkopoi* are referred to as *proïstamenoi,* "those who care for others" (Rom. 12:8; 1 Thess. 5:12), which, however, is not a technical title. See J. B. Lightfoot, "The Christian Ministry," in *Philippians,* pp. 181–269; F. J. A. Hort, *The Christian Ecclesia,* pp. 211–13; E. Best, "Bishops and Deacons: Philippians 1, 1," *TU* 102 = *SE* 4 (1968), pp. 371–76; B. Holmberg, *Paul and Power: The Structure of Authority in the Primitive Church as Reflected in the Pauline Epistles,* pp. 100, 101, 116, 117.

Introductory Thanksgiving

I thank my God for you every time I think of you; ⁴and every time I pray for you all, I pray with joy ⁵because of the way in which you have helped me in the work of the gospel from the very first day until now. ⁶And so I am sure that God, who began this good work in you, will carry it on until it is finished on the Day of Christ Jesus.

The prescript of Paul's letters is regularly followed by an introductory thanksgiving. Galatians is an exception: there was little cause for thanksgiving in the current situation of the Galatian churches. The priority Paul normally gave to thanksgiving is made explicit in Rom. 1:8: "First, I thank my God through Jesus Christ for all of you." The present thanksgiving reflects "Paul's sense of close fellowship with his Philippian friends" and is "unusually earnest" (O'Brien, p. 19). As elsewhere, Paul's giving of thanks is closely interwoven with prayer.

1:3 / The indicative **I thank** is used also in the introductory thanksgiving of Romans 1:8; 1 Corinthians 1:4; Philemon 4 (the plural "we thank" in Col. 1:3; 1 Thess. 1:2; "we must thank" in 2 Thess. 1:3; the synonymous expression "I give thanks" in 2 Tim. 1:3). In 2 Corinthians 1:3 and Ephesians 1:3 (as also in 1 Pet. 1:3) we have the more liturgical form "Let us give thanks to [lit., 'Blessed be'] the God and Father of our Lord Jesus Christ." The very thought of his Christian friends in Philippi and other places gives Paul cause for gratitude to God.

1:4 / Paul's introductory thanksgiving is repeatedly linked with the assurance of his constant prayer for the friends to whom he writes (cf. Rom. 1:9; Eph. 1:16; 1 Thess. 1:2; 2 Tim. 1:3; Philem. 4). One gets the impression that he could never think of them without praying for them; but over and above that, he prayed for them regularly and systematically both as individuals and as churches.

It is not certain whether the words **every time I pray for you all** should go closely with the following clause (as in GNB) or with the preceding clause **I thank my God for you**, in which case they would stand in parallel construction with **every time I think of you**. The repetition of **every** and **all** (one and the same root in Greek) is noteworthy; it is a characteristic feature of Paul's style throughout his correspondence and not least in this letter. There are four occurrences in verses 3 and 4, which could be brought out in the rendering: "I thank my God for you in **all** my remembrance of you at **all** times in **all** my prayer for you **all**."

His statement that he prays for them all **with joy** introduces a recurring note in this letter (cf. 1:18, 25; 2:2, 17, 18, 28, 29; 3:1; 4:1, 4, 10). In contrast to many of his other churches, the Philippian church gave Paul almost unmixed joy as he contemplated it. Evidently it harbored neither such subversive teaching as had earlier found its way into the churches of Galatia nor such ethical libertinism as was defended by some members of the Corinthian church.

1:5 / What calls forth his grateful joy more particularly here is the energetic wholeheartedness with which the Philippian Christians had cooperated with him **in the work of the gospel** since first he visited their city. While he was with them several of them had "worked hard" with him "to spread the gospel" (4:3) and after his departure they continued their active witness. They prayed for him regularly (v. 19); they maintained contact with him through messengers like Epaphroditus (2:25–30); they sent him gifts as opportunity offered—indeed, one of Paul's reasons for sending them this letter was to thank them for a gift that Epaphroditus had brought from them; here he briefly anticipates his fuller acknowledgement of it in 4:10–20. They participated generously in the Jerusalem relief fund that he organized in his Gentile mission field during the closing years of his Aegean ministry: in 2 Corinthians 8:1–5 he gives warm commendation to the liberal giving of the Macedonian churches (among which the Philippian church, of course, was included).

The fact that their cooperation in the gospel had continued without intermission **until now** suggests that nothing was happening among the Philippian Christians to cause Paul serious disquiet.

1:6 / Their eager partnership in Paul's gospel ministry was a sure sign of the work of grace that had begun to be accomplished in their lives when they first believed the saving message. Paul voices his conviction that **God, who began this good work** in them, **will carry it on** (cf. 2:13) until it reaches its consummation at the advent of Christ. Similarly in 1 Thessalonians 5:24, after praying that the readers may be preserved "free from every fault at the coming of our Lord Jesus Christ," Paul and his companions affirm, "He who calls you will do it, because he is faithful." Salvation is God's work from first to last; therefore, where it has truly been inaugurated, it will certainly be completed.

The **Day of Christ Jesus**, called "the Day of Christ" in verse 10 and in 2:16, is the time of Christ's expected appearing in glory (cf. 3:20). The expression is taken over from the OT "day of the LORD"—the day when Yahweh, the God of Israel, would vindicate his righteous cause and put down all injustice, wherever it might be found, first and foremost among his own people (cf. Amos 5:18–20). But now, by divine investment, "Jesus Christ is Lord" in the most august sense that the word can bear (2:11); the day of the LORD is therefore **the Day of Christ Jesus**. In a Christian context it is the day when the lives and actions of the people of Christ will be assessed. "The quality of each person's work will be seen when the Day of Christ exposes it" (1 Cor. 3:13); therefore, "final judgment must wait until the Lord comes" and must not be anticipated by those whose knowledge of the unseen motives and personal circumstances of others is at best imperfect (1 Cor. 4:5). Above all, **the Day of Christ Jesus** is the time when the salvation of believers, already inaugurated, will be consummated. Like their Thessalonian brothers and sisters, the Christians of Philippi had learned to wait for the Son of God "to come from heaven— his Son Jesus, whom he raised from death" (1 Thess. 1:10), and to rejoice in the "hope of salvation" because they had been chosen not to endure the divine retribution to be visited on the ungodly at the end time but "to possess salvation through our Lord Jesus Christ" (1 Thess. 5:8, 9). For believers, then, that day would be light and not darkness (by contrast with the warning of Amos 5:20 that to some it would bring "darkness and not light").

Additional Notes

1:3 / On introductory thanksgivings in Paul's letters see P. Schubert, *Form and Function of the Pauline Thanksgivings*, and P. T. O'Brien, *Introductory Thanksgivings in the Letters of Paul*. Such thanksgivings have been identified in papyrus letters of the same general period: "Paul was therefore adhering to a beautiful secular custom when he so frequently began his letters with thanks to God" (A. Deissmann, *Light from the Ancient East*, p. 181, n. 5).

The verb here is *eucharistō* (as in Rom. 1:8; 1 Cor. 1:4; Philem. 4); cf. *eucharistoumen* in Col. 1:3; 1 Thess. 1:2; *eucharistein opheilomen* in 2 Thess. 1:3; *charin echō* in 2 Tim. 1:3; *eulogētos ho theos* in 2 Cor. 1:3; Eph. 1:3.

The words **every time I think of you** (Gk. *epi pasē tē mneia hymōn*) might be rendered "every time you think of me" (if *hymōn* is subjective, not objective, genitive); cf. Moffatt: "for all your remembrance of me." P. T. O'Brien thinks it "best to understand the phrase as a reference to the Philippians' remembrance of Paul by means of their monetary support on several earlier occasions" (*Introductory Thanksgivings*, p. 23). If this is maintained, then Paul mentions three reasons for this thanksgiving: their remembrance of him, their continuous partnership in the work of the gospel (v. 5), and his confidence that this good work will be carried on to the end (v. 6). On the other hand, in every other place where Paul refers to "remembrance" (*mneia*) in his introductory thanksgivings, it is he who remembers the readers (Rom. 1:9; Eph. 1:16; 1 Thess. 1:2; 2 Tim. 1:3; Philem. 4). In the only other occurrence of *mneia* in his letters it is indeed his readers' remembrance of him that is meant, but not in an introductory thanksgiving (1 Thess. 3:6).

1:5 / The clause **because of the way in which you have helped me** is literally rendered "because of your participation (*koinōnia*)." It understands "participation" in an active sense, of the Philippians' sharing in Paul's gospel ministry, and this is certainly right. However, H. Seesemann, *Der Begriff Koinōnia im Neuen Testament*, pp. 73 f., 79, argues for a more passive sense, of the participation of believers in the saving blessings of the gospel: "your participation in the gospel" is thus a circumlocution for "your faith" (GNB's **the work of the gospel** is an interpretative amplification of "the gospel.").

3

Interlude

You are always in my heart! And so it is only right for me to feel as I do about you. For you have all shared with me in this privilege that God has given me, both now that I am in prison and also while I was free to defend the gospel and establish it firmly. [8]God is my witness that I tell the truth when I say that my deep feeling for you all comes from the heart of Christ Jesus himself.

A transition from the thanksgiving of verses 3–6 to the intercession of verses 9–11 is provided by these personal words in which Paul addresses the Philippians directly and speaks of his deep affection for them.

1:7 / They have shown themselves so much at one with him that "it is only natural" (Moffatt) that he should feel about them as he does. The **privilege** or "grace" of apostolic ministry had been divinely granted to Paul (cf. Rom. 1:5), but he rejoices when his converts share it with him. Their partnership in his gospel witness meant much to him when he was free to move around; it meant, if anything, even more to him now that he was **in prison**. It should not be inferred from the GNB rendering that his opportunity **to defend the gospel and establish it firmly** was greater when he was at liberty than in his present restricted situation. He had come to accept that the interests of the gospel required him to be where he was right then: while he was under house arrest he knew himself to be at the post of divinely appointed duty for "the work of defending the gospel" (v. 16) and he looked forward to the rare opportunity of defending and establishing it before the highest officers of state when his case came up for hearing shortly. So long as he was in the place where God intended him to be, the ministry with which he had been entrusted would prosper. This assurance was strengthened in him by the steadfastness with which his Philippian friends showed themselves to be his partners in his imprisonment and in his continued gospel witness.

1:8 / In moments of intense emotion Paul was prone to invoke **God** as his **witness** (cf. Rom. 1:9; 2 Cor. 11:11, 31; 1 Thess. 2:5). Here the emotion is deep affection. The calling of **God** to **witness** does not suggest that some of the Philippians needed to be assured of this; Paul is never reticent about his love for his converts (cf. 2 Cor. 12:15; Gal. 4:19; 1 Thess. 2:8). But the terms he uses in addressing the Philippians "show a depth not plumbed elsewhere" (O'Brien, p. 29). His yearning for them **comes from the heart of Christ Jesus himself**—it is an utterly selfless affection. "As it is not Paul, but Jesus Christ, that lives in Paul, so it is not by Paul's heart, but by the heart of Jesus Christ, that Paul is moved" (Bengel, ad loc.).

The unity of the Philippian church in its relations with Paul is emphasized; they **all** shared in his ministry and they were **all** embraced in his heart's affection.

Additional Notes

1:7 / **You are always in my heart** (Gk. *dia to echein me en tē kardia hymas*) might equally well be rendered "I am always in your heart" (cf. NEB: "because you hold me in such affection"). Either rendering fits the context; perhaps the word order slightly favors the former.

The "privilege" (Gk. *charis*, "grace") granted to Paul is mentioned again in 1 Cor. 15:10; Gal. 2:9; Eph. 3:7, 8, 9 ("God gave me this privilege of taking to the Gentiles the Good News about the infinite riches of Christ, and of making all people see how God's secret plan is to be put into effect").

The words **to defend the gospel and to establish it firmly** (Gk. *en tē apologia kai bebaiōsei tou euangeliou*) might have a forensic connotation, in view of Paul's impending appearance in court.

1:8 / The phrase **my deep feeling** represents the verb *epipothō*, which Paul uses repeatedly of longing to see his friends, as in Rom. 1:11, 1 Thess. 3:6, 2 Tim. 1:4 (the noun *epipothia* is used in the same way in Rom. 15:23); cf. Phil. 2:26 (of Epaphroditus's longing to see his Philippian friends); 2 Cor. 5:2 (of Christians' longing to be clothed with their "home which comes from heaven"). Here, however, it is used, without a dependent infinitive, of Paul's affectionate yearning for his friends (cf. 2 Cor. 9:14, of the deep love which, as Paul hopes, the Jerusalem church will conceive for his Gentile converts at the reception of their gift; also 2 Cor. 7:7, 11, where the noun *epipothēsis* is used of the Corinthian Christians' feeling for Paul). See C. Spicq, "*Epipothein*. Désirer ou chérir?" *RB* 64 (1957), pp. 184–95; *Notes de Lexicographie Néo-Testamentaire*, 1 (Fribourg: Éditions Universitaires, 1978), pp. 277–79.

From the heart of Christ Jesus himself, lit. "in the bowels of Christ Jesus," the bowels (Gk. *splanchna*) being used, as frequently, of the seat of the emotions (like "heart" in v. 7); cf. 2:1.

4

Intercessory Prayer

I pray that your love will keep on growing more and more, together with true knowledge and perfect judgment, ¹⁰so that you will be able to choose what is best. Then you will be free from all impurity and blame on the Day of Christ. ¹¹Your lives will be filled with the truly good qualities which only Jesus Christ can produce, for the glory and praise of God.

The introductory thanksgiving, which itself included an element of prayer, is now followed by an intercessory prayer (strictly speaking, a prayer report). The subject matter of this prayer is identical with the subject matter of the letter as a whole; here are concentrated the main concerns to which Paul gives fuller expression throughout the letter.

1:9 / **I pray**, which catches up "I pray" in verse 4 (although a different Greek word is now used), may mean "I am praying at this moment" (which was no doubt true in any case) or (more probably) "I pray for you regularly, and this is what I pray for"—**that your love will keep on growing more and more**. For Paul, "the Spirit produces love" before all else in the lives of which he takes possession (Gal. 5:22); "God has poured out his love into our hearts by means of the Holy Spirit" (Rom. 5:5). If such love increases among the Philippian Christians, it will remove those threats to their unity of heart and purpose that arise from occasional clashes of personality and temperament. Paul returns to the subject in 2:2, where he urges his readers to make him "completely happy by 'sharing the same love.'"

This love, he trusts, will be accompanied by **true knowledge and perfect judgment**. Paul was not blind to the dangers of emotion uncontrolled by intelligence. He was resolved, by his own account, to pray and sing "with my spirit, but . . . also with my mind" (1 Cor. 14:15), and he was equally concerned that he and his converts should love in spirit and mind alike.

It is love that fosters the growth of **true knowledge** and discernment or spiritual perception. Knowledge, divorced from love, "puffs a person up with pride," whereas "love builds up" (1 Cor. 8:1). But if love is indispensable, **true knowledge and perfect judgment** are necessary. The truth of the gospel is liable to be subverted where ignorance and faulty judgment provide a foothold for the unsound teaching against which the Philippians are put on their guard in chapter 3.

1:10 / When so many competing forms of doctrine and ways of life are presented for acceptance (as they certainly were in the eastern Mediterranean world of the first century), true knowledge and perfect judgment will enable Christians **to choose what is best** (for the expression cf. Rom 2:18). This might mean "to know what is good or expedient" as against "empty subtleties and speculations" (Calvin, ad loc.) or (as the GNB rendering suggests) to discern "the best among the good" (Bengel, ad loc.). Both kinds of discrimination are necessary. Such discernment comes with mature experience. A classic NT text on this is Hebrews 5:14, with its reference to spiritually mature people "who through practice are able to distinguish between good and evil." Without this faculty of discrimination one could not develop "a sense of what is vital" (Moffatt). It is the effect, not of a logical process of moral philosophy, but of growing insight into the character and will of God.

It is important in view of **the Day of Christ**, the day of review and reward for his people (cf. v. 6), that they should **be free from all impurity and blame**. They cannot be so on that day unless they lead pure and blameless lives here and now. Choosing what is best therefore includes pre-eminently choosing what is ethically best. Similarly the prayer in 1 Thessalonians 5:23 that God may keep his people "free from every fault at the coming of our Lord Jesus Christ" involves his making them "holy in every way" at this present time.

1:11 / The **truly good qualities** that Paul desires to see reproduced in the Philippians' **lives** make up "the fruit (or 'harvest') of righteousness," as the phrase is literally rendered—essentially identical with those graces which, according to Galatians 5:22, 23, make up the "fruit (or 'harvest') of the Spirit." These **qualities** are the spontaneous product of the new life implanted within them, a life based on "the righteousness that is given through faith in Christ" (3:9). It is because of their union with him by faith that they will display those **qualities which only Jesus Christ can produce** and which were manifested perfectly in his own character and action. There is no room for self-congratulation here.

In such lives God will be glorified. The words **for the glory and praise of God** are part of the construction of the sentence, but at the same time they serve the purpose of a doxology concluding the period of thanksgiving and prayer.

Additional Notes

1:9 / On intercessory prayer in Paul's letters see G. P. Wiles, *Paul's Intercessory Prayers*.

I pray: Gk. *proseuchomai*, whereas in v. 4 the noun *deēsis* is used. The more general sense of prayer is expressed by *proseuchomai* (with the noun *proseuchē*); *deēsis* (with the verb *deomai*) denotes the petitionary element in prayer. See 4:6.

True knowledge renders Gk. *epignōsis* (a compound of *gnōsis*), used in NT only of moral and religious knowledge. The adjective **true** is probably intended to convey the force of the prefix *epi-*; "the compound *epignōsis* has become a technical term for the decisive knowledge of God which is implied in conversion to the Christian faith" (R. Bultmann, *TDNT* 1, p. 707, s.v. *ginōskō*, etc.).

Perfect judgment renders Gk. *aisthēsis* ("perception"), not found elsewhere in NT. Here it denotes moral insight; cf. *aisthētēria* ("sense organs") in Heb. 5:14 of the moral faculties trained "to distinguish between good and evil."

1:10 / **Free from all impurity** renders Gk. *eilikrinēs* ("unmixed" and therefore "pure"), here (as in 2 Pet. 3:1) in the moral sense (cf. the noun *eilikrineia* in 1 Cor. 5:8; 2 Cor. 1:12; 2:17). The adjective rendered **free from . . . blame** is *aproskopos*, which may have either an intransitive force ("not stumbling") or a transitive force ("not causing others to stumble"), the reference in the one as in the other being ethical. The force is probably intransitive here; in 1 Cor. 10:32 it is transitive (GNB: "cause no trouble"). The only other NT occurrence of the adjective is in Acts 24:16, where it is used of Paul's consistently "clear conscience" (GNB).

1:11 / For fruit or harvest used in an ethical sense cf. Prov. 11:30; Amos 6:12; Eph. 5:9; Heb. 12:11; James 3:18. Here the "fruit" or "harvest" of righteousness (Gk. *karpos dikaiosynēs*) might conceivably be the fruit which consists in righteousness (*dikaiosynēs* being construed as genitive of definition), but it is more in accord with the analogy of similar expressions and with Pauline thought to understand it as the fruit which springs from the gift of righteousness or justification that God by his grace bestows on believers. While the participle "filled" (Gk. *peplērōmenoi*) is commonly treated as passive, there is a good case for taking it in the middle voice, as in NEB: "reaping the full harvest of righteousness" (cf. G. B. Caird, ad loc.).

There is a curious variant at the end of v. 11, where instead of **for the glory and praise of God** the "western" codices F G (with Ambrosiaster) read "for glory and praise to me" and P[46] reads "for the glory of God and praise to me." The reading "to me" must be understood in the sense of 2:16 ("I shall have reason to be proud of you on the Day of Christ"); even so, it is out of place here, although J.-F. Collange (ad loc.) thinks it "surprising enough in character to be original" (he compares "praise" in a similar eschatological context in 1 Cor. 4:5).

5

Paul's Present Situation

I want you to know, my brothers, that the things that have happened to me have really helped the progress of the gospel. ¹³As a result, the whole palace guard and all the others here know that I am in prison because I am a servant of Christ. ¹⁴And my being in prison has given most of the brothers more confidence in the Lord, so that they grow bolder all the time to preach the message[a] fearlessly.

a. the message; *some manuscripts have* God's message.

The Christians of Philippi were deeply concerned about Paul. They cherished a warm affection for him; they knew that he was now in custody awaiting trial and that his case was due to come up for hearing soon before the supreme tribunal of the empire. How was he faring right now? And what would be the outcome of the hearing when once it took place? What, moreover, would be the effect of its outcome on **the progress of the gospel** throughout the Roman world?

Paul knows what is in their minds, and he proceeds to reassure them, to impart to them something of the confidence that fills his own heart as he contemplates the situation.

1:12 / That the apostle to the Gentiles should be in chains might well have been regarded as a blow to **the progress of the gospel** that he was commissioned to proclaim. But no: whatever might be Paul's own situation, the word of God was not in chains (cf. 2 Tim. 2:9). Indeed, Paul's presence in Rome as a prisoner awaiting trial had **really helped the progress of the gospel**. He was a distinguished prisoner, a Roman citizen exercising his prerogative to have his case heard by the emperor, and he made sure that everyone who came in touch with him knew that it was on account of the gospel that he was under house arrest, and not because of subversive political activity or criminal conduct.

1:13 / The **whole palace guard**, he says, **and all the others** who have anything to do with my case **know that** it is "in Christ" that I have been taken into custody. Here we have a further instance of the "incorporative" use of the phrase "in Christ" that was considered briefly in the exposition of verse 1. It is not simply that Paul's imprisonment is due to his being **a servant of Christ** (GNB); that is true, but in his eyes it is part of his life in Christ, to whom he is united by faith; it is, especially, part of his sharing in the sufferings of Christ (cf. 3:10). Of course, the members of the **guard** and **the others** to whom he refers would not see it from his point of view, but they could not fail to realize that it was Paul's being a Christian that had landed him where he now was.

The **palace guard** is, literally, the "praetorium," that is, the praetorian guard, the emperor's bodyguard. The word "praetorium" has a variety of meanings according to the context (cf. Mark 15:16 par. Matt. 27:27 and John 18:28 ff. for the praetorium in Jerusalem; Acts 23:35 for the praetorium in Caesarea), but as has been argued in the Introduction, its most probable meaning here is the praetorian guard in Rome. Having made his appeal to the emperor, Paul was the emperor's prisoner (although he preferred to think of himself as "the prisoner of Christ Jesus"), and while he waited for his case to be heard, he "was allowed to live by himself with a soldier guarding him" (Acts 28:16). It was natural that the soldier (relieved by a comrade every four hours or so) should be a member of the imperial bodyguard. News about this extraordinary prisoner would naturally spread through the praetorian barracks.

In addition to the soldiers, there were **others** who were interested in Paul—notably the officials charged with preparing his case for the hearing before the emperor. He claims no converts among either group, but he is filled with encouragement because in this way the gospel had become a topic of conversation in the capital, at the heart of the empire.

1:14 / Not only that, but all this gave fresh encouragement to the Christians of Rome. When Paul arrived in their city as a prisoner for the gospel's sake, some of them perhaps wondered how safe it would be for them to be known as those who professed the same faith as he did. According to Luke, the leaders of the Jewish community in Rome judged it best to know nothing about Paul or his case (Acts 28:21). But when the gospel became a talking point because of Paul's presence in Rome, the Christians exploited the situation and began to bear their public witness with greater confidence and vigor. When Paul says that this is true of **most of the brothers**, he does not mean that there was a minority that refused to seize this opportunity for evangelization; he means that so many did so that their action characterized the Roman church as a whole. Nothing could have given Paul greater delight.

Additional Notes

1:12 / **I want you to know** is called a "disclosure formula" by J. L. White, *The Form and Function of the Body of the Greek Letter*, pp. 2–5, etc.; he adduces many examples of the use of such a formula to mark the transition from introductory thanksgiving to the body of the letter. Cf. also J. T. Sanders, "The Transition from Opening Epistolary Thanksgiving to Body in Letters of the Pauline Corpus," *JBL* 81 (1962), pp. 348–62. Paul commonly words the formula negatively: "I do not wish you to be ignorant" (Rom. 1:13, etc., where GNB obscures the negative construction).

1:14 / The phrase **in the Lord**, which GNB construes with **more confidence** (so J. B. Lightfoot, ad loc.), is to be taken rather with **the brothers**, "the brothers in the Lord" being "Christian brothers" (cf. C. F. D. Moule, *IBNTG*, p. 108). There may be a slightly different nuance of meaning between **in the Lord** and "in Christ"; "one becomes in the Lord what one already is in Christ" (M. Bouttier, *En Christ*, pp. 54–61; cf. C. F. D. Moule, *The Origin of Christology*, p. 59: "what you are is 'in Christ,' and what you are to become is 'in the Lord' ").

Preach the message: although the added genitive "of God" is absent from P^{46} and the majority of later witnesses, its attestation is impressively strong.

6

Various Motives for Gospel Witness

PHILIPPIANS 1:15–17

Of course some of them preach Christ because they are jealous and quarrelsome, but others from genuine good will. [16]These do so from love, because they know that God has given me the work of defending the gospel. [17]The others do not proclaim Christ sincerely, but from a spirit of selfish ambition; they think that they will make more trouble for me while I am in prison.

This paragraph is described by Dibelius (ad loc.) as an "excursus"; Paul adds, in passing, to what he has just said that not all of those who have seized the opportunity for gospel witness were moved by equally worthy sentiments. But at least the opportunity has been seized and that is cause for satisfaction.

1:15 / Not all the Roman Christians who were preaching the gospel so energetically were animated by a spirit of fellowship with Paul. The house-churches of the city represented a wide variety of Christian outlook. There were Jewish Christians and Gentile Christians. There were some (in both categories) who were in entire sympathy with Paul and his policy; there were some who shared the suspicion with which he was viewed by his Judaizing opponents in other places; there were some of a Gnosticizing tendency who reckoned Paul's understanding of the gospel to be curiously immature and unenlightened. There were others, no doubt, who were not sure where they ought to stand in relation to him. Here, however, Paul seems to have in mind people who preach what he recognizes as the genuine gospel, whatever their motives may be.

Why should some preach the gospel in a **jealous and quarrelsome** spirit? Perhaps they were envious of Paul's achievement in carrying the message through so many provinces in such a brief space of time and thought that they could at last gain a march on him now that he was confined. Perhaps they regarded themselves as followers of some other leader, to whom (in their eyes) Paul was a rival; now that Paul was no longer free to move around, their own leader's cause could make better progress. Was there already a "Cephas" party in Rome as there had been some years earlier in Corinth (1 Cor. 1:12)?

Those, on the other hand, who preached **from genuine good will** were glad to think, as they did so, that they were sharing in Paul's ministry; in them Paul welcomed the same spirit of partnership as he praised in the Philippian Christians.

1:16 / Paul amplifies his references to the two kinds of preachers, and does so in the form of a chiasmus.* He enlarges first (in v. 16) on those who preached **from genuine good will** (who were mentioned last in v. 15) and then (in v. 17) on those who preached in a **jealous and quarrelsome** spirit (who were mentioned first in v. 15). The former were actuated by **love** for Paul. They recognized that God had sent him to Rome for this very purpose—**the work of defending the gospel**. As in verse 7, his impending opportunity to defend the gospel before Caesar's tribunal is probably in his mind: it is for this, he says, that I am posted here in Rome. If Paul, despite his restrictions, was promoting the interests of the gospel, those people of **good will** could do no less: they must play their part along with him.

1:17 / But what of those whose preaching sprang from no sincere motives **but from a spirit of selfish ambition**? They were evidently jealous of Paul's record and prestige as a preacher of the gospel. Anything he could do they could do better; they would let it be seen that they came behind him in no respect. The news of what they were doing, they thought (and hoped), would fill Paul with chagrin and frustration. It was galling enough for Paul to be deprived of his liberty: it would be more galling still for him to learn how those who did not wish him well were forging ahead with their presentation of the gospel.

If we find it difficult to credit that followers of Christ could actually find satisfaction in thus rubbing salt into Paul's wounds, it may be because we fail to realize how controversial a figure Paul was, even within the Christian fellowship, and how deep and bitter was the opposition maintained by some to his gospel interpretation and missionary policy.

But if they thought Paul would be annoyed or resentful, they mistook

---

*Chiasmus is a figure of speech by which parallel terms in adjacent clauses or sentences are placed in reverse order (e.g., "he created them male and female/male and female created he them").

their man. If they were more successful than he in propagating the gospel, that was all to the good in Paul's eyes. His pre-eminent concern was that the saving message might "continue to spread widely and be received with honor" (2 Thess. 3:1). He could treat unfriendly attitudes with relaxed indifference: what did it matter, so long as Christ was being preached?

Additional Notes

1:15 / W. Schmithals presents the extraordinary argument that only if the references are to groups *in Philippi* "are the remarks in vv. 15–17 significant and pertinent, for as a reference to the place where Paul is imprisoned they must have been just as puzzling to the Philippians as they are for us" (*Paul and the Gnostics*, p. 75). Paul is here giving the Philippians information about his own affairs that they did not possess, and he implies throughout the letter that the Philippian church as a whole supported him in his missionary enterprise.

T. W. Manson suggested that the reference here was to the partisanship in the church of Corinth, which Paul, he believed, had recently left and with which he was currently engaged in correspondence (*Studies in the Gospels and Epistles*, pp. 161 f.). T. Hawthorn has argued that the distinction is between those who preach in a spirit of apocalyptic antagonism to the state and those who in their preaching manifest the same attitude of good will as Paul does in Rom. 13:1–7; the former would certainly **make more trouble** for Paul ("Philippians i. 12–19 with special reference to *vv.* 15. 16. 17," *ExpT* 62 [1950–51], pp. 316 f.)

1:16 / The chiasmus is obliterated by the majority of later manuscripts, which (together with D¹ and *Psi*) transpose vv. 16 and 17 (cf. KJV).

1:17 / **Not . . . sincerely** (Gk. *ouch hagnōs*) is construed by J.-F. Collange (ad loc.) with **they think** (*oiomenoi*): "their judgment is not pure . . . , i.e., is not free from ulterior motives." This paraphrase of *ouch hagnōs* is good, but it goes better with **proclaim Christ** (cf. NEB: "the others . . . present Christ from mixed motives").

From a spirit of selfish ambition (Gk. *ex eritheias*, in antithesis to *ex agapēs*, from love, in v. 16). For *eritheia*, cf. 2:3. The word originally meant doing something for hire or wages, but came to denote a mercenary attitude, and in the NT is always used in a bad sense, of party spirit and the contention to which it leads. R. Jewett links the people referred to here with those described in 2:21 as concerned only with their own affairs; he thinks they were missionaries who held up the "divine man" (*theios anēr*) as an ideal and felt that the humiliating spectacle of Paul in prison gave the lie to this ideal and endangered their mission ("Conflicting Movements in the Early Church as Reflected in Philippians," *NovT* 12 [1970], pp. 362–90).

The free rendering **make more trouble for me while I am in prison** conceals a variation in reading: "thinking to *stir up* (Gk. *egeirein*, read by the principal Alexandrian and 'western' witnesses) affliction in my imprisonment" (lit. "to my chains") or "thinking to *add* (*epipherein*, read by the majority of later manuscripts with D² and *Psi*) affliction to my imprisonment." The former is preferable.

7

Life or Death?

PHILIPPIANS 1:18–26

It does not matter! I am happy about it—just so Christ is preached in every way possible, whether from wrong or right motives. And I will continue to be happy, [19]because I know that by means of your prayers and the help which comes from the Spirit of Jesus Christ I shall be set free. [20]My deep desire and hope is that I shall never fail in my duty, but that at all times, and especially right now, I shall be full of courage, so that with my whole being I shall bring honor to Christ, whether I live or die. [21]For what is life? To me, it is Christ. Death, then, will bring more. [22]But if by continuing to live I can do more worthwhile work, then I am not sure which I should choose. [23]I am pulled in two directions. I want very much to leave this life and be with Christ, which is a far better thing; [24]but for your sake it is much more important that I remain alive. [25]I am sure of this, and so I know that I will stay. I will stay on with you all, to add to your progress and joy in the faith, [26]so that when I am with you again, you will have even more reason to be proud of me in your life in union with Christ Jesus.

P aul contemplates death or acquittal as the outcome of his impending trial with equal equanimity. His own preference would be to depart this life and be with Christ, but he knows that it is more important for his friends' sake that he should be spared to be with them a little longer.

1:18 / Paul's reaction to those who are stirring up trouble for him is far removed from the anathema invoked on those agitators who, several years earlier, invaded the churches of Galatia and taught his converts a "different gospel" from that which they had heard from him. True, his ill wishers in Rome were not intruding into a sphere of missionary service that was not their own, and there is no hint of any defect or subversive element in what they preached. Whatever their motives were—whether (on the one hand) their activity was a cloak for ambitions of their own or a cover for diminishing Paul's standing or (on the other hand) it was the outcome of a pure desire to spread the saving message—the important point was that Christ was being preached. This acknowledgment on Paul's part sets the preachers in a different category from the type that (as he puts it elsewhere) "preaches a different Jesus, not the one we preached" (2 Cor. 11:4). Even so, Paul has mellowed; he shows more of the "gentleness and kindness of Christ" than he had been able to show when he invoked these graces in his remonstrance with disaffected members of the Corinthian church (2 Cor. 10:1). Perhaps his two years of imprisonment in Caesarea, followed by a further spell under house arrest in Rome, had taught him new lessons in patience.

There is a striking similarity between Paul's attitude here and Luther's often-quoted words from the preface to the Letter of James in his German New Testament of 1522: "That which does not teach Christ is not apostolic, even if Peter or Paul taught it. Again, that which does preach Christ is apostolic, even if Judas, Annas, Pilate or Herod did it." What matters is the content of the preaching, not the identity of the preacher.

Paul rejoices, then, and will go on rejoicing, not only in the fact that Christ is being preached more and more, but in all his circumstances and prospects.

1:19 / Paul sees the hand of God so manifestly at work in the situation which he has just described that he is left in no doubt that he is in the place where God wishes him to be in the fulfillment of his apostolic commission. With such confidence, he can apply to his own present state the words of Job 13:16, "this will turn out for my salvation." The GNB rendering of Job's words, "It may even be that my boldness will save me," could be related to what Paul goes on to say in verse 20 about his being **full of courage**. When he says that the present state of affairs will work out for his salvation, he is not thinking so much of immediate acquittal and discharge from custody—as might be suggested by GNB's **I shall be set free**—but (like Job) of his vindication in the heavenly court, his final salvation. This is assured whether he receives a favorable or an unfavorable verdict before Caesar's tribunal (cf. the confidence expressed in 2 Tim. 4:8 in the award of "the Lord, the righteous Judge").

It is plain, indeed, from the words that follow that his "ultimate destiny is intimately connected with his present dilemma" (R. W. Funk, in Farmer et al., eds., p. 262). He is sure that their spiritual welfare requires his survival in mortal body; he knows that he will remain on earth in order to continue his fruitful work. The **prayers** of his Philippian friends will contribute to this, together with **the help which comes from the Spirit of Jesus Christ**. But this is an expression of confidence, not the assertion of something which he has received by divine revelation or the like. He has in fact been given no revelation about the outcome of his trial.

1:20 / Paul's **deep desire and hope** is not for his own safety but for the progress of the gospel, the perseverance of his converts, and the accomplishment of God's redeeming purpose. This is one of the two Pauline occurrences of the noun (Gk. *apokaradokia*) here rendered **deep desire**; in Romans 8:19 it is used for the "eager longing" with which all creation waits "for God to reveal his sons." In that context it is coupled with repeated mentions of the realization of the *hope* of the ages, "that creation itself would one day be set free from its slavery to decay and would share the glorious freedom of the children of God" (Rom. 8:21). Paul's own **deep desire and hope** are caught up into the prospect of that consummation; indeed, Paul knows that his ministry has a special part to play in speeding its arrival. Therefore he hopes and prays **that I shall never fail in my duty**—literally, "that I shall be put to shame in nothing." Christian hope and being put to shame are mutually exclusive (cf. Rom. 5:5). The only thing that could put Paul to shame would be failure to win his Lord's approval; that is why he kept "the Day of Christ" before him in all that he planned and did. The declaration of the gospel is the **duty** entrusted to him; he is eager to be faithful to that trust and do nothing unworthy of it, especially when he stands before Caesar. Personal humiliation is not what Paul fears; he had endured plenty of that already in the service of Christ and was likely to endure more. But he knows that he will not be **put to shame** if **honor** is brought **to Christ** through him, and especially through his demeanor and defense of the gospel in the supreme court.

What he needs is complete **courage** to "speak boldly" (as the word is rendered with reference to the same occasion in Eph. 6:19, GNB). To proclaim the gospel courageously is the antithesis of being ashamed of it (cf. Rom. 1:16). Paul's constant ambition is that in his **whole being**, more especially in his body—that is, in whatever happens to him on the physical plane, whether life or death—the glory of Christ will be promoted. Should it be for the advancement of Christ's cause that Paul is sentenced to death and executed, then welcome death! But if it is for the advancement of Christ's cause that Paul should be acquitted and granted a further lease of mortal life, then welcome life!

1:21 / He views either prospect with equanimity. Indeed, if he had nothing but his personal choice to consider, the prospect of **death** might be preferable: **death** could be nothing but sheer gain to anyone for whom **life**

meant **Christ**. The GNB rendering, **Death, then, will bring more**, prompts the question: "More of what?" The answer could only be, "More of Christ." Paul's existence was life in Christ, with Christ living in him (cf. Gal. 2:20); death would bring no cessation or diminution of that existence but would rather enhance it with the experience of being **with Christ** (v. 23) in a closer communion than he had known while still in the body. If **life** means **Christ**, it must be exhilaratingly wonderful to be alive; "yet even for such a life, precisely for such a life, **to die is gain**" (F. W. Beare, ad loc.). If death meant (even temporarily) less of Christ than was enjoyed in mortal life—above all, if it meant (even temporary) annihilation—it would be absurd to speak of it as "gain."

Paul no doubt meant that for the man or woman in Christ to die would be gain, whatever form death took. But the death that he has specially in mind for himself in the present situation is execution in consequence of an adverse judgment in the imperial court. If such a death in the service of Christ crowned a life spent in the service of Christ, it would be gain not to Paul alone but to the cause of Christ throughout the world.

1:22 / A continuation of mortal life would mean **more worthwhile work** for him to do, or it might mean an opportunity to reap more fruit from the work that had been interrupted by his arrest and imprisonment, as well as from the work that he had been doing during his imprisonment. A literal rendering of his words would be, "But if [the outcome for me will be] to live in the flesh, this is the fruit of labor for me," and this could be understood more ways than one. It could point to fruitful labor in the future (as GNB takes it) or to the fruit of labor already done (as NEB takes it, following J. B. Lightfoot: "what if my living on in the body means that I could reap the fruit of my toil!").

So, early death and continued life alike had their attractions, and if the choice between the two were left to him, he would find difficulty in making up his mind. The choice, however, did not lie with him.

1:23 / **I am pulled in two directions**, he says; more literally, "I am hemmed in on both sides." If he had only his own interest to consider, then it would be **a far better thing** for him **to leave this life and be with Christ**; and this was his personal desire.

Paul speaks in several of his letters of the resurrection of the believing dead at the time of Christ's advent (cf. 3:20, 21). He has less to say about the state of the individual believer immediately after death, but what he does say is quite plain. So far as can be judged from his correspondence, he did not grapple with this question until it began to become more probable, as he viewed the situation, that he would die before the advent of Christ than that he would live to witness it. He did not pretend to know when the advent would take place, but a change of perspective can be traced as he grew older: whereas in his earlier letters he tends to identify himself with those who will survive to the coming of the Lord, in his later letters he tends to identify himself with those who will be raised from the dead then.

The change of perspective can be discerned between 1 and 2 Corinthians: in 1 Corinthians 15:52 he says that "when the trumpet sounds, the dead will be raised, never to die again, and we [the living] shall all be changed"; but in 2 Corinthians 4:14 he says that "God, who raised the Lord Jesus to life, will also raise us up with Jesus and take us, together with you [the living], into his presence." This shift in his viewpoint may have been due in part to the critical experience in the province of Asia that he describes in 2 Corinthians 1:8–10. At that time death seemed to be so certain that no way out could be seen, and when a way out was opened up, contrary to all expectation, he greeted the deliverance as an instance of God's power to raise the dead.

It is against that background that he declares his conviction in 2 Corinthians 5:1–10 that "when this tent we live in—our body here on earth—is torn down, God will have a house in heaven for us to live in, a home he himself has made, which will last forever." With this confidence, he says, we "would much prefer to leave our home in the body and be at home with the Lord." He claims no revelation as authority for this assurance, as in 1 Thessalonians 4:15 with regard to the resurrection or in 1 Corinthians 15:51 with regard to the bestowal of immortality on believers who are still alive; but he affirms his hope with a positiveness ("we know . . . we have . . .") that leaves no room for doubt.

It is the same hope that finds expression here. One who enjoys the presence of Christ in this life is not to be deprived of it when this life ends, for Christ is alive on the other side of death and because he lives on, his people live on. " 'To die' and 'to be with Christ' are therefore in large measure synonymous. Life with Christ after death is no problem for the apostle; it flows like a pure spring from the victory of Easter" (J.-F. Collange, ad loc.). No wonder, then, that Paul emphasizes how "much rather better" (piling up comparatives) it would be for him to take leave of earthly life.

1:24 / Paul, however, was the last man to put his own interests or preferences before the advantage of others. He enjoins on his readers consideration for the good of others in 2:4; the injunction would not have carried much weight if they had not known of the example that he himself set. He knew that it was "more necessary" for his converts, not least for those in Philippi, that he should continue to be available to them on earth—that he should **remain** "in the flesh" (Gk. *en tē sarki*)—that is, in mortal body.

1:25 / His knowledge that his survival would be for the benefit of his fellow Christians, and his confidence that God would do whatever was necessary for their growth in grace, combined to give him good hope that he would indeed be granted a further spell of life and apostolic activity, for their **progress and joy in the faith**. His **I know** here, as in verse 19, is the expression of faith (cf. 2 Cor. 5:1). This is more probable than that he had been given a special divine revelation to this effect (E. Lohmeyer) or had just received word of a favorable verdict in his case (W. Michaelis).

The Philippian Christians already exulted in their association with such a servant of Christ as Paul was: his release and continued ministry would give them greater cause for such exultation.

The much-debated question whether or not Paul was in fact released is perhaps, on balance, to be answered in the affirmative, but it has no bearing on the interpretation of Philippians.

1:26 / If Paul should be released and have an opportunity of seeing them again, they would **have even more reason** to "exult in Christ Jesus" on Paul's account. Paul, who rejoiced when he was able to boast about his converts (cf. 2:16; 1 Thess. 2:19; 2 Cor. 7:4; 9:2, 3), had no objection to their boasting about him (cf. 2 Cor. 1:14). Such boasting did not conflict with his resolve to boast in nothing but the cross of Christ (Gal. 6:14), for all his relations with his converts were founded on the gospel of Christ crucified, and such boasting was a genuine boasting **in union with Christ Jesus** (cf. Phil. 3:3).

The problem of relating Paul's hope expressed here of visiting his Philippian friends once more to his intention, declared in Romans 15:24, 29, of going on from Rome to Spain has been discussed in the Introduction.

Additional Notes

1:18 / **It does not matter!** renders the question *ti gar?* ("for what?"), which may mean either, "What does it matter? In either case Christ is being preached," or, "What are we to say? Only this, that Christ is being preached."

1:19 / The quotation from Job 13:16 is exact: *touto moi apobēsetai eis sōtērian.*

The help which comes from the Spirit of Jesus Christ is, lit., "the . . . supply (Gk. *epichorēgia*) of the Spirit of Jesus Christ." GNB takes "of the Spirit" (*pneumatos*) to be subjective genitive, "that which the Spirit of Jesus Christ supplies." It might, however, be objective genitive, the Spirit being that which is supplied, as in Gal. 3:5, "Does God give [*epichorēgōn*] you the Spirit . . . ?" Cf. NEB: "the Spirit of Jesus Christ is given me for support." If Paul, like Job, is looking forward to vindication in the heavenly court, then the Spirit "appears here in the Johannine role of advocate" (G. B. Caird, ad loc.). Cf. R. W. Funk, "The Apostolic 'Parousia': Form and Significance," in W. R. Farmer, C. F. D. Moule, and R. R. Niebuhr, eds., *Christian History and Interpretation*, p. 262, n. 1.

1:20 / The **courage** that Paul desires in its fullness is Gk. *parrhēsia,* "freedom of speech." W. C. van Unnik ("The Christian's Freedom of Speech in the New Testament," *BJRL* 44 [1961–62], pp. 475 f.) suggests the translation "in all openness" here, "because not the courage of the martyr, but Christ Himself will be revealed in all plainness." By making **Christ** the subject of the clause (not, as in GNB, **that . . . I shall bring honor to Christ**, but "that Christ shall be honored in my body"), Paul "brings out what is the real power of 'freedom of speech,' the fact that not only the gospel is simply proclaimed, but that the Lord of the gospel is revealed."

The phrase **with my whole being** is lit. "in my body" (Gk. *en tō sōmati mou*)—appropriately, since Paul was thinking of bodily death or life. "*Sōma* therefore does not signify the whole 'I' of Paul, but only that part of him more immediately affected by the outcome of his trial and through which he bears witness to the visible world around him" (R. H. Gundry, *"Sōma" in Biblical Theology: With Emphasis on Pauline Anthropology*, p. 37). Cf. 1 Cor. 6:20, "use your bodies for God's glory" (lit., "glorify God in your body"), where Paul is refuting the notion that bodily actions are ethically and religiously indifferent.

1:21 / On the Damascus road Christ replaced Torah as the center of Paul's life and thought; until then he might well have said, "**For what is life? To me, it is** Torah." He was now immediately and constantly aware that his own life was summed up in Christ, but he uses language similar to that of his fellow Christians: "Your real life is Christ" (Col. 3:4).

1:22 / **But if** (Gk. *ei de*) may introduce the protasis* of a conditional sentence, and so it is taken by GNB, RSV, and probably the majority of versions. In that case the apodosis* may be **then I am not sure which I should choose** (so GNB) or "that means fruitful labor for me" (so RSV, with "Yet which I shall choose I cannot tell" as an independent clause). On the other hand, *ei de* might be rendered not **but if** but "but what if" (so NEB: "but what if my living on in the body

---

*In a conditional sentence the "if" clause is called the protasis and the principal clause is called the apodosis. For example, "If he goes (protasis), he will come back (apodosis)."

may serve some good purpose?"). J. B. Lightfoot (ad loc.) proposes this last construction because "it seems to be in keeping with the abruptness of the context, and to present less difficulty than those generally adopted."

More worthwhile work renders Gk. *karpos ergou*, "fruit [harvest] of work" (cf. "fruit of righteousness" in v. 11). Here the reference is to the result (especially in the lives of his converts and other fellow believers) of Paul's ministry already accomplished or yet to be accomplished.

I am not sure renders Gk. *ou gnōrizō*. In Paul (and other NT writers) this verb is used transitively ("make known") and not intransitively ("know"); it is best to take the present occurrence as being no exception to this rule and translate, with RSV and NEB, "I cannot tell" (meaning "I cannot make known").

1:23 / The only other place where Paul uses *synechō* ("hold together," "hem in") is in 2 Cor. 5:14, "the love of Christ shuts us up (*synechei hēmas*) to this conclusion" (GNB: "we are ruled by the love of Christ").

I want very much: lit., "having the desire (*epithymia*)." J.-F. Collange (ad loc.) argues that as *epithymia* has a bad sense almost everywhere else in Paul it should be so understood here also, of a "self-centered desire," which Paul mentions only to condemn it. But the context alone can determine whether the sense of *epithymia* is bad or good, and it is as likely to have its good sense here as in 1 Thess. 2:17, where it denotes the great longing of Paul and his companions to see the Thessalonian Christians again.

To leave this life: Gk. *analysai*, of a ship weighing anchor or an army striking camp.

And be with Christ, immediately on dying, he implies. Against this O. Cullmann denies that the NT countenances "the view that the dead live even before the *parousia* beyond time, and thus at once enjoy the fruits of the final fulfilment" (*The Early Church*, p. 165). It may well be that those believers who, having died, are with Christ, still await the resurrection, as he emphasizes (cf. 3:21); but he does insufficient justice to Paul's bridging of the hiatus between death and resurrection in 2 Cor. 5:1-10. See A. Schweitzer, *The Mysticism of Paul the Apostle*, pp. 90-100, 109-13; L. S. Thornton, *Christ and the Church*, pp. 137-40; F. F. Bruce, *Paul: Apostle of the Free Spirit*, pp. 309-13.

Which is a far better thing: There is a world of difference between Paul's attitude and Jonah's petulant "I am better off dead than alive" (Jonah 4:3, 8). G. M. Lee ("Philippians I 22-3," *NovT* 12 [1970], p. 361) compares the observation of Libanius (*Oration* 17.29) that, in certain cases of soul sickness "it is better to depart (this life) than to live" (*kreitton apelthein ē zēn*), but apart from the comparative *kreitton* (cf. Paul's *pollō mallon kreisson*) the two passages have nothing in common. J. B. Lightfoot (ad loc.) refers to the frequently quoted question of Euripides (fragment 639), *tis oiden ei to zēn men esti katthanein / to katthanein de zēn* ("Who knows if life be death and death be life?") and remarks that the poet's "sublime guess . . . , which was greeted with ignoble ridicule by the comic poets, has become an assured truth in Christ"—but the connection, if any, is a very distant one.

1:24 / **That I remain alive**: lit., "remain in the flesh" (*epimenein [en] tē sarki*, where the article may hark back to *en sarki* in v. 22, "to live in the flesh" [GNB: **by continuing to live**]). For Paul to remain or to live *en tē sarki*, in mortal body, is a very different thing from living *kata sarka*, "according to the flesh"; he contrasts the two phrases in 2 Cor. 10:3. To live or act *kata sarka* is to live or act according to the standards of unregenerate humanity. J. B. Lightfoot (ad loc.), accepting the omission of *en* (with Aleph A C, etc.), suggests the translation "to abide *by* the flesh," that is, "to cling to this present life, to take it with all its inconveniences." This is somewhat strained.

1:25 / **I will stay. I will stay on**: Gk. *menō kai paramenō*, where *menō* is absolute, while *paramenō* is relative to **you all**, the dative *pasin hymin* being governed by the prefix *para*.

Your progress and joy in the faith: the phrase **in the faith** (Gk. genitive *tēs pisteōs*) qualifies both **progress** and **joy**. **Joy** (whether the noun *chara* or the verb *chairein*) is a dominant theme in this letter—the Philippians' joy (as here; cf. 2:28, 29; 3:1; 4:4), Paul's joy (cf. verses 4, 18; 2:2; 4:1, 10), and theirs and his together (cf. 2:17, 18).

1:26 / **. . . when I am with you again**: the noun *parousia* is used here in the nontechnical sense of "visit" (as in 2:12; cf. also 1 Cor. 16:17; 2 Cor. 7:6, 7; 10:10). It is not used in this letter with reference to the advent of Christ; in fact, the only Pauline letters where it is so used are 1 Corinthians (15:23), 1 Thessalonians (2:19; 3:13; 4:15; 5:23) and 2 Thessalonians (2:1, 8).

In your life in union with Christ Jesus: lit., "in Christ Jesus" (*en Christō Iēsou*). Paul was included in this union together with them; therefore, if the expression is to be amplified as in GNB, "in *our* life . . ." would be preferable.

8

Steadfastness amid Suffering

Now, the important thing is that your way of life should be as the gospel of Christ requires, so that, whether or not I am able to go and see you, I will hear that you are standing firm with one common purpose and that with only one desire you are fighting together for the faith of the gospel. ²⁸Don't be afraid of your enemies; always be courageous, and this will prove to them that they will lose and that you will win, because it is God who gives you the victory. ²⁹For you have been given the privilege of serving Christ, not only by believing in him, but also by suffering for him. ³⁰Now you can take part with me in the battle. It is the same battle you saw me fighting in the past, and as you hear, the one I am fighting still.

I t is taken for granted throughout the NT, and nowhere more so than in Paul's letters, that suffering is inevitably incurred by Christian existence in the present world. There was nothing surprising in this: Christ had suffered, and his followers—those who were "in Christ"— could expect nothing else. Paul himself, throughout his career as an apostle, knew what it meant to suffer for Christ's sake, and he prepared his converts for similar suffering. Indeed, he encouraged them with the assurance that suffering for Christ's sake proved the genuineness of their faith.

1:27 / Meanwhile, Paul's earnest desire for the Philippian Christians, as for his other converts, is that their **way of life should** continue to **be as the gospel of Christ requires**. Since their new existence was based on **the gospel of Christ**, their **way of life** should be in line with Christ's (cf. 2:5). Paul uses a verb here that strictly means "live as citizens" and is closely related to what he says later about their status as "citizens of heaven" (3:20).

A life such **as the gospel** . . . **requires** should be a life of harmony. Since they shared a common life in Christ, they should be moved by **one common purpose** and **one desire**. Only so could they effectively commend the gospel by word and action. Their witness called for strenuous endeavor and united effort; they had to contend side by side **for the faith of the gospel**. They themselves had believed the gospel, and the aim of their witness was to bring others to the same belief. In the pursuit of this aim they had to reckon with powerful and unremitting opposition; hence the call for strenuous action.

Paul would welcome the opportunity of paying them a visit and seeing them in action—and sharing in their action too. But if a visit were excluded, then he hoped to **hear** good news of their standing firm together against all opposition and bearing a united witness. It does not sound as if he expected to be executed within the next few weeks: he was prepared for the possibility of execution but expresses himself as one who expected to be around for some time yet.

1:28 / The opposition that they had to face came most probably from outside their community. It has been argued indeed by one or two scholars that Paul refers to "opponents who have made their way into the church and had some influence there" (Marxsen, *Introduction*, p. 62). J.-F. Collange (ad loc.) thinks "more precisely of itinerant Jewish-Christian preachers whom Paul takes to task more violently in 3:2 ff." But the present context (especially vv. 29 and 30) would indicate rather that the Philippian Christians were now facing the same kind of opposition that Paul himself faced when he was among them—opposition from their pagan neighbors, and not least from the authorities.

The presence of opposition, Paul assures them, shows that they are on the right path in their active gospel witness. It is a token of salvation to them, as it is a token of perdition for their opponents: **they will lose and . . . you will win**. God is the author of the gospel: those who defend it may therefore expect deliverance and victory from him as surely as those who resist it may expect to incur his judgment. Much the same thought finds fuller expression in 2 Thessalonians 1:5-10.

Don't be afraid of your enemies, says Paul (using a verb that is specially applied to the shying of a scared horse); face them with united steadfastness, and **this will prove to them** that they are in the wrong and can make no headway against you. Paul himself had been a persecutor once and could recall the steadfastness of those whom he attacked. If at the time it had seemed to him to be obstinacy rather than steadfastness, yet after his conversion he could look back and appreciate it for what it really was—evidence of the power of Christ enabling them to maintain their faith unimpaired and evidence that he himself was, albeit in all good conscience, fighting a losing battle against God.

1:29 / They had come to believe in Christ through hearing the gospel, and for that they might well be grateful to God. Did they realize that they might well be grateful to him also for granting them the opportunity of **suffering** for Christ? Did they regard such **suffering** as a **privilege**, a special favor for which God was to be thanked? That was how Paul viewed his own sufferings in the service of Christ. The risen Lord said concerning him to Ananias of Damascus, "I myself will show him all that he must suffer for my sake" (Acts 9:16), and Paul experienced the fulfillment of this prediction. But he embraced his sufferings as his share in the sufferings of Christ (Phil. 3:10); his desire indeed was that his share might be greater so that the share of his fellow believers might be less (2 Cor. 1:3–7; Col. 1:24). Nor was Paul the only one in the apostolic age to regard suffering for Christ's sake as a **privilege**; it is recorded that the original apostles, after being beaten by sentence of the Sanhedrin, "were happy, because God had considered them worthy to suffer disgrace for the sake of Jesus" (Acts 5:41). If the Philippians could view their own sufferings in this light, their joy would be the greater.

1:30 / The encouragement that Paul gave his friends was the more acceptable because it did not come from one who had no personal experience of suffering for Christ's sake. In the catalogue of apostolic hardships that he draws up in 2 Corinthians 11:23–27, he mentions that once he was "beaten with rods"—"whipped by the Romans," as the phrase is paraphrased in GNB (2 Cor. 11:25). That particular experience came his way in Philippi (Acts 16:22, 23), and his friends in Philippi could remember it well. That is how he can remind them of the **battle you saw me fighting in the past**. Christian life to him was a conflict, a conflict waged against spiritual enemies (Eph. 6:12), but waged with divine assistance. It is the same word (Gk. *agōn*) that he used at the end of his career when he spoke of himself as having "fought the good fight" (2 Tim. 4:7). You remember how I suffered imprisonment in your own city, Paul tells them in effect; I am now suffering imprisonment in the city where I am, and in Rome, as then in Philippi, I am a prisoner for Christ's sake. I am still fighting **the same battle**, as you see. And now, I hear, you are fighting it too; it is **the same battle** for you and for me. You are sharing in my ministry not only by your gospel witness but also by your endurance of affliction in the cause of the gospel.

We do not know what precise form was taken by the persecution to which the Philippian Christians were currently exposed. Paul had no need to enter into particulars that they knew only too well. What mattered was the spirit in which they accepted persecution.

Additional Notes

1:27 / **Your way of life**: Gk. *politeuesthe* (imperative), "live as citizens," then (more generally) "live as members of a community." The verb was one that would be readily understood by residents in a Roman colony. Polycarp uses it in writing to the Philippian church of his day (5:2): "if we live as citizens *[politeu-sōmetha]* in a manner worthy of him" (K. Lake translates: "if we are worthy citizens of his community"). It occurs in only one other place in NT—Acts 23:1 (in telling the Sanhedrin how he has "lived before God to this very day" Paul may have some regard to his life as a member of the people of Israel). Cf. the noun *politeuma* in 3:20, with exposition and note ad loc. See R. R. Brewer, "The Meaning of *politeuesthe* in Philippians 1:27," *JBL* 73 (1954), pp. 76–83.

As the gospel of Christ requires: lit., "worthily *[axiōs]* of the gospel of Christ." For the adverb *axiōs* with *politeuesthai* cf. Polycarp (*To the Philippians* 5:2) quoted in preceding note. It is used with *peripatein* ("conduct oneself") in Eph. 4:1 ("worthily of the calling with which you have been called"); Col. 1:10 ("worthily of the Lord"); 1 Thess. 2:12 ("worthily of God").

So that . . . I will hear: W. Schmithals (*Paul and the Gnostics*, p. 69) infers from this that Paul must have heard that all was not well in the Philippian church with regard to concord and worthy behavior and compares his "I hear" in 1 Cor. 11:18 (cf. 1 Cor. 1:11). But there is no comparison between *akouō* here (present subjunctive in a clause of purpose) and *akouō* in 1 Cor. 11:18 (present indicative). Paul had recently heard (from Epaphroditus) about the state of the Philippian church; but he had good reason to hope that what he would see for himself (if he could pay them a visit) or hear about them (at a distance) would fill him with satisfaction.

With one common purpose: lit., "in one spirit" (Gk. *en heni pneumati*). It is unlikely that the reference here is to the one Spirit of God (cf. 1 Cor. 12:13; Eph. 4:4), in view of the parallel phrase **with only one desire**, lit. "with one soul" (*mia psychē*). The verb **standing firm** is repeated (in the imperative) in 4:1, and **fighting together**, in 4:3 (where GNB gives it a weaker rendering than here). Paul likes to describe gospel witness in military and athletic terms.

For the faith of the gospel: Gk. *tē pistei tou euangeliou*, which J. B. Light-foot renders "in concert with the faith of the gospel," taking the dative as governed by the prefix *syn* in *synathlountes* (**fighting together**) and understanding **the faith** as objective, equivalent to "the teaching of the gospel"—an improbable interpretation. M. Dibelius takes the phrase to mean "the faith which is the gospel." More probably it is either the believing response to the gospel (*tou euangeliou* being then objective genitive) or the believing response which the gospel urges its hearers to make (*tou euangeliou* being subjective genitive)—there is no practical difference between these two.

1:28 / **Don't be afraid**: Gk. *mē ptyromenoi*. The verb occurs here only in the Greek Bible. It is found almost always in the passive and, apart from its use in reference to shying horses, means "let oneself be intimidated."

This will prove: lit., "which is a proof" (Gk. *hētis estin . . . endeixis*). For *endeixis* cf. Rom. 3:25, 26; 2 Cor. 8:24; but the closest parallel in sense to its present occurrence is *endeigma* in 2 Thess. 1:5 (where also the reference is to Christians' endurance of persecution as a proof of coming relief for them and of coming judgment for their persecutors). It is not immediately clear what is the antecedent of the relative pronoun *hētis* (which is attracted in gender and number to *endeixis*). GNB takes it to be the Philippians' courage; G. B. Caird (ad loc.) takes it to be "the unflinching unity of the church in the face of persecution." These two suggestions are not mutually exclusive; the Philippians' united and courageous refusal to be intimidated should convey its own message to their opponents.

Because it is God who gives you the victory: an expansion of the Greek *kai touto apo theou*, "and this from God." What is "this"? The proof (*endeixis*), says J. B. Lightfoot: "it is a direct indication from God." This is probably right (so also G. B. Caird).

1:29 / **You have been given the privilege**: Gk. *hymin echaristhē*, "it has been freely granted to you"—as an act of grace (*charis*). For another instance of the verb *charizesthai* see 2:9, of God's granting to Christ the name high over all.

Of serving Christ: lit., "for Christ's sake" (*to hyper Christou*, where the article *to* anticipates its two following occurrences before the infinitives *pisteuein*, "believe," and *paschein*, "suffer".

1:30 / **The same battle**: Gk. *ton auton agōna*. In 1 Thess. 2:2 Paul and his associates speak of their preaching the gospel at Thessalonica *en pollō agōni*, "in much conflict" (GNB: "much opposition"). See V. C. Pfitzner, *Paul and the Agon Motif: Traditional Athletic Imagery in the Pauline Literature*, *NovTSup* 16; also E. Güttgemanns, *Der leidende Apostel und sein Herr*.

9

Call for Mutual Consideration

Your life in Christ makes you strong, and his love comforts you. You have fellowship with the Spirit,[b] and you have kindness and compassion for one another. [2] I urge you, then, to make me completely happy by having the same thoughts, sharing the same love, and being one in soul and mind. [3] Don't do anything from selfish ambition or from a cheap desire to boast, but be humble toward one another, always considering others better than yourselves. [4] And look out for one another's interests, not just for your own. [5] The attitude you should have is the one that Christ Jesus had:

b. You have fellowship with the Spirit; *or* The Spirit has brought you into fellowship with one another.

P aul's concern for unity of mind and mutual consideration among the members of the Philippian church need not imply that there was an atmosphere of dissension there. The fact that two members are singled out by name and urged to agree in 4:2 could suggest (unless 4:2 belongs to an originally separate letter) that theirs was an exceptional case of conflict. We do not know what Epaphroditus had told Paul about the state of the church, but at this time Paul found sufficient evidence of quarrelsomeness and selfish ambition in some sectors of the Roman church to make him anxious that nothing of the sort should manifest itself at Philippi.

2:1 / Unity of mind is not easily cultivated when human beings of disparate backgrounds and temperaments find themselves sharing one another's company, but the resources that make such unity possible are available to the people of Christ in their fellowship with him. In his **love** there is **comfort** that more than compensates for the troubles inseparable from Christian existence in this world. From his risen life they draw encouragement and strength, for they participate in it. They have received the **Spirit** of Christ, binding them together in a **fellowship** of love; he dwells within them both as individuals and as a company of believers and through him "God has poured out his love" into their hearts (Rom. 5:5). It is the Spirit who maintains their common life in the body of Christ. The effect of this common life should be kind and compassionate hearts, but this **kindness and compassion** are first of all Christ's own. They have experienced his **kindness and compassion** and can therefore the more readily show the same qualities to **one another**.

All the conditions, in short, exist within the believing community to foster a sense of oneness and a common purpose, not only with one another, but between them and Paul. He and they are bound together in the loving fellowship of the Spirit.

2:2 / There was already sufficient evidence of oneness of purpose and mutual affection in the Philippian church to give Paul cause for joy. He has already said that his prayers for the Philippian Christians are joyful prayers (1:4). Now, he says, fill my cup of joy to the brim; **make me completely happy**. Let me hear that you share **the same disposition** and **the same love**, that you are united **in soul and mind**. He is pleading, indeed, for unanimity of heart. This is not the formal unanimity that can be maintained only by the exercise of the veto; it is that sincere unanimity of purpose in which no one would wish to impose a veto on others.

This is not a matter of making everyone see eye-to-eye or have the same opinion on every subject. Life would be very flat and dull without the give-and-take practiced when variety of opinion and viewpoint provides scope for friendly discussion and debate.

2:3 / But discussion and debate cease to be friendly when each one aims at scoring points off the others and getting his or her own way. There must be no encouragement of the spirit of "Diotrephes, who likes to put himself first" (3 John 9, RSV). **Don't do anything from selfish ambition**, says Paul; forget all thoughts of personal prestige. Concern for personal prestige and **a cheap desire to boast** spring from the root sin of pride. Pride should have no place in Christian life; what characterizes the Christian is the opposite quality of humility. Humility was not generally esteemed a virtue in pagan antiquity, in which the Greek word here translated **humble** bears the meaning "mean-spirited." The OT attitude is different: God "has no use for conceited people, but shows favor to those who are humble" (Prov. 3:34, quoted in James 4:6; 1 Pet. 5:5). Humility is specially appropriate to Christians, whose Master was, not self-consciously, but spontaneously, "gentle and humble in spirit" (Matt. 11:29). His first disciples found the lesson of humility a hard one to learn: repeatedly, when they fell to discussing which of them would be the greatest in the kingdom of God, Jesus insisted that among his followers true greatness consisted in being least of all, servant of all—"for even the Son of Man did not come to be served; he came to serve and to give his life to redeem many people" (Mark 10:45).

So, says Paul, **be humble toward one another, always considering others better than yourselves**. Rejoice in the honor paid to others rather than in that paid to yourself. The simplicity of Paul's language should not blind us to its difficulty. Those who really try to consider others better than themselves soon discover that this does not come naturally. It is too easy to introduce permissible exceptions to Paul's rule, if not as regards individuals, certainly as regards communities. There is a tendency, for example, to think one's own denomination better than others, to the point of imagining that God himself is better pleased with it than he is with others (and therefore, surely, better pleased with me for belonging to mine than he is with others for belonging to theirs). No such exceptions are permissible where true humility reigns. And, as the prophet Micah saw centuries before Paul, humility flourishes best in fellowship with God (Mic. 6:8). Or, as James Montgomery put it:

> The bird that soars on highest wing
>   Builds on the ground her lowly nest,
> And she that doth most sweetly sing
>   Sings in the night, when all things rest.
> In lark and nightingale we see
>   What honor hath humility.
>
> The saint, that wears heaven's brightest crown,
>   In lowliest adoration bends;
> The weight of glory bends him down
>   Then most, when most his soul ascends;
> Nearest the throne of God must be
>   The footstool of humility.

2:4 / To **look out for one another's interests** belongs to the foundation of Christian ethics. "Help carry one another's burdens," says Paul in another letter, "and in this way you will obey the law of Christ" (Gal. 6:2)—the law not only laid down by Christ but exemplified by Christ. Especially, as he says at greater length in Romans 15:1–3, "we who are strong in the faith ought to help the weak to carry their burdens. We should not please ourselves. Instead, we should all please our brothers for their own good, in order to build them up in the faith. For Christ did not please himself." The example of Christ is regularly Paul's supreme argument in ethical exhortation, not least in the matter of unselfish concern for the well-being of others. If Christ's example is to be followed, then it is better to be concerned about other people's rights and our own duties than about our own rights and other people's duties. When some members of the Corinthian church were so intent on defending their own rights that they had recourse to pagan judges to secure redress from their fellow Christians, Paul told them that it would be more in keeping with the way of Christ to suffer wrong without redress than to bring his name into such public disrepute (1 Cor. 6:7).

2:5 / Paul, then, urges them to have **the attitude . . . that Christ Jesus had**. This GNB rendering is probably right, but any rendering of these words involves a measure of interpretation. A rather literal translation of the sentence would be: "Think this among yourselves (Be thus minded among yourselves) which . . . also in Christ Jesus." The clause "which . . . also in Christ Jesus" lacks a verb, which has to be supplied. Further, the phrase "in Christ Jesus" may have its special Pauline sense ("in union with Christ Jesus" or "as members of Christ Jesus") or it may have its general sense, referring to something which was manifested in the person of Christ.

The GNB rendering takes "in Christ Jesus" in the latter way; so does KJV ("Let this mind be in you, which was also in Christ Jesus"). The special Pauline sense of "in Christ Jesus" was preferred by the NEB translators: "Let your bearing towards one another arise out of your life in Christ Jesus."

The words that follow, celebrating the self-emptying and self-humbling of Christ in becoming man and consenting to endure death by crucifixion, suggest strongly that his example in this regard is being recommended to his followers. Their communal life—their life "in Christ Jesus"—should be marked by those qualities that were seen in him personally; but the phrase "in Christ Jesus" in this context refers to what was seen "in him personally" rather than to their communal life (which is here expressed by the phrase "in you" or "among yourselves").

Additional Notes

2:1 / The four principal clauses in the GNB rendering of this verse are conditional clauses in the original, each being introduced by the conjunction *ei* ("if"); the apodosis to all four is the imperative clause **make me completely happy** in v. 2.

Your life in Christ makes you strong: lit., "if then there is any strengthen-

ing (Gk. *paraklēsis*) in Christ." GNB takes the phrase **in Christ** in its incorporative sense, of their common **life** as Christians. The phrase covers all four clauses
in this verse. It is **in Christ** that they have strength, **comfort**, the Spirit's **fellowship**, and mutual **kindness and compassion**. The conjunction *ei* ("if") implies
no doubt of the reality of these blessings, either in Paul's mind or in the Philippians' experience: it might be translated "As sure as . . . "

J.B. Lightfoot (ad loc.) thinks that *paraklēsis* here means "exhortation" and
paramythion (GNB: **comfort**) "incentive." This is too fine a distinction. The two
words are near-synonyms; when Paul uses the second (or its related verb *para-
mytheisthai*) it is regularly associated with the former (or with its related verb
parakalein), perhaps in order to emphasize the idea of encouragement. Cf. the
association of the two in 1 Cor. 14:3; 1 Thess. 2:12.

As for **fellowship with the Spirit**, the marginal alternative is better: "The
Spirit has brought you into fellowship with one another." Their fellowship with
one another, indeed, was the corollary of their fellowship with Christ. It is in one
Spirit that all believers in Christ have been baptized into one body (1 Cor. 12:13);
he who thus unites them to Christ unites them also one to another. It is for them
henceforth, by the cultivation of peace within their fellowship, "to preserve the
unity which the Spirit gives" (Eph. 4:3). God has called his people "to have
fellowship with his Son Jesus Christ" (1 Cor. 1:9), to participate in his risen life.
It is the Spirit who enables them to respond to this call and to enjoy this fellowship; it may therefore be called "the fellowship of the Holy Spirit" (2 Cor. 13:13)
or their joint participation in the Spirit. (See additional note on 1:5.)

The **kindness and compassion** that they have in Christ are felt **for one
another**; although the phrase **for one another** is added by GNB to complete the
sense, it expresses Paul's intention. J.-F. Collange (ad loc.) thinks the reference is
to the bonds of affection and sympathy between Paul and the Philippians. Paul
was very much aware of those bonds, but his present concern is more for the
maintenance of loving fellowship within the Philippian church. Behind **kindness** lies Gk. *splanchna* ("bowels"), translated "heart" in 1:8. Behind *compassion* lies *oiktirmoi*, plural of *oiktirmos* ("pity"). In Rom. 12:1 Paul appeals to his
readers by the *oiktirmoi* of God ("because of God's great mercy"); in 2 Cor. 1:3 he
calls God the Father of *oiktirmoi* ("the merciful Father"). The two nouns
splanchna and *oiktirmos* come together again in Col. 3:12, "clothe yourselves
with compassion" (lit., "put on bowels of compassion").

2:2 / **Having the same thoughts**, . . . **being one in** . . . **mind**: Gk. *hina to auto
phronēte*, . . . *to hen phronountes*, with repetition of the verb *phronein*, a verb
specially common in this letter (which accounts for ten out of its twenty-three
Pauline occurrences). It means "to think" in the sense of having a settled opinion
or attitude, having one's mind set in a particular way.

2:3 / **Be humble**: Gk. *en tapeinophrosynē*, "in humility," "in lowly-minded-
ness." A good first-century example of this word's currency to denote a vice, not a
virtue, comes in Josephus, *War* 4.494, where mention is made of the Emperor

Galba's "meanness" (*tapeinophrosynē*) in withholding from the praetorian guards a gift that had been promised them in his name.

2:4 / **Look out for one another's interests**: Paul may be making a more specific point, "advocating that his readers fix their gaze on the good points and qualities in other Christians; and, when recognized, these good points should be an incentive to our way of life" (R. P. Martin, ad loc.). Self-centered preoccupation with "one's own things" (*ta heautōn*) might be a mark of a "perfectionist" tendency. If indeed Paul is encouraging his friends to pay attention to the good qualities of others, this would be an appropriate preparation for his setting before them the supreme example of Christ. But equally Christ might be set before them as an example of one who placed the interests of others before his own. In the original text there is no noun to complete the sense of "one's own" (*ta heautōn*) and "those of others" (*ta heterōn*); hence KJV's "his own things" and "the things of others." What "things" Paul has in mind is a matter of interpretation. It is relevant to the interpretation that there is some (Western) evidence for the omission of "also" (*kai*) from the second part of the verse (rendered literally in KJV: "but every man also on the things of others"). If it be retained, the meaning is "look out for the interests (good points) of others as well as for your own"; if it be omitted, the meaning is "look out for the interests (good points) of others and not for your own."

2:5 / **The attitude you should have**: Gk. *touto phroneite en hymin*, "be thus minded in (among) yourselves." The interpretative problem in this verse lies partly in the supplying of a verb for the adjective clause *ho kai en Christō Iēsou* and partly in the understanding of the phrase *en Christō Iēsou*. These two issues are interrelated, for if, with J. B. Lightfoot (ad loc.), we supply the verb *ephroneito* ("was minded"), then *en Christō Iēsou* will most naturally mean "in the person of Christ Jesus"; if, on the other hand, with J. Gnilka (ad loc.), we supply *prepei* ("is fitting"), then *en Christō Iēsou* will mean "in your common life in Christ Jesus." The latter alternative does not depend on supplying *prepei* in the adjective clause (for which cf. also F. W. Beare, ad loc.); it is defended also by R. P. Martin (*Carmen Christi*, p. 71), who takes the missing verb to be *phroneite* ("you think," "you are minded") and approves of K. Grayston's rendering (EPC, ad loc.): "Think this way among yourselves which you think in Christ Jesus, i.e. as members of His Church."

E. Käsemann ("A Critical Analysis of Philippians 2:5–11") accepts this interpretation and goes farther: understanding vv. 6–11 as setting forth a drama of salvation, he takes "in Christ Jesus" in v. 5 to denote the readers' new status under the dominion of him who has been exalted as Lord over all—to denote, in other words, the realm of salvation established by Christ's victory on the cross, into which they were brought at their conversion and baptism. To think humbly is the way one ought to think (*dei phronein*) in this realm.

A persuasive defense of the view that Paul is urging his readers to manifest the same self-denying mind as Christ manifested is made by C. F. D. Moule,

"Further Reflexions on Philippians 2:5–11," in W. W. Gasque and R. P. Martin, eds., *Apostolic History and the Gospel*, pp. 264–76. He suggests the amplification *touto to phronēma phroneite en hymin ho kai en Christō Iēsou*, which he translates "Adopt towards one another, in your mutual relations, the same attitude which was found in Christ Jesus" (p. 265). This, together with his exegesis of the following verses, commends itself as an acceptable interpretation (it agrees, incidentally, with the GNB rendering). See to much the same effect E. Larsson, *Christus als Vorbild*, p. 233.

10

The Christ Hymn

He always had the nature of God,
  but he did not think that by force
    he should try to become ^c equal
    with God.
⁷Instead of this, of his own free will
  he gave up all that he had,
  and took the nature of a servant.
He became like man
  and appeared in human likeness.
⁸He was humble and walked the path
  of obedience all the way to
  death—
  his death on the cross.
⁹For this reason God raised him

  to the highest place above
  and gave him the name that is
    greater than any other name.
¹⁰And so, in honor of the name
  of Jesus
all beings in heaven, on earth, and
  in the world below^d
  will fall on their knees,
¹¹and all will openly proclaim that
  Jesus Christ is Lord,
  to the glory of God the Father.

c. become; or remain. d. WORLD BELOW: *It was thought that the dead continued to exist in a dark world under the ground.*

By printing these verses in poetical form GNB reflects the widespread recognition that here we have an early Christian hymn in honor of Christ. Like many other early Christian hymns it is cast in rhythmical prose, not in poetical meter (whether Greek or Semitic). It consists of a recital of the saving work of God in Christ, in self-humiliation followed by exaltation. He humbled himself; he was exalted by God. According to 1 Peter 1:11 the Spirit of prophecy in OT times was chiefly concerned with "predicting the sufferings that Christ would have to endure and the glory that would follow"; this is the twofold theme of the hymn now before us. Whether it was Paul's own composition or someone else's, Paul incorporates it into his present argument in order to reinforce his plea for the cultivation of a humble spirit.

2:6 / If the Philippians are urged to have "the attitude . . . that Christ Jesus had," how was his attitude shown? It was shown in his humbling himself to become man, in his humbling himself to take **the nature of a servant**, in his humbling himself to submit obediently to death—and death by crucifixion at that.

He always had the nature of God: literally, "being already in the form of God." Possession of the form implies participation in the essence. It seems fruitless to argue that these words do not assume the pre-existence of Christ. In another passage where Paul points to Christ's self-denial as an example for his people—"rich as he was, he made himself poor for your sake, in order to make you rich by means of his poverty" (2 Cor. 8:9)—his pre-existence is similarly assumed (although there Paul makes his own choice of language, whereas here he uses a form of words that are ready to hand). Elsewhere in the Pauline writings Christ is presented as the agent in creation: he is the one "through whom all things were created" (1 Cor. 8:6; cf. Col. 1:16, 17). Other NT writers agree with Paul in this presentation (cf. John 1:1–3; Heb. 1:2; Rev. 3:14); it is evidently bound up with a primitive Christian identification of Christ with the divine Wisdom of the OT (cf. Prov. 3:19; 8:22–31; also, with "word" instead of "wisdom," Ps. 33:6). First-century Christians did not share the intellectual problem involved for many today in "combining heavenly pre-existence with a human genetical inheritance" (Montefiore, *Paul the Apostle*, p. 106).

Two alternative renderings are offered of the next statement: in addition to the text, **he did not think that by force he should try to become equal with God**, we have the marginal rendering, "he did not think that by force he should try to *remain* equal with God." But these two renderings do not exhaust the possibilities. "Existing as he already did in the form of God, Christ did not regard equality with God as a *harpagmos*"— such is the literal force of the words. The interpreters' crux lies in the Greek noun *harpagmos*. This noun is derived from a verb that means "snatch" or "seize." There is no question of Christ's trying to snatch or seize equality with God: that was already his because **he always had the nature of God**. Neither is there any question of his trying to retain it by force. The point is rather that he did not treat his equality with God as an excuse for self-assertion or self-aggrandizement; on the contrary, he treated it as an occasion for renouncing every advantage or privilege that might have accrued to him thereby, as an opportunity for self-impoverishment and unreserved self-sacrifice.

Several commentators have seen a contrast here with the story of Adam: Christ enjoyed true equality with God but refused to derive any advantage from it in becoming man, whereas Adam, made man in the image of God, snatched at a false and illusory equality; Christ achieved universal lordship through his renunciation, whereas Adam forfeited his lordship through his "snatching." But it is not at all certain that this contrast was in the author's mind.

2:7 / **Instead of this**—instead of exploiting his equality with God for his own advantage—**of his own free will he gave up all that he had**. The literal translation of this clause is brief: "but he emptied himself." J. B. Lightfoot renders, " ' . . . he divested himself,' not of His divine nature, for this was impossible, but 'of the glories, the prerogatives of Deity.' " The lesson for the Philippian Christians is plain: as Christ set aside his own interests for the sake of others, so should they.

He "emptied himself" or "divested himself" specifically in that he **took the nature of a servant** (lit., "the form of a slave"). This does not mean that he *exchanged* the nature (or form) of God for the nature (or form) of a servant: it means that he displayed the nature (or form) of God *in* the nature (or form) of a servant. An excellent illustration of this is provided by the account in John 13:3–5 of what took place at the Last Supper: it was in full awareness of his divine origin and destiny, in full awareness of the authority conferred on him by the Father, that Jesus washed his disciples' feet and dried them with the towel he had tied round his waist. The divine nature was displayed, and most worthily displayed, in the act of humble service.

He became like man and appeared in human likeness: these words are misunderstood if they are taken to mean that Christ's humanity was only a semblance of humanity and not real humanity. Before the end of the first century A.D. there arose within the church a school of thought that held this very doctrine—the doctrine that came to be called Docetism (Gk. *dokēsis*, "semblance"). This doctrine was in keeping with certain current trends of thought but was rightly rejected as subversive of the foundations of the gospel. A later NT writer warns his readers against one form of this false teaching which denies that "Jesus Christ came as a human being" and stigmatizes it as the teaching of Antichrist (1 John 4:2, 3; 2 John 7). Paul had no doubt that Jesus was truly man, "the son of a human mother" (Gal. 4:4), and that he died a terribly real death by crucifixion.

He became like man probably means "he was born like other men" ("the son of a human mother," to quote Gal. 4:4 again). As for his appearing **in human likeness**, one possibility is that we have here an allusion to the one who "looked like a human being" in Daniel's vision of the judgment day, the one who received from God such power and honor that "his authority would last forever, and his kingdom would never end" (Dan. 7:13, 14). These words in Daniel may have been regarded as an anticipation of Jesus' exaltation, which is here presented as an accomplished fact (vv. 9–11).

2:8 / **He was humble**; indeed, as the clause is literally translated, "he humbled himself." A deliberate act of self-humiliation is indicated; there is little difference between "he humbled himself" here and "he emptied himself" in verse 7, unless it be that "he emptied himself" in becoming man and then, having become man, "he humbled himself" further. His whole life from the manger to the tomb was marked by genuine humility.

He **walked the path of obedience all the way to death**: the GNB rendering felicitously excludes the impression that several of the older versions might give, that it was **death** that commanded and received his obedience. It was to the will of God that his obedience was given, and even when that will pointed to suffering and death, he accepted it: "not my will," he said to his heavenly Father, "but your will be done" (Luke 22:42).

But it was in the manner of his death, **his death on the cross**, that the rock bottom of humiliation was reached. The words **his death on the cross** have not been added to a composition already existing in order to adapt it more precisely to the historical facts. They are essential to the sense, and probably to the rhythm also. The whole composition celebrates Jesus' humiliation, and his humiliation was crowned by his undergoing **death on the cross**. By the standards of the first century, no experience could be more loathsomely degrading than that.

It is difficult for us, after so many Christian centuries during which the cross has been venerated as a sacred symbol, to realize the unspeakable horror and disgust that the mention or indeed the very thought of the cross provoked. By the Jewish law anyone who was crucified died under the curse of God (Gal. 3:13, quoting Deut. 21:23). In polite Roman society the word "cross" was an obscenity, not to be uttered in conversation. Even when a man was being sentenced to death by crucifixion, an archaic formula was used that avoided the pronouncing of this four-letter word— as it was in Latin (*crux*). This utterly vile form of punishment was that which Jesus endured, and by enduring it he turned that shameful instrument of torture into the object of his followers' proudest boast. "As for me, however," said Paul (by contrast with other people's grounds of boasting), "I will boast only about the cross of our Lord Jesus Christ" (Gal. 6:14)— an incomprehensible turning upside down of all the accepted values of his day, by one who inherited both the Jewish and the Roman attitudes to crucifixion.

2:9 / The hymn goes on to celebrate the reversal of Christ's humiliation, the supreme illustration of his own words: "whoever humbles himself will be made great" (Matt. 23:11, etc.). Because he descended to the lowest depth, **God raised him to the highest place above**.

The Philippian Christians confessed Jesus as the exalted Lord. But how did he attain his present exaltation? By emptying himself, by giving up all that he had. It is not implied that eventual exaltation was the incentive for his humbling himself, or that it should be the incentive for them in following his example of humility. But, since he was the one whom they now confessed as Lord over all, his example should be decisive for them.

The wording here is not primarily intended to provide an interpretation of any particular OT passage, but it echoes some OT precedents. There is the disfigured and maltreated servant of the LORD who was nevertheless to "succeed in his task" and "be highly honored" (Isa. 52:13). There is the one "like a human being" seen in Daniel's vision, who "was given authority, honor and royal power" (Dan. 7:13, 14). So Jesus, disgraced and discredited as man, was divinely vindicated as man.

Several NT writers express the fact of Jesus' vindication and exaltation by saying that he sat down at the right hand of God (Acts 2:33; Heb. 1:3, etc.). Paul knows this expression, but seems to use it only when he is quoting a credal formula, as in Romans 8:34 and Colossians 3:1. The expression is drawn from Psalm 110:1, where the Davidic king is invited in an oracle to share the throne of Yahweh, sitting to the right side of him. According to Mark 14:62 and parallel texts, Jesus at his trial before the Jewish high priest and his colleagues told them that they would yet "see the Son of Man seated at the right side of the Almighty," occupying, that is to say, the position of highest honor in and over the universe.

In thus raising Jesus, God **gave him the name that is greater than any other name**. This is most probably the designation, "Lord," in its most sublime sense. In the Greek OT this word (*kyrios*) is used, over and above its regular meanings, to represent the personal name of the God of Israel. This personal name, usually spelled Yahweh, had come to be regarded as too sacred to be normally pronounced aloud, and so, when the Scriptures were read in public, it was replaced by another word, most often by the word meaning "Lord." (In GNB and most other English versions, "LORD" is spelled with four capital letters when it stands for the ineffable name Yahweh.) This, then, is the name that God has bestowed on Jesus—the rarest of all honors, in view of his affirmation in Isaiah 42:8, "I am the LORD, that is my name" (meaning, mine and no one else's).

Another view is that "Jesus" has become **the name that is greater**

than any other name, as though the name once placarded on the cross were now the name highly exalted in heaven. But **the name** in view here is one that he has received in consequence of his humiliation and death; the name "Jesus" was his from his birth. Even so, the name of Jesus now has the value of "Lord"; by God's decree it has become "the name high over all / In hell, and earth, and sky"—in these words Charles Wesley reproduces in reverse the threefold division of the universe in verse 10: **in heaven, on earth, and in the world below**.

2:10 / In Isaiah 45:23 the God of Israel, who has already declared that he will not share his name or his glory with another, swears solemnly by his own life, "everyone will come and kneel before me and vow to be loyal to me." Here this language is repeated, but now it is **in honor of the name of Jesus** that everyone kneels. There are parallels to this in other places in the NT: in John 5:22, 23 the Father makes the Son universal judge "so that all will honor the Son in the same way as they honor the Father," and in the vision of heaven in Revelation 5:6–14 the celestial beings around the throne of God fall down before the victorious Lamb at his appearance, and their song in celebration of his worthiness is taken up and echoed by all creation. It may well be that, in a meeting of the church, the first mention of the name of Jesus was greeted by marks of homage—the bending of knees in his honor and the confession of his lordship. The congregation thus reflected on earth the continual worship presented in heaven. But the confidence is expressed that this worship is destined to be yet more widespread—that even those who at present refuse to acknowledge, by action or word, that Jesus is Lord, will one day render that acknowledgment. There is no tension in the NT between the lordship of Christ in the church and his lordship over the cosmos.

In the phrase "in the name of Jesus" (as it is literally rendered in ASV and some other translations) the exact force of the preposition (Gk. *en*) has been debated. Worship and prayer are presented to God the Father in the name of Jesus (or through Jesus) because he is the way to the Father, the "one who brings God and mankind together" (1 Tim. 2:5). But that is not what is meant here. The sense is conveyed better in the rendering "at the name of Jesus" (so KJV, RSV, JB, NEB, NASB, NIV) or **in honor of the name of Jesus** (GNB). The power of Jesus' name, before which disease and demons fled during his earthly ministry, has been enhanced with his exaltation by God: "Angels and men before it fall, / And devils fear and fly." So Charles Wesley names (in reverse order) the inhabitants of "hell, and earth, and sky." Not only human beings, that is to say, but angels and demons, in joyful spontaneity or in reluctant fear, acknowledge the sovereignty of the crucified one—**all beings**, in fact, **in heaven, on earth, and in the world below**. But what precisely is to be understood by **the world below**? The phrase (lit., "those under the earth") may denote, as GNB margin says, the realm where "it was thought that the dead continued to exist"; it may also denote the abode of evil spirits or disobedient angels: "the angels who did not stay within the limits of their proper authority . . . are bound with eternal chains in the darkness below" (Jude 6). It may be relevant to recall how the legion expelled from the Gadarene demoniac "begged Jesus not to send them into the abyss" (Luke 8:31).

Perhaps we should not inquire too closely whether the reference is to dead human beings, or to demons, or to both groups. The language may simply be intended to convey the universality of the homage paid to Jesus. Paul elsewhere expresses the idea of universality in terms of **heaven** and **earth** (without mention of **the world below**) when he says (Col. 1:16–20) that through Christ "God created everything in heaven and on earth, the seen and the unseen things" (with the express inclusion of "spiritual powers") and also that through Christ God has "brought back to himself all things, both on earth and in heaven" (perhaps with the implicit inclusion of spiritual powers). We may compare the way in which the universality of praise to God is expressed in detail in Psalm 148.

This at any rate is affirmed: there is nothing in the whole created order that is not now "subject to the power and empire of Christ our Redeemer" (to quote the words in which the symbolism of the orb surmounted by the cross is explained in the British coronation service). As for the dead, King Hezekiah might consider that they were excluded from the privilege of praising God (Isa. 38:18); but the work of Christ has changed all this: in Paul's own words, "Christ died and rose to life in order to be the Lord of the living and of the dead" (Rom. 14:9).

2:11 / Those who kneel in honor of Jesus' name **openly proclaim** at the same time **that Jesus Christ is Lord**. He who "took the nature of a servant" has been elevated by God to be Lord of all, and **all will** confess him as such. Salvation, says Paul, is assured to those who "confess that Jesus is Lord and believe that God raised him from death" (Rom. 14:9); "no one," he says again, "can confess 'Jesus is Lord,' unless he is guided by the Holy Spirit" (1 Cor. 12:3).

"Jesus (Christ) is Lord" is the quintessential Christian creed, and in that creed "Lord" is given the most august sense that it can bear. When Christians in later generations refused to say "Caesar is Lord," they refused because they knew that this was no mere courtesy title that Caesar claimed: it was a title that implied his right to receive divine honors, and in this sense they could give it to none but Jesus. To them there was "only one God, the Father, . . . and . . . only one Lord, Jesus Christ" (1 Cor. 8:6). In the Greek OT Gentile Christians read, Yahweh was denoted either by *theos* ("God") or (most often) by *kyrios* ("Lord"); they reserved *theos* regularly for God the Father and *kyrios* regularly for Jesus.

When divine honors are thus paid to the humiliated and exalted Jesus, **the glory of God the Father** is not diminished but enhanced. When the Son is honored, the Father is glorified; for none can bestow on the Son higher honors than the Father himself has bestowed.

Additional Notes

The pioneer in presenting the thesis that vv. 6–11 form an independent composition that Paul has incorporated into his argument was E. Lohmeyer in the first edition of his commentary on Philippians (KEK, 1928) and in his monograph *Kyrios Jesus: Eine Untersuchung zu Phil 2, 5–11*. The predominant judgment on its authorship is that it was composed by someone other than Paul (see R. P. Martin, *Carmen Christi*, pp. 42–62). Pauline authorship, however, has been defended by M. Dibelius (ad loc.), W. Michaelis (ad loc.), E. F. Scott (ad loc.), L. Cerfaux, "L'hymne au Christ—Serviteur de Dieu (Phil. 2, 6–11 = Isa. 52, 13–53, 12)," pp. 425–37; J. M. Furness, "The Authorship of Philippians ii. 6–11," *ExpT* 70 (1958-59), pp. 240–43. F. W. Beare (ad loc.) sees here "not a 'pre-Pauline' hymn, but a hymn composed in Pauline circles, under Pauline influence, but introducing certain themes into the proclamation of Christ's victory which are elaborated independently of Paul."

Lohmeyer (*Kyrios Jesus*, p. 9) argued for an Aramaic original for the hymn; for attempted Aramaic retroversions see P. P. Levertoff (reproduced in W. K. L. Clarke, *New Testament Problems*, p. 148); R. P. Martin, *Carmen Christi*, pp. 40, 41; P. Grelot, "Deux notes critiques sur Philippiens 2, 6–11," pp. 185, 186. There is no need to postulate an Aramaic original; the Greek is not translation Greek. On the other hand, the Aramaic retroversions exhibit, without any forcing, appropriate structure and rhythm.

O. Hofius (*Der Christushymnus Philipper 2, 6–11*, p. 8) argues persuasively that the composition follows the pattern of those OT psalms that rehearse the saving acts of Yahweh by way of confession and thanksgiving.

2:6 / **He always had the nature of God**: Gk. *hos en morphē theou hyparchōn* ("who being already in the form of God"). For the relative pronoun *hos* used thus to introduce a christological hymn or confession cf. Col. 1:15, *hos estin eikōn tou theou tou aoratou* ("who is the image of the invisible God"); 1 Tim. 3:16, *hos ephanerōthē en sarki* ("who was manifested in flesh"). The noun *morphē* "implies not the external accidents but the essential attributes" (J. B. Lightfoot, ad loc.); it has a more substantial content than *homoiōma* in the last phrase of v. 7 or *schēma* in the first phrase of v. 8. The verb *hyparchein* "denotes 'prior existence' " (Lightfoot, ad loc.).

The meaning of *harpagmos* is disputed. According to the analogy of such formations in -*mos*, it should mean the act of snatching or seizing (*harpazein*). This is the interpretation implied in KJV "thought it not robbery to be equal with God"—a rendering that goes back to Tyndale's version of 1526 and beyond that to the Vulgate *non rapinam arbitratus est*. But there is an impressive tradition in favor of treating *harpagmos* as though it were synonymous with *harpagma*—that is (according to the analogy of such formations in -*ma*), something seized or something to be seized. So J. B. Lightfoot offers the paraphrase: "He, though existing before the worlds in the form of God, did not treat His equality with God as a prize, a treasure to be greedily clutched and ostentatiously displayed; on the contrary He resigned the glories of heaven"—adding that "this is the common and indeed almost universal interpretation of the Greek fathers, who would have the most lively sense of the requirements of the language" (*Philippians*, pp. 134, 135).

That the neuter *harpagma* could bear this sense is certain: Plutarch (*On Alexander's Fortune or Virtue* 1.8.330d) says that Alexander the Great did not treat his conquest of Asia *hōsper harpagma*, "as a prize" to be exploited for his personal enjoyment or advantage, but as a means of establishing universal civilization under one law (cf. A. A. T. Ehrhardt, "Jesus Christ and Alexander the Great," in *The Framework of the New Testament Stories*, pp. 37–43). But if this had been the sense intended here, it could easily have been expressed by *harpagma*, which was a perfectly familiar word—it occurs seventeen times in LXX, whereas *harpagmos* occurs here only in the Greek Bible, and very rarely elsewhere in Greek literature.

A powerful argument for maintaining the active force proper to *harpagmos* is presented by C. F. D. Moule ("Further Reflexions on Philippians 2:5–11," in W. W. Gasque and R. P. Martin, eds., *Apostolic History and the Gospel*, p. 272): "The point of the passage . . . is that, instead of imagining that equality with God meant *getting*, Jesus, on the contrary, *gave*—gave until he was 'empty' . . . he thought of equality with God not as *plērōsis* but as *kenōsis*, not as *harpagmos* but as open-handed spending—even to death."

For the view that a contrast is intended here between Christ and Adam see O. Cullmann, *The Christology of the New Testament*, pp. 174–81; R. P. Martin, *Carmen Christi*, pp. 161–64 (Martin traces this view back to G. Estius in 1631). D. H. Wallace ("A note on morphē") argues against it that the *morphē theou* of v. 6 (as is evident from the *morphē doulou* of v. 7) is different from the equality with God held out to Adam and Eve in Gen. 3:5. (The Greek OT does not use *morphē* but *eikōn* for the "image" of God in which Adam was created.) Another view supposes that the contrast intended is between Christ and Lucifer, who aimed to "be like the Almighty" (Isa. 14:14); to the bibliography for this view given in R. P. Martin, *Carmen Christi*, pp. 157–61, add E. K. Simpson, *Words Worth*

Weighing in the Greek New Testament (London: Tyndale Press, 1946), pp. 20–23.

2:7 / He gave up all that he had: Gk. *heauton ekenōsen* ("he emptied himself"). The use of the Greek verb here has given the name *kenosis* to a once-popular christological theory (the "kenotic" theory), which in fact has nothing to do with the meaning of the present passage. See E. R. Fairweather, "The 'Kenotic' Christology," appended note to F. W. Beare, *Philippians,* pp. 159–74.

W. Warren ("On *heauton ekenōsen,*") suggested that these two Greek words might be equivalent to Heb. *he'rāh . . . nafshô* (Isa. 53:12), "he exposed his life" (KJV: "he hath poured out his soul"). This suggestion has been taken up and elaborated with the supposition that the intervening phrase *lammāweth* ("to death") of the Hebrew text is echoed in Gk. *mechri thanatou* ("as far as death") in v. 8 below, so that **he gave up all that he had . . . all the way to death** (GNB) could be regarded practically as a variant translation for "he willingly gave his life" (Isa. 53:12, GNB). See H. W. Robinson, "The Cross of the Servant" (1926), in *The Cross in the Old Testament* (London: SCM Press, 1955), pp. 104, 105; C. H. Dodd, *According to the Scriptures,* p. 93; J. Jeremias, "Zur Gedankenführung in den paulinischen Briefen," in *Studia Paulina in honorem J. de Zwaan,* ed. J. N. Sevenster and W. C. van Unnik, p. 154 with n. 3; A. M. Hunter, *Paul and his Predecessors,* pp. 43, 44. This supposition contributes to the more general argument that the Christ hymn is an interpretation of the fourth Servant song (Isa. 52:13–53:12); it remains a supposition, attractive perhaps, but incapable of proof.

Took the nature of a servant: Gk. *morphēn doulou labōn,* where *labōn* is the simultaneous aorist participle ("he emptied himself by taking . . . "). As in v. 6, *morphē* means "not the external semblance only . . . , but the characteristic attributes" (J. B. Lightfoot, ad loc.). C. F. D. Moule points out the relevance of the word *doulos* ("slave") in this context: "slavery meant, in contemporary society, the extreme in respect of deprivation of rights . . . . Pushed to its logical conclusion, slavery would deny a person the right to anything—even to his own life and person" ("Further Reflexions," p. 268).

He became like man: Gk. *en homoiōmati anthrōpōn genomenos,* where *genomenos* probably means "born" as in Gal. 4:4 (*genomenon ek gynaikos,* "born of woman"); cf. Rom. 1:3, "he was born (*genomenou*) a descendant of David"; John 8:58, "Before Abraham was born (*genesthai*), 'I Am' "; and for the general sense Wisdom 7:1–6, where Solomon insists that he came into the world like any other man: "when I was born [*genomenos*], I began to breathe the common air."

Appeared in human likeness: Gk. *schēmati heuretheis hōs anthrōpos,* where *schēma*, without suggesting that his humanity was a mere appearance, may indicate that there was more than humanity there (he continued to have "the nature of God"). There is no emphasis on the idea of finding in *heuretheis* (aorist participle passive of *heuriskein*); the passive of *heuriskein* is here used rather like *se trouver* in French (cf. 3:9; Heb. 11:5). With *hōs anthrōpos* compare Dan. 7:13 (Theodotion), *hōs hyios anthrōpou* ("what looked like a human being"). Lightfoot (ad loc.) compares Testament of Zebulun 9:8, "you will see God in (the) fashion of man" (*en schēmati anthrōpou*)—but this comes in a Christian recension of the work and might even be dependent on the wording of this Christ hymn.

2:8 / He was humble and walked the path of obedience: Gk. *etapeinōsen heauton genomenos hypēkoos*, "he humbled himself (by) becoming obedient" (like *labōn* in v. 7, *genomenos* is simultaneous aorist participle). While F. W. Beare (ad loc.) sees a probable reference here to "submission to the power of the Elemental Spirits" (the *stoicheia*), there is no parallel to such a thought in the NT writings. Christ entered into the realm of human life that was dominated by those forces, but instead of his submitting to them, they were forced to submit to him (Col. 2:15). If A. J. Bandstra were right in taking law to be one of those forces (*The Law and the Elements of the World*, pp. 60 ff.), then it might be concluded that Christ, by being born under law (Gal. 4:4), did in some sense submit to them; but in Gal. 4:3, 9, it is legalism, not law as the revelation of God's will (to which Christ rendered glad and free obedience), that is reckoned among the *stoicheia*. Nor was it to death that Christ rendered obedience (as might be inferred from KJV); it was to the Father's will that he rendered obedience **all the way to death**.

The phrase **his death on the cross** forms the climax of the first part of the hymn. It is not a later addition calculated to christianize the composition; it is integral to the sense, and rhythmically it forms a coda to the first part as the phrase **to the glory of God the Father** does to the second part (cf. O. Hofius, *Der Christushymnus*, pp. 3–17).

Death on the cross was, in Cicero's words, "the most cruel and abominable form of punishment" (*Verrine Orations* 5.64); "the very word 'cross,' " he said, "should be foreign not only to the body of a Roman citizen, but to his thoughts, his eyes, his ears" (*Oration in Defense of C. Rabirius*, 16). See M. Hengel, *Crucifixion*.

2:9 / God raised him to the highest place above: Gk. *ho theos auton hyperypsōsen*, "God highly exalted him." The simple verb is used at the beginning of the fourth Isaianic Servant song (Isa. 52:13): "he will be exalted" (*hypsōthēsetai*). All strands of NT witness concur in celebrating Jesus' exaltation: "I have been given all authority in heaven and on earth, " he says in resurrection (Matt. 28:18); "Jesus knew that the Father had given him complete power" (John 13:3); he is depicted as "raised above the heavens" (Heb. 7:26) and as "ruling over all angels and heavenly authorities and powers" (1 Pet. 3:22); "The Lamb who was killed is worthy to receive power, wealth, wisdom, and strength, honor, glory, and praise!" (Rev. 5:12).

C. F. D. Moule ("Further Reflexions," p. 270) proposes, "despite all the weight of opinion to the contrary," to understand **the name that is greater than any other name** as "the name 'Jesus,' not the title 'Lord.' . . . God, in the incarnation, bestowed upon the one who is on an equality with him an earthly name which, because it accompanied that most God-like self-emptying, has come to be, in fact, the highest of names, because service and self-giving are themselves the highest of divine attributes." See also J. Barr, "The Word Became Flesh: The Incarnation in the New Testament," *Interp* 10 (1956), pp. 16–23, especially p. 22.

2:10 / **In honor of the name of Jesus**: "when the name of Jesus is spoken" (C. F. D. Moule, *IBNTG*, p. 78; cf. "Further Reflexions," p. 270, where he links this rendering with the identification of "Jesus" as **the name that is greater than any other name**).

All beings in heaven, on earth, and in the world below: Gk. *epouraniōn kai epigeiōn kai katachthoniōn*, three adjectives in the genitive plural, probably to be construed as of masculine (or common) gender, since it is intelligent **beings** who pay homage and make confession. But W. Carr (*Angels and Principalities*, pp. 86–89) regards it as "reasonably certain that the three adjectives are neuter rather than masculine," the reference being "not so much to beings that inhabit the three regions as to the overall notion of universality of homage to God."

There is a notable parallel (which may indeed be dependent on the present passage) in Ignatius, *To the Trallians* 9:1, where it is affirmed in a credal sequence that Jesus Christ "was truly crucified and died, in the sight of those in heaven and on earth and under the earth" (*blepontōn tōn epouraniōn kai epigeiōn kai hypochthoniōn*). Here too the adjectives appear to be masculine, since those referred to *saw* the passion of Christ. Carr may be right in thinking that by the three adjectives Ignatius denotes comprehensively "the whole inhabited universe"; but that universe is one of intelligent beings.

F. W. Beare (ad loc.) holds that the reference of all three adjectives "is certainly to *spirits*—astral, terrestrial, and chthonic." There is no good reason to limit their reference in this way, and even more emphatically none for his further statement that the proclamation of v. 11 is not "a confession of faith in Jesus on the part of *the church*" but "the acclamation of the spirits who surround his throne." It is both.

2:11 / **Jesus Christ is Lord**: Gk. *kyrios Iēsous Christos*. Cf. Acts 10:36, "Jesus Christ, who is Lord of all."

To the glory of God the Father: the coda both to the second part of the hymn (as "his death on the cross" is to the first part) and to the whole hymn. God was glorified in the humiliation of Christ as much as he is in his exaltation.

See section of For Further Reading on the Christ hymn.

Encouragement to Fidelity

So then, dear friends, as you always obeyed me when I was with you, it is even more important that you obey me now while I am away from you. Keep on working with fear and trembling to complete your salvation, [13]because God is always at work in you to make you willing and able to obey his own purpose.

After the Christ hymn, and reinforced by its contents, the apostolic exhortation is resumed.

2:12 / Christ's obedience has been stressed; his obedience should be an example to his people. Paul has no misgivings about the Philippian Christians' obedience: unlike the Corinthians in the situation reflected in 2 Corinthians 10:6, they had always shown obedience, not so much to Paul as to the Lord whose apostle he was. If it is felt to be strange that obedience should be mentioned at all in a letter from a friend to **dear friends**, it must be remembered that Paul was not only the Philippians' friend; he was to them the apostle of Jesus Christ. He does not in this letter assert his apostolic authority, as he does in some others (cf. 1 Cor. 9:1, 2; 2 Cor. 3:1–3); it was not challenged at Philippi. Yet the note of apostolic authority is evident throughout the letter.

His plea to them, then, is this: **Keep on working with fear and trembling to complete your salvation**, not only as **when I was with you**, but now much more **while I am away from you**. Their obedience involved the continual translating into action of the principles of the gospel that they had believed. The gospel brought them **salvation**—their own salvation, as Paul calls it emphatically, because it is God's free gift to them. But it needs to be worked out in practical life in view of the approaching "Day of Christ," which will **complete** their salvation (in this sense Paul says in Romans 13:11 that the salvation of Christians "is closer now than it was when we first believed"). In this context Paul is not urging each member of the church to keep working at his or her personal salvation; he is thinking of the health and well-being of the church as a whole. Each of them, and all of them together, must pay attention to this.

The seriousness with which they should treat this matter is shown by the phrase **with fear and trembling**. Certainly the attitude here recommended has nothing to do with slavish terror: as Paul assures the Christians in Rome, "the Spirit that God has given you does not make you slaves and cause you to be afraid" (Rom. 8:15). It is rather an attitude of due reverence and awe in the presence of God, a sensitivity to his will, an awareness of responsibility in view of the account to be rendered before the tribunal of Christ. In their community life they must recognize that God is present. Pagans who entered Christian meetings became quickly conscious of this: "Truly God is here among you!" (1 Cor. 14:25). All the more certainly should Christians be conscious of it.

2:13 / While Paul was alive, and especially when he was free to visit them, he made their "salvation" his concern. But Paul would not always be around. This did not mean, however, that when he was permanently absent they would be left to their own resources. **God**, he tells them, **is always at work in you**—not only in you individually but among you collectively. By his indwelling Spirit he supplies the **willing** and the **working**—both the desire **to obey his own purpose** and the power to carry it out. This is part of Paul's teaching about the Holy Spirit, even if the Spirit is not explicitly mentioned here. As he emphasizes elsewhere, the Spirit does what the law could not: the law could tell people what to do without supplying the power, or even the will, to do it; the Spirit supplies both (Rom. 8:3, 4; 2 Cor. 3:4–6). When the Spirit takes the initiative in imparting to believers the desire and the power to do the will of God, then that desire and power become theirs by his gift, and they do his will "from the heart" (Eph. 6:6).

Additional Notes

2:12 / The apostle, like the *shaliach* among the Jews, was a duly accredited messenger; so long as he kept within the terms of his commission, he exercised the authority of the person who sent him: "a man's *shaliach* is as himself" (Babylonian Talmud, tractate *Berakot* 34b). See C. K. Barrett, "*Shaliah* and Apostle," in E. Bammel, C. K. Barrett, and W. D. Davies, eds., *Donum Gentilicium*, pp. 88–102.

When I was with you . . . while I am away from you. In the Greek text these phrases are construed with **keep on working**, as is shown by the preceding negative *mē*, the negative proper to the imperative *katergazesthe*, not to the indicative *hypēkousate* (**you . . . obeyed**): **keep on working** not only as in my presence (*parousia*, as in 1:26) but now much more in my absence (*apousia*, here only in NT). The particle "as" (*hōs*) preceding "in my presence" is omitted in B and a few other witnesses; it "lays stress on the sentiment or motive of the agent" (J. B. Lightfoot, ad loc.)—"as though my presence prompted you." F. W. Beare (ad loc.) thinks that, in the setting, the contrast of "presence" and "absence" means "during my life" and "after my death"; this implication is included in Paul's wording, but the sense of the wording need not be restricted to this.

Your salvation: Gk. *tēn heautōn sōtērian* ("your own salvation"), the reflexive pronoun of the third person being extended to do duty for the second person. On the corporate sense of **salvation** here see J. H. Michael, "Work out your own Salvation," *Expositor*, series 9, 12 (1924), pp. 439–50.

With fear and trembling: Gk. *meta phobou kai tromou*, a favorite doublet in Paul's vocabulary, it seems, referring to different kinds of fear. In 1 Cor. 2:3 it is used for the misgivings with which Paul first came to Corinth, having been expelled from one Macedonian city after another; in 2 Cor. 7:15 it is used for the trepidation with which the Corinthian Christians greeted Paul's envoy Titus, so soon after they had been taken to task in the apostle's severe letter; in Eph. 6:5 it is used for the sense of reverence and duty toward Christ that should motivate Christian slaves to obey their pagan masters.

There is no support in the text or context for the view of W. Schmithals (*Paul and the Gnostics*, p. 98) that Paul is here warning his readers against the false security of those who believe that they have already attained perfection (see further on 3:12–14).

2:13 / **Is always at work**: Gk. *energein* (twice in this verse), a verb frequently used by Paul for the effectiveness of divine power (cf. the related noun *energeia*, "power," in 3:21).

To obey his own purpose: Gk. *hyper tēs eudokias*, "for the good pleasure." It is not said expressly whose "good pleasure" is meant, but it is certainly God's (since **God** is the subject of the clause). The noun *eudokia* has been used in 1:15 for the "genuine good will" with which some preach the gospel in Rome, but the sense here is rather different (despite those who think *hyper tēs eudokias* means "to promote good will"). Cf. Luke 2:14, where *en anthrōpois eudokias* means not "among men of good will" (nor even, as in GNB, "to those with whom he is pleased") but "among human beings who are the objects of God's good pleasure (saving purpose)." A similar Hebrew phrase, "sons of his/thy good pleasure" (*benê resônô/resônekā*), occurs in Qumran literature (1QH 4.32, 33; 11.9), referring "more naturally to the will of God to confer grace on those he has chosen, than to God's delighting in and approving of the goodness in men's lives" (E. Vogt, " 'Peace among Men of God's Good Pleasure' Lk. 2:14," in *The Scrolls and the New Testament*, ed. K. Stendahl, p. 117).

12

Paul's Hope of the Philippians

Do everything without complaining or arguing, [15]so that you may be innocent and pure as God's perfect children, who live in a world of corrupt and sinful people. You must shine among them like stars lighting up the sky, [16]as you offer them the message of life. If you do so, I shall have reason to be proud of you on the Day of Christ, because it will show that all my effort and work have not been wasted.

The Philippians' obedience, the working out of their salvation, depended very largely on the maintenance of love and harmony within their community. If love and harmony were maintained, their witness in the pagan environment would be effective, and Paul could look forward with confidence to the time when he would be called upon to render an account of his stewardship in respect to them.

2:14 / God's purpose for his people can be fulfilled only if they live together in unity and **do everything without complaining and arguing**. This language is borrowed from OT descriptions of the generation of Israelites that went through the wilderness under Moses' leadership after the deliverance from Egypt. Repeatedly they complained about their hardships and said they should never have left Egypt (Num. 11:1–6; 14:1–4; 20:2; 21:4, 5). Moses described them as "a sinful and deceitful nation" (Deut. 32:5, quoted in v. 15 below), "stubborn, unfaithful people" (Deut. 32:20).

2:15 / The followers of Christ should not be like that wilderness generation. Writing to his Corinthian converts, Paul had to warn them seriously against following such a disastrous example and incurring the same judgment: they "must not complain, as some of them did—and they were destroyed by the Angel of Death" (1 Cor. 10:10). But, while an admonition to pursue a contented and harmonious way of life can never come amiss, Paul knows that his Philippian friends are in better shape than that. It is not they, but their pagan neighbors, who can be described as **corrupt and sinful people**. It is for the Philippian Christians to set the surrounding world a better example, by showing themselves **innocent and pure as God's perfect children**, reflecting their Father's character, people against whose way of life no finger of reproach can be pointed. It was this that Jesus had in mind for his disciples when he called them "salt for all mankind" and urged them, by their openhanded goodness, to become true children of their Father in heaven, perfect as he is perfect (Matt. 5:13, 45, 48). The people of the wilderness generation, by contrast, were repudiated as "unworthy to be his people" (GNB) or (as RSV puts it) "no longer his children" (Deut. 32:5).

Jesus compared his followers not only to salt but also to "light for the whole world" (Matt. 5:14–16). Paul takes up this figure when he encourages the Philippian Christians to **shine among** their pagan neighbors **like stars lighting up the sky**. The word he uses means "luminaries" (Gk. *phōstēres*); it is used in the Greek version of Genesis 1:14–19 of the sun, moon, and stars that the Creator placed in the vault of heaven on the fourth day. These luminaries do not shine for their own sake; they shine to provide light for all the world. The same should be true of Christians: they live for the sake of others. The church has been called a society that exists for the benefit of nonmembers.

The **world** here is used in the same sense as in John 3:19 and 12:46, where Jesus speaks of his having "come into the world as a light" (cf. also John 1:9; 8:12; 9:5).

2:16 / Changing from figurative to literal wording, Paul tells them that their business is to **offer** their neighbors **the message of life**. They are to present the gospel by the way they live as well as by the words they speak. No one would take their **message** seriously if their way of life was at variance with it. But if they lived in such a way that their neighbors asked what enabled them to lead such **innocent and pure** lives, then they could tell them of **the message of life** that had revolutionized their attitude and conduct.

The **message of life** is so called because it proclaims the true life that is found in Christ; it tells how "the person who is put right with God through faith shall live" (Rom. 1:17; Gal. 3:11, quoting Hab. 2:4). The gospel that the apostles are commissioned to preach comprises "all about this new life" (Acts 5:20)—an expression synonymous with "this message of salvation" (Acts 13:26). Elsewhere Paul refers to this life as "eternal life in union with Christ Jesus our Lord," which is God's free gift to believers (Rom. 6:23); by "eternal life" is meant the life of the age to come (the resurrection age), received and enjoyed by believers here and now through their participation in the risen life of Christ.

Paul ordered his life in the light of the coming **Day of Christ**, when, as he knew, his apostolic service would be reviewed. He was "not at all concerned about being judged by any human standard" because, as he said, "the Lord is the one who passes judgment on me" (1 Cor. 4:3, 4). Time and again he makes it clear that he will face the day of review with confidence if his converts stand firm and live so as to bring credit to the gospel he delivered to them. When he faces the Lord from whom he received his commission on the Damascus road, he hopes that it will be sufficient for him to point to his converts and invite the Lord to assess the quality of his service by the quality of their lives. So he and his colleagues can describe the Christians of Thessalonica as "our hope, our joy, and our reason for boasting . . . in the presence of our Lord Jesus Christ when he comes" (1 Thess. 2:19). In similar vein he now assures his friends in Philippi that, if they maintain their Christian witness, **it will show that all** his **effort and work have not been wasted**; he can be **proud** of them on the great day.

The word **effort** means literally "running"; it is an instance of Paul's proneness to use athletic language to describe his ministry. Similarly in Galatians 2:2 his statement, "I did not want my work in the past or in the present to be a failure" (GNB) is literally, "lest perhaps I should prove to be running, or to have run, in vain." (See also 1 Cor. 9:24–27.) The word here used for **work** implies toil or strenuous exertion; Paul uses it again in Gal. 4:11 to express the idea of toiling in vain: "Can it be that all my work for you has been for nothing?"

For **the Day of Christ** see 1:6, 10, with comments; for the association of pride or boasting with that day see 1:26 with comments.

Additional Notes

2:14 / W. Schmithals considers that the warning against **complaining or arguing** is intelligible only as a reference to "the dissension brought into the community by the false teachers" (*Paul and the Gnostics*, p. 74). But it is easy to think of a great variety of other causes that could lead to complaining or arguing. Compare also the exhortations of 4:1–3, 8–9.

2:15 / There is a striking similarity between **so that you may be** (*hina genēsthe*) **God's . . . children** and the words in the Sermon on the Mount: "so that you may become (*hopōs genēsthe*) the sons of your Father in heaven" (Matt. 5:45). The word translated **perfect** here in GNB is Gk. *amōma*, "without blemish" (cf. Eph. 1:4; 5:27; Col. 1:22, etc.), used in LXX specially with reference to sacrificial animals. See next note.

A world of corrupt and sinful people: Gk. *geneas skolias kai diestrammenēs* ("a crooked and perverse generation"), from Deut. 32:5, where the wilderness generation is so described. The Israelites of that generation are said, in the same sentence, to be *tekna mōmēta*, "blemished (blameworthy) children"; there is a deliberate contrast here in *tekna . . . amōma*, "unblemished (blameless) children." See preceding note.

You must shine among them like stars: since the verb is in the middle or passive voice (*phainesthe*), not the active (*phainete*, which can well mean "you shine," "you give light"), it has been argued (e.g., by E. Lohmeyer, ad loc.), that it means "you appear (as lights in the world)." But the middle or passive is also attested with the meaning "shine" and in association with *phōstēres* ("luminaries") "shine" is an appropriate rendering here. In Dan. 12:3 it is said that, in the resurrection age, "the wise leaders [who had borne the brunt of persecution] will shine with all the brightness of the sky [LXX: *phanousin hōs phōstēres tou ouranou*, 'will shine like luminaries of heaven']; and those who have taught many people to do what is right will shine like the stars forever." But now those who share in Christ's risen life anticipate the ministry of the resurrection age and bear their shining witness already. For the designation "sons of light" or "children of light" applied to followers of Christ cf. Luke 16:8; John 12:36; Eph. 5:8; 1 Thess. 5:5.

2:16 / **I shall have reason to be proud**: Gk. *eis kauchēma emoi*, "for a (ground of) boasting for me"; cf. the similar use of the noun *kauchēma* in 1:26, *to kauchēma hymōn*, "your (ground of) boasting."

That all my effort and work have not been wasted: O. Bauernfeind suggests, in the light of Gal. 2:2, that the expression "running in vain" (*eis kenon trechein*) "was a common use of the apostle's" (*TDNT* vol. 8, p. 231, s.v. "*trechō*"). The word translated work (*kopian*) is a favorite of his for describing Christian service, whether his own or that of others (cf. Rom. 16:6, 12; 1 Cor. 4:12; 15:10; 16:16; Gal. 4:11; Col. 1:29; 1 Thess. 5:12); its implication of resulting weariness is conveyed in John 4:6, where Jesus at noonday sits down by Jacob's well because he is "tired out" (*kekopiakōs*) by his journey.

13

Paul's Libation on the Philippians' Sacrifice

PHILIPPIANS 2:17–18

Perhaps my life's blood is to be poured out like an offering on the sacrifice that your faith offers to God. If that is so, I am glad and share my joy with you all. ¹⁸In the same way, you too must be glad and share your joy with me.

The life of the Philippian church is viewed as an offering to God: if one thing remains to make that offering perfectly acceptable, Paul is willing that the sacrifice of his own life should be that one thing—credited to their account, not to his.

2:17 / Paul comes back to his present situation. He hopes for a favorable verdict in the imperial court, but he cannot be sure: the case might go the other way, and he might be sentenced to death. If so, the sentence would probably be carried out by decapitation. How would Paul view that prospect?

The life and service of Christians could be described as a sacrifice. Paul urges the Roman Christians to present themselves "as a living sacrifice to God, dedicated to his service and pleasing to him" (Rom. 12:1). The Philippians' monetary gift to Paul is compared to "a sweet-smelling offering to God, a sacrifice which is acceptable and pleasing to him" (Phil. 4:18). If, then, their life of **faith** is offered as a sacrifice to God, can anything be added to complete its acceptance? When a sacrifice, such as a burnt offering with its accompanying cereal offering, was presented in the temple at Jerusalem, a drink-offering or libation of wine or olive oil might be poured over it or beside it. This was added last, and completed the sacrifice. If **my life's blood is to be poured out**, says Paul, let it be poured out as a libation **on the sacrifice that your faith offers to God**. **My life's blood** is the GNB circumlocution for "I"; Paul says, "even if I am poured as a libation" (Gk. *ei kai spendomai*). He is not thinking of a literal libation of blood such as was poured out in some pagan cults (cf. Ps. 16:4, RSV: "their libations of blood"); he is thinking of the willing yielding up of his life to God.

Charles Wesley, in memorable lines, prays that his life may be a perpetual sacrifice, kindled "on the mean altar of my heart" by the flame of the Spirit:

> Ready for all thy perfect will,
>> My acts of faith and love repeat,
> Till death thy endless mercies seal,
>> And make the sacrifice complete.

Paul's imagery is similar, with one material difference: *his* death should make *their* sacrifice complete. A martyr death would be the crown of his own life of apostolic service, but he is willing that it should be reckoned not to his credit but to theirs. If so, "nothing is here for tears"; such a prospect will be sheer **joy** for him, and so should it be for them.

2:18 / Paul has said earlier that he hopes to be released so as to increase their "progress and joy in the faith" (1:25). But they must rejoice no less if matters turn out otherwise. Whatever the outcome of the trial, honor will be brought to the name of Christ (1:20), and that should give them cause for rejoicing, even if it is by Paul's death, not by his survival, that Christ is to be honored. So, he says, **you too must be glad and share your joy with me**.

Additional Notes

2:17 / For libations of wine (GNB: "wine offerings") to Yahweh cf. Hos. 9:4 and especially Sira 50:15, in the description of the temple ministry of Simon the high priest (ca. 200 B.C.):

> He reached out his hand to the cup
>> and poured a libation of the blood of the grape;
> he poured it out at the foot of the altar,
>> a pleasing odor to the Most High, the King of all.

Other OT references to libations express disapproval because of their pagan associations (cf. Jer. 7:18; 2 Kings 16:13).

For this use of *spendomai* cf. 2 Tim. 4:6 (probably a deliberate echo of the present passage), where Paul's being "poured out" is no longer a possibility to be reckoned with, but an imminent certainty; also the related verb *spondizomai* in Ignatius, *To the Romans* 2:2, where Ignatius begs the Christians of Rome not to try to avert his martyrdom in their city: "grant me nothing more than to be poured out [*spondisthēnai*] to God"; they can be the temple choir, singing while the sacrifice is being offered on the altar.

The word **offering** renders Gk. *leitourgia*, religious service (used again in v. 30 below).

J.-F. Collange (ad loc.) thinks that the reference is not to Paul's martyrdom but to his life, expended in service to God; he compares W. Michaelis (ad loc.); A. M. Denis, "Versé en libation (Phil. II, 17). Versé en son sang?" *RSR* 45 (1957), pp. 567–70 and "La fonction apostolique et la liturgie nouvelle en esprit," *RSPT* 42 (1958), pp. 617–50; T. W. Manson, *Studies in the Gospels and Epistles*, pp. 151, 152.

14

Timothy's Forthcoming Visit

PHILIPPIANS 2:19-24

If it is the Lord's will, I hope that I will be able to send Timothy to you soon, so that I may be encouraged by news about you. [20]He is the only one who shares my feelings and who really cares about you. [21]Everyone else is concerned only with his own affairs, not with the cause of Jesus Christ. [22]And you yourselves know how he has proved his worth, how he and I, like a son and his father, have worked together for the sake of the gospel. [23]So I hope to send him to you as soon as I know how things are going to turn out for me. [24]And I trust in the Lord that I myself will be able to come to you soon.

In 2:19–30 we have a section that has been called the "apostolic *parousia*" or "travelogue." Paul announces his intention of paying his readers a visit before long (v. 24) but plans to send Timothy in advance of himself.

2:19 / **If it is the Lord's will, I hope**: literally, "I hope in the Lord Jesus," where "in the Lord Jesus" may have the same "incorporative" force as similar phrases with "in" have elsewhere in Paul (cf. 1:14, 26). Paul and Timothy, as fellow Christians, participate in the risen life of Christ. Their hopes and plans are formed in the light of their union with Christ; it might almost be said that "the Lord Jesus" constitutes the sphere in which Paul and his colleagues act and think (cf. v. 24, "I trust in the Lord").

Paul hopes, then, to send Timothy to them **soon**—not immediately, it appears, but when the outcome of his trial is clearer (cf. v. 23). But, while his Philippian friends would doubtless be glad to have news of him, he was anxious to have news of them, and would take courage when it arrived. The news that he hoped to receive would reassure him that they were united in heart and purpose, able to repel threats to their Christian faith and life no matter from which quarter they came. Although the future was uncertain, he expected not only to be spared but to live long enough for Timothy to make the journey to Philippi and come back to him with news from there.

Timothy was frequently sent by Paul as his messenger, and this mission need not be identified with one mentioned elsewhere. He sent Timothy to Thessalonica from Athens (1 Thess. 3:1–5) and to Corinth from Ephesus (1 Cor. 4:17; 16:10, 11). The latter mission could have coincided with that recorded in Acts 19:22, when he sent Timothy and Erastus to Macedonia from Ephesus. Those who hold that Philippians was sent from Ephesus might identify the present mission with that of Acts 19:22; but there is no hint in Acts that Paul was at that time in custody or awaiting the outcome of a trial.

It is best to infer that Timothy had joined Paul in Rome and was again available to be sent here or there as Paul's messenger.

2:20 / When Paul describes Timothy as **one who shares my feelings** he uses a word quite similar to that which he used in verse 2 when he urged his readers to be "one in soul." Here is a man who is "one in soul" or "equal in soul" with Paul himself. Paul found Timothy to be an entirely congenial and sympathetic colleague, but here he thinks of one particular aspect of Timothy's character that strikes a responsive chord in himself: Timothy shares Paul's feelings in that he has a genuine concern for the Philippian Christians' well-being. Paul has encouraged them to "look out for one another's interests"; these words of his will be reinforced by Timothy's example when he visits them. They probably held a special place in Timothy's affection, as he had been in Philippi when the gospel was first preached and the church first planted there.

2:21 / Even among the Christians with whom Paul was in touch at the time of writing, there were too many who put their own interests before those of others, or were more **concerned** about their **own affairs** than about **the cause of Jesus Christ**. There were some indeed in Rome at the time who were preaching the gospel "from love" (1:16), but of all those who were available to Paul as messengers none was so free from self-centeredness as Timothy. For Timothy, as for Paul, **the cause of Jesus Christ** was bound up with the well-being of his people.

2:22 / **You yourselves know**: Timothy had been a member of the group that first came to Philippi with the gospel. There and elsewhere he had proved his worth as the apostle's aide-de-camp.

Paul himself had special cause to appreciate Timothy's unselfish nature. The qualities that recommended Timothy to Paul as a suitable companion and trusted representative in his apostolic ministry were qualities that might well have worked for his personal advantage had he decided to exploit them to further his own career. One can only guess the ambitions Timothy might have begun to cherish in his mind when Paul visited his home in Lystra and persuaded him to be his associate and helper. A year or two earlier Paul had been disappointed in another young man, John Mark of Jerusalem, who bade farewell to Barnabas and himself in the course of a missionary journey and went back home (Acts 13:13; 15:38). Timothy was an equally gifted young man, but Paul discerned in him the promise of greater stability, and he was not disappointed in him. Perhaps Timothy was captivated in part by the magnetism of Paul's powerful friendliness: even so, it was an act of no mean self-denial on his part to leave home and abandon other prospects to share the uncertainties and dangers of Paul's way of life. Paul greatly valued the devotion of one whom he describes as "my own dear and faithful son in the Christian life" (1 Cor. 4:17). All the service a son could render to a father Timothy performed for Paul; all the affection a father could feel for his son Paul lavished on Timothy, as the two **worked together for the sake of the gospel**. "He has served with me as a slave," says Paul (in the literal rendering of his words here)—not Paul's slave, of course, but Christ's (cf. 1:1).

2:23 / As soon as he knows **how things are going to turn out** for him, then, he will send Timothy to visit them. The result of the trial would probably become sufficiently evident some time before judgment was finally pronounced.

2:24 / And Paul is confident enough about the outcome to **trust in the Lord** that he himself will **soon** be at liberty and able to visit them. The phrase **in the Lord** has much the same force as "in the Lord Jesus" in verse 19. There is no means of knowing whether Paul's confident hope of seeing them soon was realized or not.

Additional Notes

2:19 / The designations "travelogue" and "apostolic *parousia*" have both been suggested for such a section as Phil. 2:19–30 by R. W. Funk—the former in *Language, Hermeneutic and Word of God*, pp. 264–74, and the latter in "The Apostolic *Parousia*: Form and Significance," in W. R. Farmer, C. F. D. Moule, and R. R. Niebuhr, eds., *Christian History and Interpretation: Studies Presented to John Knox*, pp. 249–68. In vv. 19–24 three characteristic features of the "apostolic *parousia*" appear: (*a*) dispatch of an emissary, with name, credentials, and purpose; (*b*) benefit accruing to Paul from the sending of the emissary; (*c*) announcement of personal visit.

If it is the Lord's will (Gk. *en kyriō Iēsou*): see additional note on 1:14.

2:20 / Timothy is here described as *isopsychos*, "equal in soul" (cf. the exhortation in v. 2 to the Philippians to be *sympsychoi*, "together in soul"). In Ps. 55(LXX 54):13 the psalmist's "colleague and close friend" is called *isopsychos*, rendering Heb. *k°erkî*, "my equal" (lit., "according to my valuation"). Erasmus paraphrases the present passage, "I will send him as my *alter ego*." G. B. Caird (ad loc.) suggests that there is much to be said for taking *isopsychos* to mean "in sympathy with your [the Philippians'] outlook."

Who really cares about you: this was no doubt true, but the verb is future (Gk. *merimnēsei*, "will care") and refers to practical help that Timothy will willingly give them when he visits them. The adverb **really** (*gnēsiōs*, "genuinely") reminds one of Paul's use of the corresponding adjective in 1 Tim. 1:2 where Timothy is addressed as his "true [*gnēsios*, 'true born'] son in the faith." "Timothy is a legitimate son, the sole authorized representative of the apostle" (J.-F. Collange, ad loc.)

2:21 / **Everyone else is concerned only with his own affairs**: lit., "all of them seek their own (interests)" (Gk. *hoi pantes . . . ta heautōn zētousin*). It is not quite clear who "all of them" are; see R. Jewett's view mentioned in additional note on 1:17. But it would have called for an exceptional share of Timothy's devotion (both to Paul and to the Philippians) for anyone else to undertake on Paul's behalf a forty days' journey on foot to Philippi and another forty days' journey back. See G. B. Caird (ad loc.).

2:24 / **I trust in the Lord**: Gk. *pepoitha . . . en kyriō*. Cf. the perfect participle *pepoithōs* in 1:6, 14, 25. For **in the Lord** cf. 1:14 and additional note on that verse.

That I myself will be able to come to you soon: according to G. B. Caird, "he cannot have had much confidence in his release, or would not have needed to send Timothy" (ad loc.). But he sent Timothy from Ephesus to Corinth in advance of himself (1 Cor. 4:17, 19) when there was no prospect of *force majeure* to prevent his own going there in due course.

15

Commendation of Epaphroditus

I have thought it necessary to send to you our brother Epaphroditus, who has worked and fought by my side and who has served me as your messenger in helping me. [26]He is anxious to see you all and is very upset because you had heard that he was sick. [27]Indeed he was sick and almost died. But God had pity on him, and not only on him but on me, too, and spared me an even greater sorrow. [28]I am all the more eager, then, to send him to you, so that you will be glad again when you see him, and my own sorrow will disappear. [29]Receive him, then, with joy, as a brother in the Lord. Show respect to all such people as he, [30]because he risked his life and nearly died for the sake of the work of Christ, in order to give me the help that you yourselves could not give.

Even before Timothy sets out, Paul has another emissary ready to go to Philippi. Epaphroditus, an emissary from the Philippian church to Paul, was now to return home immediately, without waiting to learn how Paul's case would turn out.

2:25 / Epaphroditus had come from Philippi to visit Paul, bringing him a gift from the church there (cf. 4:18). When Paul describes Epaphroditus as his fellow worker and comrade-in-arms (**who has worked and fought by my side**), he may imply that Epaphroditus had on some previous occasion been associated with him in his apostolic activity or that after delivering the Philippian church's gift to him he had stayed on and taken some share in his ministry. The strenuous character of service in the gospel is indicated by Paul's fondness for describing it in athletic or military language. The Philippian Christians may indeed have instructed Epaphroditus to stay on after delivering their gift to Paul and give him on their behalf what help he seemed to need. This may be suggested by Paul's calling him **your messenger** or "envoy" (Gk. *apostolos*). The "messengers (*apostoloi*) of the churches" had a special status as their churches' duly commissioned representatives for specific purposes (cf. 2

Cor. 8:23, GNB: "they represent the churches"). Epaphroditus may not have been vested with such a formal status by the Philippian church, but Paul speaks of him with the respect due to such an envoy: he is your *apostolos* and my *leitourgos* (a minister to my need), says Paul, choosing the latter word also as one commanding respect (it denotes a person who renders a religious service).

Probably the Philippian church had intended Epaphroditus to stay longer with Paul, **helping** him as their representative. Paul makes it plain that he is responsible for sending Epaphroditus back earlier than they expected: **I have thought it necessary**, he says, and goes on to say why.

2:26 / Some time after leaving Philippi, Epaphroditus had fallen **sick**. His sickness raises questions to which no certain answers can be given. Did he fall sick on his way to Paul, or after he had reached the place where Paul was? The usual view is that it was after his arrival, but careful consideration should be given to the possibility—indeed, the probability—that it was while he was on the way there. G. B. Caird, for example, concludes: "He fell ill on the road from Philippi to Rome, and it was his determination to complete the journey and to discharge his commission that nearly cost him his life" (ad loc.).

If (as we believe) Paul was in Rome, Epaphroditus would travel west from Philippi along the Egnatian Way. Somewhere along this road he fell ill, and his friends in Philippi got to hear of it. How they heard we do not know. Perhaps (and "perhaps" is all that can be said) he was able to send a message back to them by someone traveling in the opposite direction, warning them that he might not be able to continue the journey (at least not within reasonable time) and asking them to send someone else to the place where he was to collect the gift and take it on to Paul in Rome. The Philippian Christians were naturally concerned about Epaphroditus, but had difficulty in finding a replacement for him: they could only hope he would recover in time to complete the journey.

Epaphroditus did recover and was able to complete the journey to Rome, but he knew that his friends in Philippi would be anxious about him and may well have blamed himself for causing them anxiety. In spite of being **very upset** over this, he was eager to stay with Paul and be of service to him, as he had been instructed to do. But Paul knew that the sooner Epaphroditus returned to Philippi, the happier Epaphroditus himself and his friends there would be, so he sent him back, exonerating him in their eyes from all responsibility for returning so soon.

2:27 / He was certainly ill, Paul adds; indeed, his illness nearly proved fatal. Until they received the letter, the Philippians may not have known how serious Epaphroditus's illness was. It did not matter if they knew it now, for it was Epaphroditus who took the letter to them, and they could see for themselves that he was safe and well.

Paul had been sorry indeed that Epaphroditus should run the risk of death in his eagerness to save him on behalf of the Philippian church. He would have had **an even greater sorrow**—"sorrow upon sorrow"—if Epaphroditus had actually died. His recovery was a token of God's mercy to Epaphroditus himself, but it was a token of God's mercy to Paul also, as Paul viewed it.

2:28 / Now that Epaphroditus had recovered, he would willingly have remained in Rome and served Paul further, but Paul said, "No: our friends back in Philippi have been very anxious about you and will be relieved to see for themselves that you have quite recovered. Besides, I am giving you a letter for them to tell them how things are going with me here and to thank them for the gift you brought me from them." Paul himself would be the more relieved to think of the mutual joy that Epaphroditus and his friends in Philippi would experience when they were safely reunited. It was ultimately because of their love for him that both Epaphroditus and the other Christians in Philippi had been upset and anxious, and Paul's love for them moved him to relieve their concern as soon as possible. His **own sorrow** at being the involuntary cause of their concern would thus **disappear**.

2:29 / So then, says Paul, "welcome him in the Lord with great joy." This is not the only occasion on which Paul bespeaks a welcome for one of his letter-carriers: he similarly asks the Roman Christians to receive Phoebe "in the Lord's name, as God's people should" (Rom. 16:2). But Epaphroditus does not need to be introduced to the Philippian Christians. He is one of them, and is sure to be received **with joy** on his return—to be received "in the Lord," as a fellow member of the believing community, or, as GNB aptly expands it, **as a brother in the Lord**. Even if part of his commission had perforce to remain unfulfilled, Paul says, "Welcome him nevertheless: it is I who am sending him home."

It is people like Epaphroditus who are worthy of **respect** and esteem in the church. Paul uses the same kind of language in commending Stephanas and his family to the Corinthian Christians. Because they "have given themselves to the service of God's people," he begs the church of

Corinth "to follow the leadership of such people as these, and of anyone else who works and serves with them"; mentioning some others of the same character, he adds, "Such men as these deserve notice" (1 Cor. 16:15–18). The Philippians already had their "church leaders and helpers" (1:1); Epaphroditus by his self-sacrificing service had shown himself well qualified to be added to their number.

This direction of Paul's is completely in line with the teaching of Jesus, according to whom greatest honor among his followers belongs to the one who renders the lowliest service (Mark 10:42–45; Luke 22:24–27; cf. John 13:13–15).

2:30 / Epaphroditus (together with others like him) must be honored, Paul repeats, **because he risked his life and nearly died for the sake of the work of Christ**. Epaphroditus expended himself in service to his fellow Christians of Philippi, doing on their behalf what they as a body were unable to do (they could not all make the journey to Rome to visit Paul). He expended himself equally in service to Paul, ministering to him not only on his own account but also as the representative of the Philippian church. Paul and the Philippian church were alike engaged in their gospel partnership (1:5): by serving them both, Epaphroditus was expending himself in the cause of Christ.

Paul did not set out deliberately to present three examples of the self-renouncing attitude "that Christ Jesus had" (v. 5). But in fact this is what he has done. His own readiness to have his martyrdom credited to the spiritual account of his Philippian friends, Timothy's unselfish service to Paul and genuine concern for other Christians, Epaphroditus's devotion to his mission at great risk to his health and (as it might have been) to his life—all these display the unselfconscious care for others enjoined at the beginning of this chapter and reinforced by the powerful example of Christ's self-emptying.

Additional Notes

2:25 / R. W. Funk ("The Apostolic *Parousia*: Form and Significance," in Farmer, Moule, and Niebuhr, *Christian History*, p. 250) considers vv. 25–30 to be attached to the "apostolic *parousia*" proper (vv. 19–24) as a secondary but related passage. Elements characteristic of the "apostolic *parousia*" found in vv. 25–30 are (*a*) despatch of an emissary, with name, credentials, and purpose; (*b*) the emissary's eagerness to see the recipients; (*c*) benefit accruing to the recipients from the sending of the emissary; (*d*) benefit accruing to Paul from the sending of the emissary.

I have thought it necessary: Gk. *anankaion de hēgēsamēn*, where *hēgēsamēn* is probably to be taken as epistolary aorist (i.e., the time perspective is that of the readers, not of the writer). Cf. *epempsa* (v. 28).

Epaphroditus, meaning "lovely" (derived from Aphrodite), was a very common personal name; cf. Josephus's patron Epaphroditus, to whom his later works were dedicated (*Ant* 1.8; *Life* 430; *Against Apion* 1.1; 2.1, 296). Epaphras of Colossae (Col. 1:7; 4:12; Philem. 23) bears a name which is a shortened form of Epaphroditus, but there is no reason to identify the two men.

Who has worked and fought by my side: Gk. *synergos* and *synstratiōtēs*, two of Paul's well-loved compounds with *syn-* (cf. 4:3, *sy(n)zygos*, "yokefellow"). He uses *synergos* ("fellow worker") also of Priscilla and Aquila (Rom. 16:3), Urbanus (Rom. 16:9), Timothy (Rom. 16:21; 1 Thess. 3:2), Titus (2 Cor. 8:23), Philemon (Philem. 1), as well as others more comprehensively (Phil. 4:3). As for *sy(n)stratiōtēs* ("fellow soldier"), he applies that term also to Archippus of Colossae (Philem. 2). Elsewhere he refers to the gospel ministry as a military campaign (*strateia*, as in 2 Cor. 10:4) and speaks of himself and his colleagues as waging (spiritual) warfare (*strateuesthai*, as in 1 Cor. 9:7; 2 Cor. 10:3).

Who has served as your messenger in helping me: a happy rendering of the hendiadys* "your messenger (*apostolos*) and minister (*leitourgos*) to my need." For the somewhat sacral *leitourgos* cf. *leitourgia* in 2:17, 30. In Rom. 15:16 Paul is the *leitourgos* of Christ Jesus to the Gentiles, discharging a "priestly service" (*hierourgein*); in Rom. 13:6 even secular rulers are "ministers (*leitourgoi*) of God."

2:26 / On the timing of Epaphroditus's illness see W. J. Conybeare and J. S. Howson, *The Life and Epistles of St. Paul*, p. 722; B. S. Mackay, "Further Thoughts on Philippians," *NTS* 7 (1960–61), p. 169; C. O. Buchanan, "Epaphroditus' Sickness and the Letter to the Philippians," *EQ* 36 (1964), pp. 157–66.

Very upset: Gk. *adēmonōn*, used of Jesus in Gethsemane in Mark 14:33 par. Matt. 26:37 ("anguish came over him"), "representing the distress which follows a great shock" (H. B. Swete, *The Gospel According to St. Mark*, p. 342).

2:28 / **I am all the more eager, then, to send him**: Gk. *spoudaioterōs oun epempsa auton*, where *epempsa* is epistolary aorist (cf. *hēgēsamēn* in v. 25) and *spoudaioterōs* emphasizes Paul's initiative in sending him back.

W. Schmithals suggests that, over and above Paul's avowed reasons for sending Epaphroditus back, he perhaps wanted to post in the Philippian church a man he could trust, one who would see to it that he got accurate reports on the situation there (*Paul and the Gnostics*, pp. 70, 71). This suggestion is bound up with Schmithals's view that Paul was disturbed by Gnosticizing tendencies in the Philippian church.

2:30 / **He risked his life**: Gk. *paraboleusamenos tē psychē*, lit., "having gambled with his life" (this is the only NT occurrence of *paraboleuesthai*).

---

*A hendiadys is a figure of speech in which a single idea is expressed by means of two terms joined by "and." For example, "with might and main."

The work of Christ: the variant reading "the work of the Lord" is found in a number of witnesses to the text, including Aleph A P Psi (perhaps under the influence of 1 Cor. 15:58; 16:10). According to J. B. Lightfoot "the work" with no genitive (as in C) is the original text.

In order to give me the help that you yourselves could not give: lit., "in order to fill up your deficiency of ministry to me" (Gk. *hina anaplērōsē to hymōn hysterēma tēs pros me leitourgias*). The *leitourgia* would include the gift mentioned in 4:10–20, brought to Paul by Epaphroditus (cf. the verb *leitourgēsai* used of monetary gifts in Rom. 15:27) but was not exhausted by it; that was a ministry that the Philippian Christians could and did render, but the personal ministrations Paul received from Epaphroditus in Rome (as their *leitourgos* to Paul's need, v. 25) could not be rendered by them in person, and those ministrations are included in the *leitourgia* here.

16

First Conclusion:
Call to Rejoice

In conclusion, my brothers, be joyful in your union with the Lord. I don't	mind repeating what I have written before, and you will be safer if I do so.

"With this communication about Epaphroditus now the epistle seems to be at an end" (Ewald, ad loc.). If so, nothing remains but a final word of greeting. The reader is therefore prepared for **In conclusion**.

3:1 / **In conclusion**: the natural inference from this phrase (drawn by most commentators) is that Paul is on the point of finishing his letter. If the letter be regarded as a unity, it must be assumed that something suddenly occurred to him which prompted the warning of verse 2 with its sequel.

The exhortation to **be joyful** is expressed in a word (Gk. *chairete*) which is also a common form of greeting: "hail" or (less often) "farewell." The language here, **In conclusion, my brothers, be joyful** . . . (Gk. *to loipon, adelphoi mou, chairete* . . .), is very similar to that in 2 Corinthians 13:11 (Gk. *loipon, adelphoi, chairete*), where the sense is certainly "In conclusion, brothers, farewell" (GNB: "And now, my brothers, goodbye!"). The main reason for not taking the present words in the same sense lies in the added phrase "in the Lord" (Gk. *en kyriō*). Here, as clearly in 4:4 (*chairete en kyriō*), the most natural rendering is "rejoice in the Lord." It is unnecessary to overload the wording by translating *en kyriō* as "in your union with the Lord"; "the Lord" may simply be the object of their rejoicing. **Be joyful in** . . . **the Lord** echoes an exhortation repeated in the Psalms (cf. Pss. 32:11; 33:1). The people of God rejoice in him because he is their "exceeding joy" (Ps. 43:4, where GNB paraphrases "you are the source of my happiness"); cf. Rom. 5:11, "we rejoice in God" (GNB: "we rejoice because of what God has done"). It is not necessary to give "in the Lord" its incorporative sense here.

The question now arises: what is it that Paul has **written before** and does not **mind repeating**? The reference might be to the exhortation to rejoice given already in 2:18 (cf. also 1:25; 2:28, 29), but it is difficult to see how a repeated exhortation to rejoice would make life **safer** for the Philippians. G. B. Caird explains that joy "is a safeguard against the utilitarian attitude which judges people and things wholly by the use that can be made of them" (ad loc.). On the other hand F. W. Beare (ad loc.), regarding 3:2–4:1 as part of another Pauline letter that has been editorially interpolated between 3:1 and 4:2, takes the reference here to be Paul's call for unity, already voiced in general terms in 2:1–4 and now about to be repeated with respect to two named individuals in 4:2. Yet another possibility is that the second half of 3:1 goes closely with the warning of 3:2 and refers to a similar warning given in an earlier letter, now lost (cf. J. H. Michael, ad loc.). On the whole, in spite of some difficulty, it seems best to understand **what I have written before** as the call for joy in 2:18 and elsewhere.

Additional Notes

3:1 / In *The New Testament: An American Translation* the first clause is rendered: "Now, my brothers, goodbye, and the Lord be with you"; cf. E. J. Goodspeed, *Problems of New Testament Translation*, pp. 174, 175. "The Lord be with you" is an excessively free rendering of *en kyriō*, "in the Lord."

On the significance of **In conclusion** and the relevance of **what I have written before**, see (in addition to the commentaries and NT introductions) W. Schmithals, *Paul and the Gnostics*, pp. 71–74; he treats 3:2–4:3 and 4:8, 9 as part of a separate Pauline letter and argues against the division of v. 1 so as to relate its second sentence to what immediately follows, as suggested by R. A. Lipsius, E. Haupt, and P. Ewald (ad loc.).

You will be safer if I do so: lit., "for you it is safe" (Gk. *asphales*). V. P. Furnish ("The Place and Purpose of Philippians iii," *NTS* 10 [1963–64], pp. 80–88) argues that the adjective *asphales* (not found elsewhere in Paul) means here "specific" or "dependable" (as in Acts 25:26) and (unconvincingly) that "to write the same things" (*ta auta graphein*) means "to give the same admonitions in writing as Timothy and Epaphroditus have been instructed to give you orally" (not, as in GNB, **repeating what I have written before**).

The words *emoi men ouk oknēron, hymin d' asphales* ("not irksome for me, and safe for you") may well form an iambic trimeter (quoted by Paul from some source or other), even if a purist would object to the caesura in the penultimate spondaic foot, as violating the "law of the final cretic."

17

Warning Against "Workers of Iniquity"

Watch out for those who do evil things, those dogs, those men who insist on cutting the body. ³It is we, not they, who have received the true circumcision, for we worship God by means of his Spirit and rejoice in our life in union with Christ Jesus. We do not put any trust in external ceremonies.

After "In conclusion" in verse 1, it comes as a surprise to find this warning which, together with the later warning of verses 18 and 19, forms a substantial part of the letter in its present form. It is by way of contrast with those against whom the warnings are given that Paul sets forth his own procedure and purpose in life (vv. 7–14).

3:2 / Who now are **those who do evil things**, the **dogs** against whom Paul puts his readers on their guard? They are certainly identical with the **men who insist on cutting the body** (all three expressions denote the same people) and these last words provide the surest clue to their identity. In the original they represent a single noun, devised by Paul as a derogatory wordplay on "circumcision" (Gk. *peritomē*) and rendered in older English versions as "concision" (Gk. *katatomē*). Paul sometimes uses the word "circumcision" as a collective noun, as when Peter is called an apostle "to the circumcision," meaning, as GNB puts it, "to the Jews" (Gal. 2:7–9). Here the word "concision" is similarly used, of those **who insist on cutting the body**—"the mutilation party," we might say.

For Paul, circumcision is a sacral term, applied not only in its literal sense but also to the purification and dedication of the heart. There is OT precedent for this in Deuteronomy 10:16 (GNB: "be obedient to the LORD") and Jeremiah 4:4 (GNB: "dedicate yourselves to me"), where emphasis is laid on the circumcision of the heart as what God really desires. Paul's older contemporary Philo of Alexandria agrees that circumcision signifies "the cutting away of pleasure and all passions and the destruction of impious glory," but disagrees with those who maintain that the external rite may be discontinued if the spiritual lesson is practiced (*Migration of Abraham*, 92). Here, therefore, Paul applies to those who insist on the external rite a disparaging parody of the sacral word—a parody that links literal circumcision with those pagan cuttings of the body that were forbidden by the law of Israel (Lev. 19:28; 21:5; Deut. 14:1; cf. 1 Kings 18:28).

But it is not to Jews in general that he refers here so scathingly, nor yet to those Jewish Christians who may have continued to circumcise their sons in accordance with ancestral custom. The people against whom Gentile Christians needed to be put on their guard, and whom Paul elsewhere denounces in the same kind of unsparing terms as he uses here, are those who visited Gentile churches and insisted that circumcision was an indispensable condition of their being justified in God's sight. This insistence was conceivably part of a campaign to bring Paul's Gentile converts under the control of the mother church in Jerusalem. Paul was certainly at pains to emphasize his converts' independence of Jerusalem; but his basic objection was that the insistence on circumcision undermined the gospel that proclaimed that God in his grace justified Jews and Gentiles alike on the ground of faith in Christ, quite apart from circumcision or any other legal requirement. The Judaizers, then, are the **men who insist on cutting the body**—"the Snippers," as H. W. Montefiore aptly translates the dismissive term.

In calling them **those who do evil things**, Paul may be echoing the phrase "workers of iniquity" (GNB: "wicked people," "evil men") which some of the OT psalmists used to describe their enemies (cf. Pss. 5:5; 6:8; etc.); he refers to the same class of interlopers in 2 Corinthians 11:13 as "deceitful workmen" (GNB: "who lie about their work"). To his mind, they were doing the devil's work by subverting the faith of Gentile believers. In calling them **dogs**, he was perhaps throwing back at them a term of invective by which they described uncircumcised Gentiles; it was all the more apt if he pictured them as prowling round the Gentile churches trying to win members to their own outlook and way of life.

It is not implied that such people had already made their way into the fellowship of the Philippian Christians, but it was quite likely that they would attempt the same tactics in Philippi as they had used in Corinth (cf. 2 Cor. 11:4–6, 12–15, 20), and the Philippian Christians are forewarned against them.

3:3 / **It is we, not they**, says Paul, **who have received the true circumcision**: literally, "For *we* are the circumcision" (another instance of "circumcision" as a collective noun). True circumcision, "the circumcision made by Christ" (Col. 2:11), is a matter of inward purification and consecration. Those **who have received** this **circumcision** render to God true heart devotion: they **worship** him **by means of his Spirit** (lit., "worship by the Spirit of God"). This is the teaching conveyed by Jesus to the Samaritan woman: "God is Spirit, and only by the power of his Spirit can people worship him as he really is" (John 4:24). Such people **rejoice in** their **life in union with Christ Jesus**—more literally and concisely, they "boast in Christ Jesus"; he is the object of their exultation (there is no need to give the phrase "in Christ Jesus" its incorporative force here). More than once Paul quotes Jeremiah 9:24 in the form "Let him who boasts, boast in the Lord" (1 Cor. 1:31; 2 Cor. 10:17, where GNB renders "Whoever wants to boast must boast about what the Lord has done"). He probably alludes to the same text here: for Paul, "the Lord" is **Christ Jesus**.

External ceremonies are henceforth irrelevant. Physical circumcision has been replaced by the circumcision of the heart which "is the work of God's Spirit, not of the written Law" (Rom. 2:29). The word rendered **external ceremonies** is literally translated "flesh" (Gk. *sarx*); Paul uses this word not only in its ordinary sense but also to denote unregenerate human nature and sometimes to include practically everything, apart from God, in which people mistakenly put their trust.

Additional Notes

3:2 / "It will always appear extraordinary," wrote H. J. Holtzmann, "that the letter actually first finds its center at the very point where it seems to be moving towards the end" (*Einleitung in das Neue Testament*, p. 301). The abrupt transition to a note of warning has been variously explained—by changing impressions affecting Paul's attitude as he dictated the letter (R. A. Lipsius, ad loc.), by a belated stimulus from Timothy (P. Ewald, ad loc.), by a fresh report that had just reached Paul (J. B. Lightfoot, *Philippians*, p. 69).

Watch out is the rendering of Gk. *blepete*, which is similarly used in warning in several NT passages; cf. Mark 4:24; 8:15; 12:38; 13:5, 9; 1 Cor. 8:9; Gal. 5:15; Col. 2:8; etc. It can, of course, mean simply "look at," "pay attention to" (cf. G. D. Kilpatrick, "*Blepete* Philippians 3:2," in M. Black and G. Fohrer, eds., *In Memoriam Paul Kahle*, pp. 146–48), but in the present context a more urgent sense is indicated.

Dogs were regarded as unclean animals (cf. Rev. 22:15) because they were not particular about what they ate. J. B. Lightfoot (ad loc.) quotes *Clem. Hom.*

2.19, where (with reference to Matt. 15:26) Gentiles are said to be called **dogs** because their habits in the matter of food and conduct are so different from those of the Israelites.

The idea that the **men who insist on cutting the body** are Jews who have no commitment to the Christian faith (cf. E. Lohmeyer, ad loc.) may be ruled out because Paul does not use such opprobrious language in speaking of his own natural kinsfolk; moreover, there does not seem to have been any substantial Jewish community in Philippi (see p. xvi). As for the view of W. Schmithals (*Paul and the Gnostics*, pp. 65–91) that they were Jewish Christian Gnostics, *hē katatomē* would have been a most imprecise and misleading way of designating such people. As with so many other features of Schmithals's interpretation, Gnosticism has to be read into Phil. 3:2 in order to be read out of it.

3:3 / **We worship God by means of his Spirit**: Gk. *hoi pneumati theou latreuontes* ("who worship by the Spirit of God"), for which there is a rather less well attested variant *hoi pneumati theō latreuontes* (so KJV: "which worship God in the spirit"). GNB seems to combine both readings.

18

Paul's Former Code of Values

I could, of course, put my trust in such things. If anyone thinks he can trust in external ceremonies, I have even more reason to feel that way. ⁵I was circumcised when I was a week old. I am an Israelite by birth, of the tribe of Benjamin, a pure-blooded Hebrew. As far as keeping the Jewish Law is concerned, I was a Pharisee, ⁶and I was so zealous that I persecuted the church. As far as a person can be righteous by obeying the commands of the Law, I was without fault.

When Paul claims that he could put up a better record "in the flesh" than most people, if he still attached any importance to this sort of thing (which he does not), he means not only **external ceremonies** but a wide range of heritage, endowment, and achievement. The contemplation of this wide range once filled him with deep satisfaction, but this is no longer so.

3:4 / If an orthodox pedigree and upbringing, followed by high personal attainment in the religious and moral realm, ensured a good standing in the presence of God (as was implied by the people against whom Paul's warning is directed), Paul need fear no competition. There is a close affinity between his words here and 2 Corinthians 11:21 ff., where ("talking like a fool") he lists things in which he might boast, if boasting were appropriate, and then dismisses the idea of boasting in such things as utter madness. This suggests that the opponents whom he now has in view are of the same order as those whom he castigates in 2 Corinthians 11:12–15, and it would be easy to believe that the present warning was written about the same time as 2 Corinthians 10–13. Even if such people had not yet infiltrated the church of Philippi, they might well try to do so. It is not so certain as W. Schmithals thinks (*Paul and the Gnostics*, p. 73) that Paul's language reflects an attempt already made to undermine his authority in the eyes of the Philippians.

3:5 / Paul now lists seven things which at one time would have given him confidence before God.

I was circumcised when I was a week old: literally, "on the eighth day," as every male Israelite child had to be, according to the terms of God's covenant with Abraham (Gen. 17:12). He was a Jew by birth, not a proselyte from paganism who would have been circumcised at the time of his conversion.

I am an Israelite by birth. Having been born into the chosen race and admitted into the covenant community by circumcision, he inherited all the privileges that belonged to that community—privileges he enumerates in Romans 9:4, 5.

Of the tribe of Benjamin. Paul evidently attached some importance to his membership of this tribe; he mentions it also in Romans 11:1. Benjamin was the only son of Jacob born in the holy land (Gen. 35:16–18). When the Davidic monarchy was disrupted after Solomon's death, the tribe of Benjamin, situated on the northern frontier of Judah, was retained as part of the southern kingdom. After the return from the Babylonian exile there were resettlements in Jerusalem and the surrounding territory of members of the tribe of Benjamin (Neh. 11:7–9, 31–36). From some of these Paul's family may have traced its descent. His parents may have given him the name Saul (cf. Acts 7:58; 13:9; etc.) after Israel's first king, the most illustrious member of the tribe of Benjamin in Hebrew history.

A pure-blooded Hebrew: literally, "a Hebrew from Hebrews" (Hebrew son of Hebrew parents). This implies something more than his being "an Israelite by birth," as in 2 Corinthians 11:22, where he says of his opponents, "Are they Hebrews? So am I. Are they Israelites? So am I." "Hebrews" in the special sense (as probably in Acts 6:1) were Jews who normally spoke Aramaic with one another and attended synagogues where the service was said in Hebrew (as distinct from Hellenists, who spoke only Greek). According to Luke, Paul heard the heavenly voice on the Damascus road address him in Hebrew (Acts 26:14) and could address a hostile Jerusalem crowd impromptu in Hebrew (Acts 21:40; 22:2); in both these places "Hebrew" may be used in a wider sense to include Aramaic. Unlike many Jews of the dispersion, Paul's family apparently avoided as far as possible assimilation to the culture of their Tarsian environment.

I was a Pharisee. The party of the Pharisees made special conscience of **keeping the Jewish Law** in minute detail, although all members of the covenant community were under an obligation to keep it. The Pharisees, who first appear in history late in the second century B.C., seem to have been the spiritual heirs of the Hasidaeans or pious groups who played a noble part in defense of their ancestral religion when Antiochus Epiphanes (175–163 B.C.) set himself to abolish it (cf. 1 Macc. 2:42; 7:14; 2 Macc. 14:6). At an earlier date those pious groups receive honorable mention in Malachi 3:16–4:3; their devotion to the divine law is illustrated by Psalm 119.

The term Pharisees means "separated ones"; it has been variously explained, but among those so designated it probably emphasized their separation from everything that might convey ethical or ceremonial impurity. They built up a body of oral tradition, which was designed to adapt the ancient precepts of the written law to the changing situations of later days and thus safeguard their principles against being dismissed as obsolete or impracticable. In this they were distinguished from their chief rivals, the Sadducees, who maintained the authority of the written law alone and who also rejected the Pharisees' belief in the resurrection of the dead and in the existence of orders of angels and demons (cf. Acts 23:8). They banded themselves together in local fellowships. Josephus, who claims to have regulated his own life by Pharisaic rule from the age of nineteen, reckons that there were some six thousand Pharisees in his day (*Ant.* 17.42).

Paul's membership in the party of the Pharisees is attested by Luke, who reports him as saying that he was "brought up . . . as a student of Gamaliel" (Acts 22:3), the leading Pharisee of his day (cf. Acts 5:34), as telling the younger Agrippa that he had lived "from the very first . . . as a member of the strictest party of our religion, the Pharisees" (Acts 26:5), and as claiming before the Sanhedrin to be "a Pharisee, the son of Pharisees" (Acts 23:6), implying that he was not the first member of his family to be associated with the party or (less probably) that he was the pupil of Pharisees.

I was so zealous . . . : zeal for God was an honorable tradition in Israel, and at this period was not confined to the party of militant nationalists who came to be known as the Zealots. The precedent for godly zeal had been set by Phinehas (Num. 25:7–13; Ps. 106:30, 31), Elijah (1 Kings 19:10, 14) and Mattathias, father of Judas Maccabaeus (1 Macc. 2:24–28). Paul describes himself in Galatians 1:13, 14, as having been "much more devoted [zealous] to the traditions of our ancestors" than most of his youthful contemporaries and as providing supreme evidence of that devotion or zeal by the ruthlessness with which he "persecuted . . . the church of God" and did his best "to destroy it." If in 1 Corinthians 15:9 (cf. 1 Tim. 1:13, 14) his persecution of the church, viewed from a later Christian perspective, was the sin of all sins, rendering him quite unworthy of the grace that yet called him to be an apostle; nevertheless when he was actively engaged in the work of persecution he regarded it as his most acceptable service to God. When in Romans 10:2 he describes his fellow Israelites as "deeply devoted to God," adding that "their devotion is not based on true knowledge," he is drawing a pen portrait of the man he himself once was, endeavoring by his persecuting zeal to set up his own way of getting right with God.

In fact, **as far as a person can be righteous by obeying the commands of the Law**, he says, **I was without fault**. This is Paul's Christian assessment of his pre-Christian attainment, made from the perspective of nearly thirty years of apostolic ministry. No Jew could have achieved more in devotion to his ancestral heritage. The parents of John the Baptist are commended because they "obeyed fully all the Lord's laws and commands" (Luke 1:6). High commendation indeed, and Paul also had earned it. To gain such commendation was once his ambition, but now the great reversal of accepted values had altered everything.

With Paul's attainment may be compared that of the rich man who assured Jesus that he had kept all the commandments of God since his boyhood (Mark 10:20) or, more relevantly, Paul's own claim before the Sanhedrin to have maintained a good conscience before God his whole life long (Acts 23:1; cf. 24:16). To conform with the righteousness required by the law called for infinite painstaking, but (as Paul had proved) it was not impossible. He made the grade, only to discover that it did him no good.

Additional Notes

3:4 / The twofold **I** (**I could . . . put my trust . . . I have even more reason . . .**) is emphatic (Gk. *egō*). Cf. the repeated "So am I" (Gk. *kagō*=*kai egō*) of 2 Corinthians 11:22. W. Schmithals thinks Paul is defending himself against Gnostics who represent him as a mere man of flesh, lacking the Christ spirit, and therefore no apostle of Christ but at best an apostle of men (*Paul and the Gnostics*, pp. 90, 91). There is nothing in the text to support this. He is rather defending himself against Judaizers who try to diminish his status in order to exalt their own superior authority.

3:5 / **Of the tribe of Benjamin**. It is one of the "undesigned coincidences" between Acts and the Pauline letters that only in the latter do we read that Paul belonged to **the tribe of Benjamin** and only in the former do we read that his Jewish name was Saul. Early Christian writers traced a connection between Paul's persecuting zeal and the words about Benjamin in Jacob's blessing of his sons (Gen. 49:27): "Benjamin is like a vicious wolf. Morning and evening he kills and devours" (cf. Hippolytus, *On the Blessing of Jacob*, ad loc.; cf. *ANF* 5, p. 168).

A pure-blooded Hebrew: on Hebrews and Hellenists see C. F. D. Moule, "Once More, Who Were the Hellenists?" *ExpT* 70 (1958–59), pp. 100–102; F. F. Bruce, *Paul: Apostle of the Free Spirit*, pp. 42, 43.

As far as keeping the Jewish Law is concerned: lit., "according to law" (Gk. *kata nomon*). The omission of the definite article before "law" is common in Paul; it may reflect the Jewish tendency to treat the corresponding Hebrew word *tōrāh* almost as a proper noun, and therefore not requiring the article, when the law of Moses is meant.

I was a Pharisee: on the Pharisees see Josephus, *War* 2. 162–66; *Ant.* 18.12–15. "Pharisees" most probably represents Aram. *pᵉrîshayyâ*, Heb. *pᵉrûshîm*, "separated ones" (especially in a moral sense). For the Hebrew word cf. a later rabbinical commentary, *Leviticus Rabba*, where the injunction, "Be holy, because I, the LORD your God, am holy" (Lev. 19:2) is amplified: "As I am holy, so you also must be holy; as I am separate, so you also must be separate [*pᵉrûshîm*]." The Pharisees were particularly scrupulous is observing the Jewish food laws and the rules about tithing. They tithed garden herbs as well as grain, wine, and olives (cf. Matt. 23:23; Luke 11:42), and avoided eating food that was subject to tithing unless they were sure that the tithe had been paid on it. See W. D. Davies, *Paul and Rabbinic Judaism*; E. P. Sanders, *Paul and Palestinian Judaism*; and E. Rivkin, *A Hidden Revolution*.

3:6 / In Gal. 1:14 Paul calls himself a zealot (Gk. *zēlōtēs*) for the ancestral traditions; in Acts 22:3 he tells a Jewish audience in Jerusalem that, before his conversion, he was a zealot for God "as are all of you who are here today"; in Acts 21:20 the elders of the Jerusalem church tell Paul that all its members are zealots for the law. In none of these places is the noun used in its party sense (as it is, perhaps, in Luke 6:15; Acts 1:13). The party of the Zealots shared the principles of the Pharisees, but insisted in addition that it was impermissible for Jews living in the holy land to pay taxes to a pagan ruler (like the Roman emperor).

19

Paul's Present Code of Values

Philippians 3:7–11

But all those things that I might count as profit I now reckon as loss for Christ's sake. ⁸Not only those things; I reckon everything as complete loss for the sake of what is so much more valuable, the knowledge of Christ Jesus my Lord. For his sake I have thrown everything away; I consider it all as mere garbage, so that I may gain Christ ⁹and be completely united with him. I no longer have a righteousness of my own, the kind that is gained by obeying the Law. I now have the righteousness that is given through faith in Christ, the righteousness that comes from God and is based on faith. ¹⁰All I want is to know Christ and to experience the power of his resurrection, to share in his sufferings and become like him in his death, ¹¹in the hope that I myself will be raised from death to life.

What Paul formerly regarded as achievement he now acknowledges to have been failure. What he would formerly have regarded as worthless and indeed pernicious he now recognizes to be the only achievement worth pursuing—the personal knowledge of Jesus as Lord, sharing the experience of his death and resurrection.

3:7 / It was but reasonable to take pride, as Paul once did, in such a catalogue of merit. If a reader suspects that Paul still feels some pride in being able to present such a record of past achievement, all such suspicion is swept away by what Paul now says: **all those things that I might count as profit**, and did once count as profit, **I now reckon as loss for Christ's sake**—that is, for the sake of gaining Christ. From the credit side of the ledger they have been transferred to the debit side; they are not merely seen to be valueless and irrelevant, but he would be better off without them. Perhaps the very recollection of such attainments could now be harmful if it carried with it the temptation to put some confidence in them again. Christ alone must be the object of Paul's confidence, and **for Christ's sake** all these former objects of confidence have lost the value they once had. Paul had learned that, in spite of them all, his only ground of acceptance before God was ground that he shared with the rawest convert from paganism: faith in Christ. He does not deny that it was a great privilege to have been born a Jew and have access to the oracles of God (Rom. 3:1, 2); he does deny that one can rely on such a privilege as a basis of divine approval.

3:8 / In truth, not only Paul's personal heritage and achievement but **everything** in the world has been transvalued by Christ. So **much more valuable** was **the knowledge of Christ Jesus my Lord** that, by comparison with it, **everything** else was not merely valueless but had negative value. Whatever existed outside of Christ and the gospel that he had commissioned Paul to make known throughout the world was a dead loss, the sort of thing to be **thrown** . . . **away**, like so much **garbage**, the merest street-sweepings. When he entered the service of Christ on the Damascus road, that meant the renunciation of all that he had chiefly prized up to that moment; it was a renunciation well worth making.

The knowledge of God was of paramount value in the eyes of the great prophets of Israel (cf. Hos. 6:6); for Paul the knowledge of God was supremely mediated through Christ, and in being so mediated it was immensely enriched. "Knowledge" (Gk. *gnōsis*) was a current term in the religious and philosophical vocabulary of Paul's day; the "knowledge" that was widely sought and esteemed was partly intellectual, partly mystical. Some forms of the current cultivation of "knowledge" developed into the systems of thought that appear in the second century under the general designation of "Gnosticism." Such "knowledge" was pursued in the Corinthian church, and Paul was not impressed by it: "such knowledge," he said, "puffs a person up with pride, but love builds up" (1 Cor. 8:1). A community was helped to grow to maturity much more by love of God and love of one's fellows than by the pursuit of knowledge. The **knowledge of Christ Jesus my Lord** is personal knowledge: it includes the experience of being loved by him and loving him in return—and loving, for his sake, all those for whom he died. It is not certain that here, as in his Corinthian correspondence, Paul is contrasting this personal **knowledge of Christ** with inferior forms of knowledge: he is assuredly emphasizing that it is the only form of knowledge worth having, a knowledge so transcendent in value that it compensates for the loss of everything else.

To know Christ and to **gain Christ** are two ways of expressing the same ambition. If Christ is "the key that opens all the hidden treasures of God's wisdom and knowledge" (Col. 2:3), to know him means to have access to those treasures; but to know him for his own sake is what matters to Paul most of all.

Paul had never known the earthly Jesus. If, during Jesus' ministry, Paul had learned anything about his teaching and activities, he would have disapproved. After Jesus' arrest and execution, Paul thought of him with repulsion as one on whom, by the very nature of his death, the curse of God rested: "Anyone who is hanged on a tree is under God's curse" (Gal. 3:13). Those who proclaimed such a person to be the Lord's anointed, as the disciples of Jesus did, were blasphemers; the well-being of Israel demanded their extinction. And, quite apart from Paul's antipathy to all that Jesus stood for, how can one enjoy a personal relationship with someone who has died and whom one never knew?

When God chose, on the Damascus road, to reveal his Son to Paul, the Son of God at the same time introduced himself to Paul: "I am Jesus," he said. Immediately Paul was captivated by him and became his bondslave for life. "What shall I do, Lord?" he asked him, and his whole subsequent career was one of obedience to the answer that his question drew forth (Acts 22:7–10). In that moment Paul knew himself to be loved by the Son of God who, as he was to say, "loved me and gave his life for me" (Gal. 2:20). For him henceforth the "first and great commandment," to love the LORD his God, was honored in his love for Christ, the image of God: "the person who loves God is known by him" (1 Cor. 8:3). A relationship of mutual knowledge and love was established there and then between the apostle on earth and his exalted Lord, and to explore the fullness of this relationship was from now on Paul's inexhaustible joy. For him, in short, life was Christ—to love Christ, to know Christ, to **gain Christ**: "Christ is the way, and Christ the prize."

3:9 / To **gain Christ** means to **be completely united with him**, to enjoy faith-union with him (and therefore also with the rest of his people); compare NEB: "for the sake of . . . finding myself incorporate in him." Paul was intensely aware and appreciative of his one-to-one relationship with the risen Christ, but it was not an exclusive relationship: "I knew that Christ had given me birth / To brother all the souls on earth" (John Masefield, "The Everlasting Mercy"). He was already "in Christ" but here he speaks of his ambition "to be found in him" (as his words are literally rendered). The aorist tense of the verbs "gain" and "be found" suggests that he is again looking forward to the Day of Christ. But his ambition "to be found in him" on that great day can be realized only if he is continuously and progressively living in union with him during this mortal existence, and to this end Paul gladly jettisons everything else, including his formerly prized **righteousness . . . gained by obeying the Law**.

The man who had attained full marks in competing for legal **righteousness** now threw that **righteousness** overboard, for he had found a better **kind**. What good had legal **righteousness** done him after all? It had not saved him from the sin of persecuting the followers of Christ. Anyone who sought legal **righteousness** could no doubt claim it as his **own**, but it was fatal to imagine that such a **righteousness**, which was inevitably self-righteousness, could establish a claim on God.

But with the better **righteousness that is given through faith in Christ** there is no question of establishing a claim on God; it is God himself who gives this righteousness. It **comes from God and is based on faith**. **Faith in Christ** is the means by which sinners appropriate it; they are "put right with God through . . . faith in Christ, and not by doing what the Law requires" (Gal. 2:16). It is good to do what the Law requires, but that is not the way to receive the **righteousness** that God bestows. Paul's trusted foundation of legal **righteousness** collapsed beneath his feet on the Damascus road, when he suddenly saw himself to be the chief of sinners; but in that same instant he received **through faith** in the Son of God the new and durable foundation of **righteousness** freely bestowed by God's grace. Now, and forever after, he knew himself to be accepted by God for Christ's sake.

3:10 / **All I want is to know Christ**: once more Paul states his ambition. He had lived with the knowledge of Christ for many years, but he found in Christ an inexhaustible fullness; there was always more of him to know. So much was this knowledge a matter of interpersonal union that **to know Christ** meant **to experience the power of his resurrection**. If the love of God is supremely demonstrated in the death of Christ (Rom. 5:8), his **power** is supremely demonstrated in the **resurrection** of Christ, and those who are united by faith with the risen Christ have this **power** imparted to them. "This power working in us is the same as the mighty strength which he used when he raised Christ from the dead" (Eph. 1:19, 20); it is the **power** which, among other things, enables the believer to ignore the dictates or enticements of sin and to lead a life of holiness which pleases God.

If, on one plane, Paul shared the **power** of Christ's risen life, on another plane he shared **his sufferings**. To suffer for Christ, he has said already (1:29), is a privilege; moreover, to suffer for him is to suffer with him. "We have a share in Christ's many sufferings" (2 Cor. 1:5), he says in the letter that perhaps more than any other discloses this aspect of Paul's apostleship. In Paul's eyes, the **sufferings** he endured for Christ's sake in the course of his apostolic service represented his share in the **sufferings** of Christ, and to accept them as such transfigured and glorified them. It was also his hope that, by absorbing as many of these afflictions as possible in his own person, he would "complete what still remains of Christ's sufferings on behalf of his body, the church" (Col. 1:24) and leave less for his fellow Christians to endure. Thus he might make some personal recompense for the zeal with which he had once made the people of Christ suffer and so persecuted Christ himself (cf. Acts 9:4, 5). Nor does he show any spirit of self-pity in speaking thus: it was an honor to **share in** the **sufferings** of Christ and so to enter into closer personal fellowship with him.

To **become like** Christ **in his death** was for Paul partly self-identification with Christ crucified, partly a matter of daily experience, partly an anticipation of bodily death, which would more probably than not take the form of martyrdom for Christ's sake (as in the event it did).

So far as self-identification with Christ is concerned, the dying with Christ enacted in baptism at the outset of Paul's Christian career (Rom. 6:2–11) was no make-believe; it exercised a decisive influence on him from then on: "I have been put to death with Christ on his cross, so that it is no longer I who live, but it is Christ who lives in me" (Gal. 2:19, 20).

So far as daily experience was concerned, Paul could say, "I face death every day!" (1 Cor. 15:31). He could speak of "carry[ing] in our mortal bodies the death [or rather the 'dying'] of Jesus, so that his life also may be seen in our bodies" (2 Cor. 4:10). And if he should one day face the executioner for Jesus' sake, that would crown his likeness to Christ **in his death**. Death, and especially such a death as that, would (as he has said in 1:21) be sheer gain for one to whom life meant Christ.

There were no doubt some people in the Gentile churches (not necessarily in the church of Philippi) who viewed Paul's hardships, including his present imprisonment, as a sign that he had not yet reached that stage of spiritual perfection that they themselves claimed to have attained (cf. 1 Cor. 4:8). Paul views them quite differently: they are for him the indispensable conditions of identification with Christ in glory: "If we share Christ's suffering, we will also share his glory" (Rom. 8:17).

3:11 / Experiencing **the power** of Christ's **resurrection** here and now was not a substitute for looking forward to the resurrection of the body, as some of Paul's Corinthian converts appear to have thought (1 Cor. 15:12). Christ's resurrection, the power of which was imparted to his people even in their present mortal life, involved the hope for those who died believing in him "that God, who raised the Lord Jesus to life, will also raise us up with Jesus" (2 Cor. 4:14). Paul will return to this later (vv. 20, 21). Here he speaks personally: if one who faced death daily for Christ's sake was liable to end mortal life as a martyr for him, so one who experienced **the power of his resurrection** day by day could look forward with certainty to sharing his **resurrection** after death. The **hope** of which Paul speaks is no uncertain hope for him, but one that is sure and wellfounded. If his language implies any uncertainty—"if only I may finally arrive at the resurrection from the dead" (NEB)—it may lie in Paul's belief that, even at this late stage in his career, he might not pass through death after all but still be alive at the coming of Christ. But all the signs pointed to his having to undergo death, and a violent death in all probability. His assurance, however, was that if "Christ has been raised from death," this is "the guarantee that those who sleep in death will also be raised" (1 Cor. 15:20). "We know," he says in 2 Corinthians 5:1, "that when this tent we live in . . . is torn down, God will have a house in heaven for us to live in, a home he himself has made, which will last forever."

The GNB rendering, **in the hope that I myself will be raised from death to life**, does not bring out the clear implication of Paul's wording: that the resurrection of believers is a resurrection that brings them out of the realm where the rest of the dead are.

Additional Notes

3:7 / I now reckon: Gk. *hēgēmai* ("perfect"); the reference is not particularly to his conversion experience, as it would be if the aorist *hēgēsamēn* had been used. (In v. 8 **I reckon** represents the present *hēgoumai*.)

Paul's language here is different from the adaptation of the bookkeeping terminology of profit and loss occasionally found elsewhere. Cf. Aristotle, *Nicomachean Ethics* 5.4.13, where justice is said to be the mean between profit and loss (no one gets more or less than is due); also *Pirqe Abot* 2.1, where Rabbi Judah the Prince (ca. A.D. 200) is credited with the precept: "Reckon the loss incurred by the fulfillment of a commandment against the reward secured by its observance, and the gain acquired by a transgression against the loss it involves."

3:8 / Not only those things: Gk. *alla menounge kai* ("Yes indeed; I even . . ."). Gk. *alla kai* is reinforced by the compound particle (*men, oun,* and *ge*), which emphasizes its progressive sense (cf. M. E. Thrall, *Greek Particles in the New Testament*, pp. 15,16).

F. W. Beare (ad loc.) has a helpful discussion of **the knowledge of Christ Jesus my Lord**. Paul's language here cannot be accounted for in terms either of the Hebraic or of the Hellenic background of *gnōsis*: rather, he makes "a new, creative fusion of the Hellenic with the Hebraic, which issues in a distinctively *Christian* synthesis far richer than either, though it is the heir of both." In this synthesis, it should be added, the most important element was the personal knowledge of Christ that Paul had already gained; he expands its significance in v. 10. See R. Bultmann, *TDNT* vol. 1, pp. 689–714, s.v. *"ginōskō," "gnōsis,"* etc.; J. Dupont, *Gnosis: La connaissance religieuse dans les épîtres de saint Paul*; B. E. Gärtner, "The Pauline and Johannine Idea of 'to know God' against the Hellenistic Background," *NTS* 14 (1967–68), pp. 209–31.

I have thrown everything away: Gk. *ta panta ezēmiōthēn* (passive), lit., "I have been fined everything"; "I have been deprived of all that I have," which may imply such penalization or disinheritance as he had suffered because of his commitment to Christ as well as his willing renunciation of all for Christ's sake.

3:9 / To **be completely united with him** is, lit., "that I may be found (*hina . . . heurethō*) in him." For the use of the passive of *heuriskein* as a surrogate for the verb "to be" or "to become" cf. 2:7. See also E. D. Burton, *The Epistle to the Galatians*, p. 125 (in a note on Gal. 2:17). If it be asked at what time Paul hopes to be found in Christ, the answer may be "on the Day of Christ"; but he knows that he will be found in Christ then only if he lives in Christ now.

The **righteousness that comes from God** is "God's way of putting people right with himself" (Rom. 3:21)—a right relationship with God received by divine grace and not achieved **by obeying the Law**. It **is given through faith in Christ**: Gk. *dia pisteōs Christou*, where GNB is certainly right in treating *Christou* as objective genitive, although some wish to treat it as subjective genitive and render the phrase, "through Christ's faithfulness" (cf. Rom. 3:22, 26; Gal. 2:16). See J. A. Ziesler, *The Meaning of Righteousness in Paul*; F. F. Bruce, *The Epistle to the Galatians*, pp. 138–40 (in a note on Gal. 2:16).

3:10 / **All I want is to know Christ**: Gk. *tou gnōnai auton*, "in order to know him," where the aorist infinitive follows the precedent of the aorists *kerdēsō* (**I may gain**) and *heurethō* ("I may be found") in vv. 8, 9. It is with the knowledge of Christ to be experienced in this life that Paul is here concerned (as in v. 8, **the knowledge of Christ Jesus my Lord**). It is pointless to say that "Paul undoubtedly borrows from the Gnostics in describing the *gnōsis Christou Iēsou* as a distinctive mark of the Christian" when it is conceded, almost in the same breath, that the content of vv. 8–11 "is very different from Gnosticism" since "Paul is not describing individual experiences but the character of Christian existence in general" (R. Bultmann, *TDNT* vol. 1, pp. 710, 711, s.v. *"ginōskō," "gnōsis,"* etc.). It might be, as W. Schmithals, says, that Paul here "sets the true knowledge of Jesus Christ in opposition to the 'contradictions of what is falsely called knowledge' " (*Paul and the Gnostics*, p. 92), if it were clear that Paul had in mind proponents of such a rival *gnōsis* (see notes on vv. 18, 19 below).

On Paul's desire **to share in** Christ's **sufferings** see B. M. Ahern, "The Fellowship of His Sufferings (Phil 3: 10)," *CBQ* 22 (1960), pp. 1–32; also H. Seesemann, *Der Begriff KOINŌNIA im Neuen Testament*.

3:11 / **In the hope that**: Gk. *ei pōs*, "if perhaps," "if by any means," introducing a clause of purpose where the attainment of the purpose is not altogether within the subject's power; cf. Acts 27:12, of the sailors' hope of making Phoenix and spending the winter there; Rom. 1:10, of Paul's prayer that it may be possible for him at last to visit Rome; 11:14, of his hope to promote the salvation of his fellow Jews by moving them to covet a share in the gospel blessings so much enjoyed by Gentile believers. See BDF, #375.

The noun *exanastasis*, "resurrection," is unparalleled in NT; the addition of the prefix *ex-* before the regular form *anastasis* (used, e.g., in v. 10) reinforces the significance of the preposition *ek* in the following phrase *ek nekrōn*, "out from among dead ones," and emphasizes that the end-time bodily resurrection of the just is in view, not simply a present spiritual resurrection. It "is intended unmistakably to convey the realism of the resurrection from among the physically dead, but it makes sense only if it is distinguished from another interpretation" (J. Gnilka, ad loc.)—the other interpretation being presumably that against which Paul makes a full statement of the doctrine of resurrection in 1 Cor. 15. Again, this may be so; we cannot be sure.

20

Paul's Ambition

I do not claim that I have already succeeded or have already become perfect. I keep striving to win the prize for which Christ Jesus has already won me to himself. ¹³Of course, my brothers, I really do not[e] think that I have already won it; the one thing I do, however, is to forget what is behind me and do my best to reach what is ahead. ¹⁴So I run straight toward the goal in order to win the prize, which is God's call through Christ Jesus to the life above.

e. not; *some manuscripts have* not yet.

Whatever others may claim for themselves; Paul knows that he has not attained perfection yet. So long as mortal life lasts, there is further progress to be made. Not until the end of the race is the prize awarded.

3:12 / Paul now passes from the language of accountancy to that of athletic endeavor (cf. 2:16). He is running a race; he has not yet breasted the tape or won **the prize**, and he must keep on running until he does so. Some of his converts elsewhere imagined that they had attained perfection and entered into their kingly glory already: Paul tells them ironically that he wishes their claims were true, because then it would be true for him as well, but he knows that he is still exerting himself amid the dust and heat (1 Cor. 4:8–13). If some of his Philippian friends are tempted to make similarly premature claims of spiritual achievement, what he now says may be helpful to them. He illustrates the true nature of Christian existence on earth by reference to himself. His growing knowledge of Christ, his sharing here and now both in his sufferings and in the power of his risen life, are bringing him nearer the goal, but so long as he is in the body, that goal still lies ahead. He will never in this life attain perfection in the sense that no further spiritual progress is possible and nothing is left to aim at beyond the point he has reached. The purpose for which **Christ Jesus** grasped him on the Damascus road remains for Paul to grasp.

Paul recalls his conversion as the occasion on which a powerful hand was laid on his shoulder, turning him right round in his tracks, and a voice that brooked no refusal spoke in his ear: "You must come along with me." Paul was conscripted into the service of Christ, but never was there a more willing conscript. The passion of his life from that hour on was to serve this new Master and fulfill the purpose for which he had conscripted him—to "lay hold on that," as he put it, "for which also I was laid hold on by Jesus Christ" (ASV). Every phase of Paul's subsequent life and action, every element in his understanding and preaching of the gospel, can be traced back to the revelation of Jesus Christ that was granted to him there and then.

3:13 / No indeed, he says, I do not imagine that I have gained perfection yet or fully attained the purpose for which I was summoned into the service of Christ; that is why I still press on. He speaks of himself as a runner with but one object in view: to finish the race and win the prize. A competitor in a race does not look over his or her shoulder to see how much ground has been covered already or how rivals are getting on: the runner keeps eyes fixed on the winning post. **What is behind me** is that part of the race that has been completed so far, but it will not help a runner to outstrip the others for the first nine-tenths of the way only to falter and be overtaken in the last lap.

When Paul did contemplate what he had achieved in apostolic service, it was only to reinforce his resolution to go on as he had begun. When he recorded the completion of his ministry "all the way from Jerusalem to Illyricum," it was to announce his plan to travel to Spain and repeat in the western Mediterranean the program he had accomplished in the eastern Mediterranean. So long as opportunity offered "to proclaim the Good News in places where Christ has not been heard of," his task remained unfinished (Rom. 15:19–24).

3:14 / **I run straight toward the goal**, he says, using a noun (Gk. *skopos*) not found elsewhere in the NT. There is a **prize** to be awarded, and he aims to secure it; he looks forward to hearing the president of the games call him up to his chair to receive it. On a special occasion in Rome this call might come from the emperor himself; how proudly the successful athlete would obey the summons and step up to the imperial box to accept the award! For Paul, the president of the games was none other than his Lord; **the prize** was **God's call through Christ Jesus to the life above** or, more simply, "the upward call of God in Christ Jesus" (RSV). In similar language Paul can speak later of the wreath of victory "which the Lord, the righteous Judge, will give me on that Day" (2 Tim. 4:8).

The word translated **prize** (Gk. *brabeion*) is used in 1 Corinthians 9:24, "many runners take part in a race, but only one of them wins the prize." But there is no such exclusiveness about this prize; it will be given, as Paul goes on to say about the wreath of victory in 2 Timothy 4:8, "not only to me, but to all those who wait with love for him to appear." Paul aims to win his prize, but there is a prize for everyone who finishes this race; Paul recommends his example to his readers (1 Cor. 9:24), so that they may make his ambition their own.

And what can **the prize** be but that final gaining of Christ for the sake of which, as Paul has said, everything else is well lost?

Additional Notes

3:12 / **That I have already succeeded**: lit., "that I have already obtained" (*elabon*); the verb is transitive, but the object is not expressed. The object is the ambition that he has stated at length in vv. 8–11, the ultimate and complete "gaining" of Christ, not to be distinguished from **the prize** of which he goes on to speak.

Become perfect: "been perfected" (*teteleiōmai*). It may be that Paul is borrowing a term from the mystery religions (cf. 4:12), in which the person admitted to the highest grade was said to have been "perfected"; but as he uses it, the word has no mystery connotation here. Nor is he thinking primarily of his coming martyrdom, although Ignatius (*To the Ephesians* 3:1) uses a synonymous term as he contemplates exposure to the wild beasts in the arena: "I have not yet been perfected [*apērtismai*] in Jesus Christ," he says; but he welcomes the prospect of martyrdom, whatever form it may take, "only that I may attain [*epitychō*] to Jesus Christ" (*To the Romans* 5:3). Paul's outlook is saner: the perfection that he has not yet reached will be his when the time comes for him "to leave this life and be with Christ." (1:23).

Before **or have already become perfect** the manuscripts P^{46} and D*, with Irenaeus (Latin translation) and Ambrosiaster, insert the clause "or have already been justified" (*dedikaiōmai*). This would be an un-Pauline use of the verb "justify": Paul knew that, together with all believers in Christ, he had been "justified by faith" (Rom. 5:1, etc.; cf. v. 9 above). It resembles rather the Ignatian use: Ignatius, speaking of the hardships endured by him on his way to Rome, says, "I am not hereby justified" (*dedikaiōmai*), implying that he will at last be justified when he has undergone a martyr's death (*To the Romans* 5:1).

I keep striving: Gk. *diōkō*, "I pursue," "I follow on."

To win the prize: Gk. *ei kai katalabō*, "if indeed I may lay hold of . . ."; the use of *ei* ("if") to introduce a clause of purpose is similar to that in v. 11, "in hope that . . ." (Gk. *ei pōs*). GNB supplies **the prize** as the antecedent to **for which**; the antecedent is not expressed in the original, and probably something less specific, like "the purpose," might be supplied, in keeping with *eph' hō*, "with a view to which."

97

Christ Jesus has already won me to himself: Gk. *katelēmphthēn hypo Christou Iēsou*, "I was laid hold of by Christ Jesus." The translator must find an appropriate verb to cover both senses of *katalambanein* (*katalabō . . . katelēmphthēn*). It is difficult to improve on the KJV choice of the verb "apprehend." For the significance of Paul's experience of being "apprehended by Christ Jesus" in relation to his subsequent ministry see J. Dupont, "The Conversion of Paul, and Its Influence on his Understanding of Salvation by Faith," in W. W. Gasque and R. P. Martin, eds., *Apostolic History and the Gospel*, pp. 176–94; G. Bornkamm, "The Revelation of Christ to Paul on the Damascus Road and Paul's Doctrine of Justification and Reconciliation," in R. Banks, ed., *Reconciliation and Hope*, pp. 90–103; S. Kim, *The Origin of Paul's Gospel*.

3:13 / The variant reading "not yet" (*oupō*) for **not** (*ou*), mentioned in GNB footnote, has early and wide attestation, but is more likely to have replaced an original **not** than vice versa.

3:14 / The **goal** or *skopos* was so called because the competitor kept his eye fixed on it (*skopein*, "look"). The "upward call" to the victor came in Greek contests from the *agōnothetēs*, in the Panhellenic games (like those at Olympia) from the *hellēnodikai*.

21

Spiritual Maturity

All of us who are spiritually mature should have this same attitude. But if some of you have a different attitude, God will make this clear to you.	[16]However that may be, let us go forward according to the same rules we have followed until now.

Paul knows that not all his friends assess Christian issues as he himself does. He does not force his own assessment on them, but gives them helpful advice.

3:15 / GNB is right in rendering *teleioi* ("perfect") by **spiritually mature** here. It has been widely maintained that the reference is to those who claimed to have attained perfection in the sense that Paul has just disclaimed for himself (v. 13). But Paul now includes himself among the "perfect" just as in Romans 15:1 he includes himself among the "strong" ("we who are strong"). The repetition of a word or its derivative in a different sense within a short interval is a common literary phenomenon. There is no need to write the word in its present occurrence within quotation marks, as though Paul were not committing himself to its use. To be sure, if any of his readers claimed to be perfect in a sense that could not be achieved short of the Day of Christ, there may be a word of admonition for them: it was a mark of the **spiritually mature** to recognize that such perfection was unattainable during mortal life.

> Let no man think that sudden in a minute
>   All is accomplished and the work is done;
> Though with thine earliest dawn thou shouldst begin it
>   Scarce were it ended in thy setting sun.
>   (F. W. H. Myers, "Saint Paul")

But more positively, the Christ-centered ambition expressed by Paul should characterize every **spiritually mature** believer. No doubt Paul's ambition, from the moment of his conversion, was to serve Christ and "be found in him"; but it took time for him to appreciate by experience what was involved in the pursuit of this ambition. Having attained spiritual maturity, however, he "no longer frets about weaknesses, failures and frustrations," whether in himself or in others (Montefiore, *Paul the Apostle*, p. 30).

If some of Paul's readers felt bound to admit that they could not express their ambition or attitude in Paul's terms, let them not despair or resign themselves to eking out a second-rate Christian existence. Let the matter be committed to God, and **God will make this clear to you**. Paul will not scold them or express disappointment that they have made such poor progress. He aims rather to encourage them.

GNB omits the word "also" that is present in the original: **God will make this** also (*kai touto*) **clear to you**. On the supposition that Paul is taking issue with those who claimed a premature perfection, the "also" might mean that, over and above the "visions and revelations" they boasted of having received (cf. 2 Cor. 12:1), there were matters of practical Christian living that they required to have revealed to them. Otherwise, the point may be that, since they have accepted the divine revelation that leads to the attitude characteristic of spiritual maturity, they may trust God to give them whatever further revelation is necessary to remove any remaining inadequacies or inconsistencies in their Christian outlook.

3:16 / If **the . . . rules** they **have followed until now** are the guidelines for Christian living which Paul habitually recommended to his converts—if they are, as he puts it elsewhere, "the principles which I follow in the new life in union with Christ Jesus and which I teach in all the churches everywhere" (1 Cor. 4:17)—then let them continue to follow those rules, and the desired spiritual growth will manifest itself. To those who walk in the light they already have, more light will be given.

There is no word in the Greek text here corresponding to **rules**; this rendering may have been influenced (and properly so) by the similar wording of Galatians 6:16, where the noun "rule" (Gk. *kanōn*) does occur: "As for those who follow this rule in their lives, may peace and mercy be with them . . . !"

To the question how Paul's reference to **rules** can be squared with his denial of any place for law in Christian life, let it be said that (1) these **rules** are not regulations; they have rather the nature of guidelines or principles, and (2) over against "law" in the legal sense Paul sets "the law of Christ"—that is, the way of life exemplified by Christ and recorded for the imitation of his followers. The **rules** implied here, then, are the principles of living involved in "the law of Christ," among which the carrying of one another's burdens takes a leading place (Gal. 6:2). Paul encourages the Philippian Christians to continue to march forward as a united community, shoulder to shoulder, according to the teaching which they had received from him since first he brought them the gospel.

Additional Notes

3:15 / **Spiritually mature**: Gk. *teleioi*, "perfect." W. Lütgert (*Die Vollkommenen im Philipperbrief und die Enthusiasten in Thessalonich*, p. 19), W. Schmithals (*Paul and the Gnostics*, pp. 99–104), and others take the people so designated to be those of a Gnosticizing tendency, like the self-styled "spiritual persons" (*pneumatikoi*) at Corinth (cf. 1 Cor. 2:13, 15; 3:1, etc.). According to them, Paul's ostensible association of himself with them in the first person plural is at most a *captatio benevolentiae*. This is a strained interpretation of his words.

Should have this same attitude: Gk. *touto phronōmen*, "let us be thus minded." In Aleph, L, and a few other manuscripts the indicative *phronoumen* is read: "we are thus minded" (but this variant has no claim to serious consideration). The attitude in question is explained by Chrysostom as readiness to "forget what is behind"; he adds, playing on the double sense of "perfect" (*teleios*): "it is the mark of one who is perfect not to consider himself perfect" (*Homilies on Philippians*, 12). To **have a different attitude** may mean to have a wrong attitude; the adverb *heterōs* "seems to have the meaning 'amiss' " (J. B. Lightfoot, ad loc.).

God will make . . . clear: lit., "will reveal" (Gk. *apokalypsei*). Gk. *kai touto* ("this also") might mean "this indeed," as though the sense were: "*This* is the revelation you need; not revelations as understood in Gnosticizing schools" (cf. Schmithals, *Paul and the Gnostics*, p. 104).

3:16 / **Let us go forward** . . . : lit., "let us march by the same (rule as we have followed) to the point we have already reached" (*eis ho ephthasamen*). With *tō autō* ("the same") several witnesses read *kanoni* ("rule"), but the weight of the evidence favors its omission (although it represents the implied meaning). Cf. Gal. 6:16, "as many as will march by this rule" (Gk. *hosoi tō kanoni toutō stoichēsousin*), the influence of which is probably to be discerned on those authorities that add "rule" (*kanoni*) here. The verb *stoichein* (rendered **go forward** in GNB) means "stand in line" or "march in line"; the implication is that this is not a matter of individual attainment, but one in which the whole community should move forward together.

22

Imitation of Paul

Keep on imitating me, my brothers. Pay attention to those who follow the right example that we have set for you.

T here are many itinerant teachers whose example it would be unsafe to follow. Paul recommends his own example and that of others who, like him, adhere to the way of Christ.

3:17 / If Paul's precept is not clear enough, let his example be followed.

The "imitation of Paul" is a remarkable and recurring theme in his letters. He taught his converts by precept, spoken and written, how they ought to live; but a living example could be more telling than many words. If they desire to see Christian life in action, Paul directs their attention to his own conduct, as he does here: "join in imitating me."

For a man like Paul to take this line meant that he had to be exceptionally careful about his conduct, lest his example be a spiritual stumbling-block to others or even, without his intending it, lead them into sin. He urged his converts to be equally careful: "Live in such a way as to cause no trouble either to Jews or Gentiles or to the church of God. Just do as I do: I try to please everyone in all that I do, not thinking of my own good, but of the good of all, so that they might be saved. Imitate me, then, just as I imitate Christ" (1 Cor. 10:32–11:1).

These last words are crucial: it was not that Paul wished to set his own life up as an ethical standard; he presented Christ as the absolute standard, in action and teaching alike. He himself was to be imitated only insofar as he imitated Christ, but the imitation of Christ was an exercise he cultivated daily. He knew that many of his converts would imitate him in any case, and he knew that, if his example led them astray, he would have to answer for it on the Day of Christ. Hence the care with which he practiced unremitting self-discipline, lest he himself be "disqualified after having called others to the contest" (1 Cor. 9:27). See also 4:9 below.

Nor was it only his own example that he recommended. There were others who followed the same way of life and shared the same attitudes and principles: Timothy and Epaphroditus have been mentioned in this regard in 2:19–30. Men and women of their quality also presented examples that might be followed with confidence.

Additional Notes

3:17 / **Pay attention**: Gk. *skopeite*, "look," "watch." In Rom. 16:17 this verb is used in the sense "watch and avoid"; here it is used in the sense "watch and follow."

The right example that we have set for you: lit., "as you have us for an example." In Greek "us" (*hēmas*) occupies an emphatic position as the last word in the sentence; it is probably implied that a different example is set by others—namely, those against whom a warning is issued in vv. 18, 19.

See W. P. DeBoer, *The Imitation of Paul.*

23

Warning Against Enemies

I have told you this many times before, and now I repeat it with tears: there are many whose lives make them enemies of Christ's death on the cross. ¹⁹They are going to end up in hell, because their god is their bodily desires. They are proud of what they should be ashamed of, and they think only of things that belong to this world.

P aul warns the Philippians against those whose example is morally harmful, not helpful.

3:18 / GNB rightly indicates that it was the behavior of the people now referred to that made them **enemies of Christ's death on the cross**. The men who tried to impose the Jewish law on Paul's Gentile converts in the Galatian churches implied by their teaching (according to Paul) that Christ's death was pointless and ineffectual (Gal. 2:21) and in that sense might have been called "enemies of the cross," but nothing is said against their moral standards. The "enemies of the cross" denounced here are described in different terms from those people against whom the Philippians are put on their guard in verse 2 and need not be identified with them. It is useless to insist in this connection that "entities must not be multiplied beyond what is necessary" (the principle known as Occam's razor), as though that dictated the identification of the two groups: real life is more complicated than logical argument.

It is evident from his general correspondence that Paul at times had to wage war on at least two fronts—at Corinth, for example, against ascetics on the one hand, who would have liked to forbid marriage (1 Cor. 7:1), and against libertines on the other hand, whose slogan was "everything is permissible" (1 Cor. 6:12). The grace of God is received in vain equally by those who continue to live under law and by those who think they should "continue to live in sin so that God's grace will increase" (Rom. 6:1). In verses 18 and 19 Paul is concerned about people who took the latter line, in practice and teaching alike. Christ endured his **death on the cross** to free believers from sin and reconcile them to God (Rom. 6:7; 2 Cor. 5:18–

21); those who deliberately indulge in sin and repudiate the will of God deny all that the cross of Christ stands for.

Paul had warned the Philippian Christians against such people before—whether by word of mouth or in writing we cannot say. If he now repeats his warning, it is because he knows it to be necessary. Such people were exerting their influence in many churches, and they might make an appearance in the Philippian church, if they had not done so already. It is not suggested that the Philippian church was inclined to countenance them, but Paul knew how insidious their arguments were and how disastrous their example could be.

3:19 / Such people, says Paul, are "bound for destruction"; this is a better rendering than GNB's **they are going to end up in hell**, for **hell** is not necessarily identical with "destruction" and nowhere in his surviving writings or in his recorded words does Paul ever use any of the Greek words for **hell**. They are going to be destroyed, and those who follow their bad example are likely to share their fate.

Their god is their bodily desires is literally "whose god is the belly"; compare Romans 16:18, where the Roman Christians are warned against undesirable characters who "are not serving Christ our Lord, but their own appetites" ("appetites" there renders the same noun, Gk. *koilia*, as **bodily desires** renders here). The rendering **bodily desires** is apt, because it indicates that gluttony is not the only vice with which the people in question are charged. Similarly in 1 Corinthians 6:13, where Paul quotes the libertine epigram, "Food is for the stomach [*koilia*], and the stomach [*koilia*] is for food," the context makes it plain that sexual license, not freedom from food restrictions, is the subject under discussion. If **their god is their bodily desires**, that means that **their bodily desires** are their ultimate concern; they do not say so expressly, but that is the implication of their way of life.

They are proud of what they should be ashamed of (lit., "whose glory is in their shame"—a good instance of oxymoron): this confirms our understanding of the preceding clause. There is no hint at circumcision here, as though "their shame" denoted the part of the body that bore the seal of circumcision; a specific example of the situation deplored by Paul is provided in 1 Corinthians 5:2, where an irregular sexual union within the church that not only contravened Jewish law but also shocked the pagan sense of propriety (even in the permissive climate of Corinth) was regarded by some church members as rather a fine assertion of Christian liberty. "It is not right for you to be proud!" said Paul in that situation

(1 Cor. 5:6), because they were proud of what they should have been ashamed of. A century and a half later Hippolytus of Rome speaks of a group called the Simonians who "actually congratulate themselves on their promiscuity, because (they say) that is what is meant by perfect love" (*Refutation of Heresies* 6.19.5).

Such people had no awareness of the call to Christians to exhibit a higher standard of behavior than that which their neighbors observed; they were content to **think only of things that belong to this world**. There was, in fact, no reason to think that they had ever been touched by the grace of God proclaimed in the gospel; their lives were far from yielding the fruit of the Spirit.

Additional Notes

3:18 / Before "the enemies of the cross of Christ" P^{46} inserts "watch out for" (Gk. *blepete*, borrowed from v. 2). Polycarp quotes the phrase "enemies of the cross" (*To the Philippians*, 12:3); earlier in the same letter he declares that "whoever does not confess the testimony of the cross is of the devil" (7:1).

The identity of these **enemies** is disputed. W. Schmithals sees in them the same Jewish Christian Gnostics as he discerns in "those who do evil things" of v. 2; like their counterparts in Corinth, they "put 'knowledge' in place of 'the folly of the cross' " (*Paul and the Gnostics*, p. 107). W. Lueken (ad loc.) thinks of Christians who cannot break loose from the old familiar pagan immorality (similarly E. Haupt (ad loc.), and T. Zahn, *Introduction to the NT* i, p. 539); E. Lohmeyer (ad loc.) considers them to be lapsed or apostate Christians; H. Appel more precisely (and correctly) identifies them as professing Christians who misuse the doctrine of grace as an occasion for libertinism (*Einleitung in das NT*, p. 57).

3:19 / These **enemies** are bound for "destruction" (Gk. *apōleia*), the word used in 1:28 of the destiny of the church's persecutors. Cf. the participial phrase *hoi apollymenoi*, "those who are on the way to destruction," used in 1 Cor. 1:18; 2 Cor. 2:15; 4:3 of those who reject the gospel. In 1 Cor. 1:18 it appears in a context that speaks of the cross as being "robbed of its power" (1 Cor. 1:17).

A verbal parallel to the clause "whose god is their belly" comes in Euripides, *Cyclops* 334, 335, where the Cyclops says, "I offer sacrifice to no god but myself, and to this belly of mine, the greatest of divinities" (*kai tē megistē gastri tēde daimonōn*). Schmithals thinks the words point to "disregard for the rules concerning food" (*Paul and the Gnostics*, p. 109); but Paul himself shared that disregard. J.-F. Collange (ad loc.) suggests that the description is of self-worshipers who contemplate their own navels (not a natural meaning for *koilia*).

In contrast to those who **are proud of what they should be ashamed of** Paul speaks of himself and his associates as having "put aside all secret and shameful deeds" (2 Cor. 4:2). (In Jude 13 libertine teachers are compared to "wild waves of the sea, with their shameful deeds showing up like foam.") J. A. Bengel (*Gnomon*, ad loc.) and some later writers have understood the reference here to be to circumcision, as though Gk. *aischynē* ("shame") were synonymous with *aidoia*, but this sense is poorly attested for *aischynē*.

The **things that belong to this world** (Gk. *ta epigeia*, "the earthly things") may be contrasted with "the things that are in heaven, where Christ sits on his throne at the right side of God," on which Christians are directed to set their hearts (Col. 3:1, 2). This, in effect, is what Paul now goes on to say.

24

Heavenly Citizenship and Hope

We, however, are citizens of heaven, and we eagerly wait for our Savior, the Lord Jesus Christ, to come from heaven. ²¹He will change our weak mortal bodies and make them like his own glorious body, using that power by which he is able to bring all things under his rule.

True believers are citizens of heaven, where their Lord now is, and when he comes from there he will equip his people with bodies like his own, fitted for full entry upon their heavenly heritage.

3:20 / In saying that "our citizenship is in heaven," Paul uses the noun *politeuma*, not found elsewhere in the NT, but related to the verb *politeuesthai*, which he has used in 1:27 to denote the Philippian Christians' "way of life," with special reference to their responsibility as members of a community. So here, if they **are citizens of heaven**, their way of life should be in keeping with their citizenship.

There may be an allusion here to the constitution of Philippi. Since Philippi was a colony of Rome, its *politeuma*, the register of its citizens, was kept in Rome, its mother city (Gk. *mētropolis*). No doubt only a minority of the church membership possessed this citizen status, but the constitution of the city would be well enough known to them all. Moffatt's translation, "But we are a colony of heaven," could express the general sense quite well. As citizens of a Roman colony were expected to promote the interests of their mother city and maintain its dignity, so citizens of heaven in an earthly environment should represent the interests of their true homeland and lead lives worthy of their citizenship. This citizenship was theirs already; they did not have to wait for it. But they did **eagerly wait for** their **Savior, the Lord Jesus Christ, to come from heaven**. This expectation was a constant element in the primitive apostolic preaching: the Thessalonian converts, for example, were taught to wait for the Son of God "to come from heaven—his Son Jesus, . . . who rescues his people from the coming judgment" (1 Thess. 1:10).

It would be pressing Paul's language here too far to infer from it that he himself expected to be still alive to greet the appearing Savior. In 1:20–24 he expects rather to die before the advent of Christ, and in verse 11 above he hopes to "be raised from death to life." So, in saying now that **we eagerly wait for our Savior**, he expresses the attitude of Christians in general, without special reference to his personal prospects.

3:21 / When the Savior comes, **he will change our weak mortal bodies**. A fuller statement is given in 1 Corinthians 15:42–53. Whether believers have died or are still alive at the time of the advent, they will have to undergo a change in order to inherit God's eternal kingdom. Those who have died will receive a "spiritual body" to replace the "natural body" that has disintegrated; the mortality of those who are still alive will "be changed into what is immortal." Both the dead who are raised and the living who are changed, having hitherto worn "the likeness of the man made of earth" (the first Adam, according to the narrative of Gen. 2:7), will henceforth "wear the likeness of the Man from heaven."

This last statement is expressed here in slightly different wording when Paul says that Christ will make **our weak mortal bodies** (lit., "our body of humiliation") . . . **like his own glorious body** (lit., "his body of glory")—that is, his glorified body. The bodies that the people of Christ will wear in the age to come will belong to the same heavenly order as his own resurrection body. "All of creation waits with eager longing for God to reveal his sons" (Rom. 8:19) because their revelation as the sons and daughters of God will be their participation in the glory in which he who is the Son of God par excellence will then be revealed. "Your real life is Christ," says Paul to the Colossian Christians, "and when he appears, then you too will appear with him and share his glory!" (Col. 3:4).

The **power by which he is able to bring all things under his rule** is the power he shares with the Father. The almighty power of the Father, demonstrated in his raising his Son from death (see comment on v. 10 above, "the power of his resurrection") is exercised by the Son in virtue of the authority he has received to give life to whom he chooses (cf. John 5:21, 25–29). The raising of his people to resurrection life is one phase of the Son's exercise of this God-given authority: "Christ must rule," says Paul to the Corinthians, "until God defeats all enemies and puts them under his feet" (1 Cor. 15:25, echoing Pss. 8:6; 110:1).

Paul did not know, nor did he pretend to know, when the advent would take place. Something has been said about his own changing perspective in the comment on 1:23. The so-called delay of the *parousia* involved no such agonizing reappraisal for him and his theology as has often been supposed. The certainty of the advent is accepted by faith; its timing is inaccessible to curious calculation. Each successive generation of the church has the privilege of living as though it were the generation that will greet the returning Christ.

Additional Notes

3:20 / On Roman citizenship see A. N. Sherwin-White, *Roman Society and Roman Law in the New Testament*, pp. 78–80 and *The Roman Citizenship*; on its relevance to Phil. 3:20 see E. Stauffer, *New Testament Theology*, pp. 296, 297. For the heavenly metropolis cf. Gal. 4:25 ("the heavenly Jerusalem is free, and she is our mother"). For Gentile analogues see Plato, *Republic* 9.592B (on the pattern of the ideal city laid up in heaven); and Marcus Aurelius, *Meditations* 3.11 ("dear city of God").

E. Lohmeyer (ad loc.) draws attention to the rhythmic structure of the words beginning **we eagerly wait for our Savior**, as though Paul were quoting a Christian hymn or confession without necessarily committing himself to every one of its details (so also E. Güttgemanns, *Der leidende Apostel und sein Herr*, pp. 246, 247; J. Becker, "Erwägungen zu Phil 3, 20–21," *TZ* 27 [1971], pp. 16–29). Moreover, the word **Savior** (Gk. *sōtēr*) does not appear elsewhere in the Pauline corpus apart from Eph. 5:23 and the Pastoral Letters. But the wording of Phil. 3:20, 21 (especially as regards the **body** in v. 21) is completely consistent with Paul's general teaching; see R. H. Gundry, *"Soma" in Biblical Theology*, pp. 177–83.

J.-F. Collange (ad loc.), R. P. Martin (ad loc.), and others point to a striking series of parallels between this passage and 2:6–11. Among those others M. D. Hooker sees 3:20, 21 as carrying on the line of thought in 2:6–11: in 2:6–8 we have a description of Christ's becoming like us, in 2:9–11 we have an account of what he now is, in 3:20, 21 we are told how, by the power bestowed on him, he will make us like himself ("Interchange in Christ," *JTS* n.s. 22 [1971], pp. 356, 357; and "Philippians 2:6–11," in *Jesus und Paulus*, ed. E. E. Ellis and E. Grässer, p. 155).

When Paul says that "our citizenship is already (Gk. *hyparchei*) in heaven" and yet points forward to its consummation at the advent of Christ, he illustrates the interplay of realized and future eschatology in the NT; on this and other features of the present passage see A. T. Lincoln, *Paradise Now and Not Yet*, pp. 87–109.

3:21 / The "body of our humiliation" (*sōma tēs tapeinōseōs hēmōn*) is identical with the "natural (lit., 'soulish') body" (*sōma psychikon*) of 1 Cor. 15:44, so called because it is inherited from the first Adam, who became a "living soul" (*psychē zōsa*, Gen. 2:7, LXX). The "spiritual body" (*sōma pneumatikon*) of 1 Cor. 15:44 is so called because Christ, the "last Adam," became in resurrection a "life-giving spirit" (*pneuma zōopoioun*, 1 Cor. 15:45). In 1 Cor. 15:42–50, as in the present passage, it is to Christ's resurrection body that the believer's body is to be conformed.

With **making them like** (Gk. *symmorphon*, "conformable") may be compared "being conformed [*symmorphizomenos*] to his death" in v. 10 above. "Since we have become one with him in dying as he did, in the same way we shall be one with him by being raised to life as he was" (Rom. 6:5).

Through the **power** (Gk. *energeia*) **by which he is able to bring all things under his rule** he fulfills what is said of man in Ps. 8:6 ("You [God] appointed him ruler over everything you made; you placed him over all creation") and to the Davidic king in Ps. 110:1 ("Sit here at my [God's] right side until I put your enemies under your feet"). See 1 Cor. 15:24–28; Heb. 2:5–9.

On the imminence and "delay" of the advent see A. L. Moore, *The Parousia in the New Testament*, pp. 108–74; also S. S. Smalley, "The Delay of the Parousia," *JBL* 83 (1964), pp. 41–54.

Exhortation to Stand Firm

So then, my brothers, how dear you are to me and how I miss you! How happy you make me, and how proud I am of you!—this, dear brothers, is how you should stand firm in your life in the Lord.

4:1 / Paul once more expresses his joy and pride in his Philippian friends and encourages them afresh to be steadfast in their Christian life (cf. 1:27). More particularly in the present context he encourages them to be steadfast in resistance to those influences against which he has just warned them—influences that would undermine their Christian stability. But the delight he finds in these friends as he addresses them and calls them to mind suggests that those harmful influences had not made serious inroads among them, as they had done in some other churches.

Additional Notes

4:1 / **How I miss you** renders the verbal adjective *epipothētos*, "longed for." While this form does not appear elsewhere in NT, the verb *epipothein* is commoner: it has occurred twice earlier in this letter—in 1:8, where Paul speaks of his "deep feeling" or longing for them all (see additional note 1:8), and in 2:26, where he speaks of Epaphroditus's anxiety to see them.

How happy you make me, and how proud I am of you—lit., "my joy and crown"; cf. 1 Thess. 2:19, where Paul and his companions, with an eye on the advent of Christ, call the Thessalonian believers their "joy or crown of exultation" (GNB: "our joy, and our reason for boasting of our victory"). In both places the "crown" is the *stephanos*, the wreath awarded to the victor in the games (not the *diadēma*, the symbol of sovereignty).

Fresh Plea for Unity

Euodia and Syntyche, please, I beg you, try to agree as sisters in the Lord. ³And you too, my faithful partner, I want you to help these women; for they have worked hard with me to spread the gospel, together with Clement and all my other fellow workers, whose names are in God's book of the living.

Two members of the church are begged by name to reach a common mind as fellow Christians, and another of Paul's co-workers is urged to help them in this regard.

4:2 / **Euodia** and **Syntyche** were evidently two very active members of the Philippian church, probably foundation members. From the fact that (in a letter meant to be read to the church) Paul begs each of them by name to **try to agree as sisters in the Lord**, it may be inferred that the disagreement between them, whatever its nature, was a threat to the unity of the church as a whole (especially in view of their prominence and influence). But from the fact that only two members are thus singled out by name, it may also be inferred that such personal dissension was exceptional in that particular fellowship.

4:3 / Who is singled out as Paul's **faithful partner**, or "true yokefellow"? Plainly it was someone whom it was not necessary to name: everyone, including the person so addressed, would know who was intended.

One very attractive suggestion is that Luke was the person so addressed. If Luke was the author of Acts, or at any rate of the "we" narrative, it can be inferred that he was in Philippi for part or most of the time between the first evangelization of the city and Paul's brief visit to it before setting out on his last journey to Jerusalem (cf. Acts 16:17 with 20:5). If, then, this part of the letter falls within that period (as its affinities with 2 Corinthians might suggest), Luke might well be the **faithful partner**. Otherwise, the partner's identity must be a matter of even more random speculation.

The **faithful partner** is urged to lend a helping hand to Euodia and Syntyche, so that their valuable contribution to the life and witness of the community may not be impaired by their failure to agree. Paul pays the two women a striking tribute when he says that they **worked hard with** him **to spread the gospel**. He uses a forceful athletic term: "they contended side by side with me," he says (the same verb, *synathlein*, has appeared in 1:27, "**fighting together** for the faith of the gospel"). This does not suggest that Paul's female co-workers played a minor part as compared with their male counterparts.

As Paul remembers them, he thinks of other co-workers who contributed nobly to the common endeavor. Clement, who is mentioned by name, is otherwise unknown: since his name is Latin, he may conceivably have been a citizen of Philippi. Of all these **fellow workers** Paul remarks that their **names are in God's book of the living**—the burgess roll of the heavenly commonwealth. The **book of the living** is an expression found in the OT for those who survive a disaster and enjoy a renewed spell of life on earth, as in Isaiah 4:3, "everyone who is left in Jerusalem, whom God has chosen for survival" (lit., "everyone who has been recorded for life in Jerusalem"). (Cf. also Exod. 32:32; Ps. 69:28; Ezek. 13:9.) In Daniel 12:1 and the NT the figure is used rather for those who are admitted to eternal life, whose "names are written in heaven" (Luke 10:20; cf. Heb. 12:23). The malediction of Psalm 69:28 ("May their names be erased from the book of the living") is reversed in Revelation 3:5 for fearless confessors who win the spiritual victory: "I will not remove their names from the book of the living." At the last assize in Revelation 20:11–15 the "book of the living" (cf. Rev. 13:8; 17:8) is opened, and "whoever did not have his name written in the book of the living was thrown into the lake of fire."

But Paul may denote here something more than the possession of eternal life (which is the heritage of every believer); the implication may be that the gospel service rendered by his co-workers is recorded, along with their names, in the **book of the living**.

Additional Notes

4:2 / Paul says, "I beseech Euodia, and I beseech Syntyche"; his repetition of the verb "I beseech" (Gk. *parakalō*) with each of their names, as though he were personally addressing first one and then the other ("Please, Euodia; please, Syntyche . . ."), is noteworthy.

To agree: Gk. *to auto phronein*, rendered "having the same thoughts" in 2:2a. There is nothing to suggest that the disagreement had anything to do with

114

Gnostic agitation, as though the two women endangered the unity of the church "by opening their assemblies—perhaps as leaders of house churches—to the Gnostics" (W. Schmithals, *Paul and the Gnostics*, pp. 112–14).

It is fruitless to try to identify either of them with Lydia of Acts 16:14, 40, as though Lydia were not a personal name but meant "the Lydian woman" (cf. the mention of Thyatira in Acts 16:14).

4:3 / The **faithful partner** is identified with Luke by M. Hájek ("Comments on Philippians 4:3—Who Was '*Gnesios Syzygos*'?" *Communio Viatorum* 7 [1964], p. 261–62) and T. W. Manson. The adjective **faithful** (Gk. *gnēsios*) has suggested Timothy to some, such as J.-F. Collange and G. Friedrich (cf. the adverb *gnēsiōs* in 2:20, with additional note *ad loc.*). Timothy could have been given his instructions by word of mouth, before he set out for Philippi, but their inclusion in the letter would ensure that when it was read publicly in church his authority to take action in this matter would be recognized. This latter consideration would apply to Epaphroditus, who is favored by Marius Victorinus and J. B. Lightfoot. Many commentators take Syzygos to be a personal name, and not the common noun meaning **partner**: so K. Barth, P. Benoit, P. Ewald, J. Gnilka, E. Haupt, J. J. Müller, K. Staab. But G. Delling points out (*TDNT* vol. 7, pp. 748–50) that Syzygos is unattested as a personal name; his own preference is for Silas (Silvanus), Paul's colleague in the evangelization of Philippi.

The fact that Gk. *syzygos* (like Eng. **partner**) sometimes bears the meaning "spouse" has prompted some to see this meaning here—as though Paul had a wife resident in Philippi (who but Lydia?) and begged her to help settle the disagreement between Euodia and Syntyche. This interpretation was apparently approved by Clement of Alexandria (*Strom.* 3.6.53.1) and defended by Erasmus; cf. also E. Renan, *St. Paul*, p. 76; S. Baring Gould, *A Study of St. Paul* (London: Isbister, 1897), pp. 213–16. But the adjective **faithful** or "genuine" (*gnēsie*, vocative) that qualifies *syzygos* here is certainly masculine. The idea belongs to romantic fiction rather than to historical exegesis.

W. Schmithals suggests that the prescript (now lost) of the letter to which this section originally belonged was addressed to an individual by name (e.g., a community leader or one of the Philippian "firstfruits"); this individual would then be the **faithful partner** (*Paul and the Gnostics*, pp. 76, 77). It is best to recognize that the identity of the **faithful partner** was perfectly well known to the Philippian church but can only be guessed at by us.

Repeated Call to Rejoice

> May you always be joyful in your
> union with the Lord. I say it again:
> rejoice!

Paul repeats and emphasizes the exhortation of 3:1.

4:4 / The adverb **always** makes it plain that this is no mere formula of farewell; the verb **be joyful** has its full sense. Compare 1 Thessalonians 5:16, "be joyful always." As in 3:1, the rendering **in your union with the Lord** probably overloads the sense of "in the Lord"; the Lord is to be the object of their joy.

I say it again: literally, "I will say it again"; the verb is unambiguously in the future tense (*erō*). "I have said it once," Paul means, "and I will say it a second time" (for emphasis).

Additional Note

4:4 / In *The NT: An American Translation* this verse is rendered "Good-bye, and the Lord be with you always. Again I say, good-bye." Cf. its rendering of 3:1, with E. J. Goodspeed, *Problems of NT Translation*, pp. 174, 175.

Encouragement to Faith

Show a gentle attitude toward everyone. The Lord is coming soon. ⁶Don't worry about anything, but in all your prayers ask God for what you need, always asking him with a thankful heart. ⁷And God's peace, which is far beyond human understanding, will keep your hearts and minds safe in union with Christ Jesus.

The assurance of the Lord's nearness, confidence in approaching God in prayer and thanksgiving, and the ensuing sense of peace at heart will be manifested in an attitude of Christian courtesy to all.

4:5 / The **gentle attitude** inculcated here belongs to a Christlike character. Paul in 2 Corinthians 10:1 speaks of the "gentleness" or "forbearance" (GNB: "kindness") of Christ, where (as in Wisdom 2:19) the patient bearing of abuse may be included. A **gentle attitude** knows how to give way graciously and not insist on one's rights. Matthew Arnold's rendering of the word as "sweet reasonableness" has passed into general currency. When Shakespeare's Portia says to Shylock (in *Merchant of Venice* 4.1),

> Though justice be thy plea, remember this:
> That, in the course of justice, none of us
> Should see salvation . . . I have spoke thus much
> To mitigate the justice of thy plea,

she is recommending to him the cultivation of that **gentle attitude** which "is an attribute of God himself."

Christians, who have been beneficiaries of God's gentleness, should show the same quality in their dealings with others.

The Lord is coming soon is something Paul might very well have said (cf. 3:20), in the spirit of Jesus' direction to his disciples to be "like servants who are waiting for their master" (Luke 12:46). But what he actually says is "The Lord is near," which may imply nearness in place as well as nearness in time. "The LORD is near" is a recurring assurance to his people in the OT (cf. Ps. 34:18; also Pss. 119:151; 145:18). If time alone were in view, then it might be thought that the assurance is more valid for those living only a short time before the unknown date of his advent than for those living a longer time before it; but in the sense that Paul's words probably bear here the Lord is always equally near his people, continually "at hand" (KJV). "Christ, then, is ever at our doors; as near eighteen hundred years ago as now, and not nearer now than then, and not nearer when He comes than now" (Newman, p. 241).

4:6 / Because "the Lord is near," his people need not **worry about anything**. This is in line with Jesus' own teaching to his disciples: "do not be worried about the food and drink you need in order to stay alive, or about clothes for your body . . . do not worry about tomorrow: it will have enough worries of its own" (Matt. 6:25–34). Christian existence in a pagan world was full of uncertainties: persecution of one kind or another was always a possibility, and the impossibility of membership in guilds which were under the patronage of pagan divinities was bound to involve economic disadvantage. But if the Lord was near, there was no cause for anxiety. Jesus had encouraged his disciples to have done with anxiety because their heavenly Father, who fed the birds and clothed the grass with flowers, knew their needs and was well able to supply them (Matt. 6:26–32 par. Luke 12:24–30). Similarly Paul says, **in all your prayers ask God for what you need**. He uses three different Greek words for "prayer" here; compare the more literal RSV: "in everything by prayer and supplication with thanksgiving let your requests be made known to God." There are slight differences of nuance between one word and another, but the main effect of the use of all three is to emphasize the importance in Christian life of constancy in believing and expectant prayer. Like his Master, Paul takes it for granted that an essential element in prayer is asking God for things, with the same trustful spirit as children show when they ask their fathers for things. In the prayer Jesus taught his disciples to use when addressing their heavenly Father, the provision of his children's daily bread is included along with the establishment of his kingdom on earth.

Moreover, a grateful remembrance of past blessings is a safeguard against anxiety for the future: it adds confidence to the prayer for continued blessings. Hence the importance of **a thankful heart** in all true prayer.

4:7 / If they paid heed to this encouragement, then, in place of anxiety they would enjoy **peace** of heart. Jesus, in John 14:27, bequeathes to his disciples his "own peace," which he gives them "not . . . as the world does." So here, the peace that God's children receive is **God's peace, which is far beyond human understanding**. It "surpasses all imagination" (F. W. Beare); it exceeds all that human wisdom can plan. This **peace** will "stand garrison" over their **hearts and minds** and keep anxiety and other intruders out: it will preserve them **safe in union with Christ Jesus**.

God's peace may mean not only the peace that he gives (cf. Rom 5:1) but the serenity in which he lives: God is not subject to anxiety.

Additional Notes

4:5 / **Gentle attitude**: Gk. *epieikes*, neuter adjective; cf. the abstract noun *epieikeia*, "gentleness," in 2 Cor. 10:1 (GNB: "kindness"). Aristotle describes *epieikeia* as that which is not only just but even better than justice (*Nicomachean Ethics* 5.10.6). There are occasions when strict insistence on the letter of the law (as with Shylock's pound of flesh) would lead to injustice; *epieikeia* recognizes those occasions and knows how to act when they arise. "For the right inculcation of the method and secret of Jesus, we need the *epieikeia*, the sweet reasonableness, of Jesus" (M. Arnold, *Literature and Dogma* [London: Smith, Elder, 1900], p. 225). See also R. Leivestad, "The Meekness and Gentleness of Christ," *NTS* 12 (1965–66), pp. 156–64.

The Lord is coming soon: Gk. *ho kyrios engys*. The adverb *engys* may mean "near" either in place or in time; the context is normally decisive.

4:6 / **In all your prayers**: of the three words for "prayer" used in this sentence the first (*proseuchē*) is a general term for prayer to God; the second (*deēsis*) emphasizes the element of petition or entreaty in prayer; the third (*aitēma*) means the thing that is asked for.

4:7 / **Will keep . . . safe**: Gk. *phrourēsei*, "will guard," "will garrison." A different figure is used in Col. 3:15, where the peace of Christ is to "arbitrate" (Gk. *brabeuein*) in the readers' hearts (GNB: "The peace that Christ gives is to guide you in the decisions you make").

In union with Christ Jesus: lit., "in Christ Jesus" (*en Christō Iēsou*).

29

Second Conclusion:
Food for Thought

PHILIPPIANS 4:8–9

In conclusion, my brothers, fill your minds with those things that are good and that deserve praise: things that are true, noble, right, pure, lovely and honorable. ⁹Put into practice what you learned and received from me, both from my words and from my actions. And the God who gives us peace will be with you.

In thought and action alike the readers are urged to concentrate on those things that are both good in themselves and beneficial to all.

4:8 / **In conclusion, my brothers**: practically the same wording as in 3:1.

If "the mind is dyed the color of its waking thoughts," then what one thinks about gives character to life. As good food is necessary for bodily health, so good thoughts are necessary for mental and spiritual health. **Fill your minds**, then, says Paul, **with those things that are good and that deserve praise**; that is, "take them into account" or "give them weight in your decisions" (F. W. Beare). Then, more specifically, he lists six things that can be so described (in the Greek text this sixfold list precedes the summarizing mention of "whatever is good and praiseworthy"). Set your minds on such things, he says, and having set your minds on them, plan to act accordingly—**things that are**

(1) **True**. This could be a warning against indulgence in mental fantasies or baseless slanders. But even some things that are factually true are not healthy things to dwell on: **things that are true** have the moral qualities of uprightness and dependability, of reality as opposed to mere appearance.

(2) **Noble**. This word (Gk. *semnos*) is particularly common in the Pastoral Letters; this is its only NT occurrence outside those three documents. A mind that concentrates on ignoble matters is in danger of becom-

ing ignoble itself. Nobility is the converse of that vulgarity which debases all moral currency and is incompatible with the mind of Christ.

(3) **Right**, or righteous (Gk. *dikaios*). The propriety of righteous thoughts and plans needs no emphasizing: God himself is righteous and loves righteousness in his people (Ps. 11:7). The converse to this is found in the wicked man who "makes evil plans as he lies in bed" in order to carry them into action when daylight comes (Ps. 36:4; cf. Amos 8:4–6).

(4) **Pure**. The word (Gk. *hagnos*) has the general sense of innocence (as in 2 Cor. 7:11) or the special sense of chastity (as in 2 Cor. 11:2). Purity of thought and purpose is a precondition of purity in word and action, as opposed to "matters of sexual immorality or indecency or greed" which should not even be mentioned among God's people (Eph. 5:3).

(5) **Lovely**. (Gk. *prosphilēs*). **Lovely** things are those that commend themselves by their intrinsic attractiveness and agreeableness. They give pleasure to all and cause distaste to none, like a welcome fragrance.

(6) **Honorable**. (Gk. *euphēmos*). A thing is **honorable** in this sense if it deservedly enjoys a good reputation. The mind that dwells on such things rather than on those that are disreputable has much in common with the love that takes more pleasure in what is to other people's credit than in what is to their discredit (1 Cor. 13:6).

There is a rhythmic quality about the Greek text of verse 8 (as there is in the familiar KJV rendering: "Whatsoever things are true . . . "). This suggests that Paul may be quoting some well-known words of ethical admonition. The virtues listed are not specifically Christian; they are excellent and commendable wherever they are found. But in a Christian context such as they are given here they take on the distinctive nuances associated with the mind of Christ.

Such things, then, are to be pondered and planned; the results will be beneficial for life and action.

4:9 / Once again the note of the imitation of Paul is struck. By teaching and example Paul had shown his converts how to live and act, thus imparting to them the ethical tradition that stemmed from the teaching and example of Jesus. If they put these lessons **into practice**, then their conduct will be the outward expression of the habits of mind inculcated in verse 8.

Thus **the God who gives us peace will be with** them. He is "the God of peace"; it is not only that he gives us peace; peace belongs to his very character. He is "the author of peace and lover of concord"; dissension and strife are "works of the flesh" (Gal. 5:20). To have the God of peace himself is even better than having the peace of God (v. 7). "The God of peace" is a recurring designation of God in the NT—especially in Paul's letter closings (Rom. 15:33; 16:20; 2 Cor. 13:11; 1 Thess. 5:23) and also in Hebrews (13:20).

Additional Notes

4:8 / **In conclusion, my brothers** (Gk. *to loipon, adelphoi*): the pronoun "my" (Gk. *mou*) is absent here, whereas it is expressed in 3:1. On the repetition of *to loipon* see pp. xxvii and 74 above.

Fill your minds with: Gk *logizesthe*, "reckon," "take into reckoning."

Those things that are good: lit., "if there is any goodness" (Gk. *aretē*, "virtue," "excellence," not found elsewhere in Paul).

Noble: Gk. *semnos*, "dignified." The quality of *semnotēs*, according to Aristotle, is "a mild and seemly gravity" (*Rhetoric* 2.17.4); it is the mean between *areskeia*, obsequiousness, subservience, and *authadeia*, incivil stubbornness (*Eudemian Ethics*, 2.3.4).

Honorable: J. B. Lightfoot (ad loc.) suggests an active meaning for this adjective (*euphēmos*): "fair speaking" rather than "well spoken of."

4:9 / **Received**: Gk. *parelabete*. Here we should probably recognize the verb *paralambanein* in the sense "receive by tradition" (the correlative being *paradidonai*, "deliver as tradition"), as in 1 Cor. 15:1; Gal. 1:9; Col. 2:6; 1 Thess. 4:1. The tradition (*paradosis*) of Christ in the NT has three main components: (1) a summary of the gospel story, whether it takes the form of preaching (*kērygma*) or confession of faith (*homologia*); (2) a narration of the deeds and words of Christ; (3) ethical and procedural guidelines for Christian living. It is the third of these categories of tradition that is in view here. See R. P. C. Hanson, *Tradition in the Early Church*; F. F. Bruce, *Tradition Old and New*.

In the presentation of Paul's example here, as in 3:17, W. Schmithals discerns a polemical note, as though Paul were warning the Philippians against what they might have "learned and received and heard and seen" in others (*Paul and the Gnostics*, pp. 112, 113).

30

Paul's Sufficiency

In my life in union with the Lord it is a great joy to me that after so long a time you once more had the chance of showing that you care for me. I don't mean that you had stopped caring for me—you just had no chance to show it. [11]And I am not saying this because I feel neglected, for I have learned to be satisfied with what I have. [12]I know what it is to be in need and what it is to have more than enough. I have learned this secret, so that anywhere, at any time, I am content, whether I am full or hungry, whether I have too much or too little. [13]I have the strength to face all conditions by the power that Christ gives me.

Paul now comes to one of his main reasons for writing. If this note (4:10–20) was an integral part of the main letter, he has reserved it to the end to give it prominence–his expression of thanks for the gift that Epaphroditus had brought him from the Philippian church.

4:10 / **In my life in union with the Lord it is a great joy to me**: more simply, "I rejoiced greatly in the Lord," meaning "I gave joyful thanks to the Lord" (when I received your gift). Paul is grateful to the Philippian Christians for the gift they have sent, but his **joy** arises chiefly from the evidence it supplies of their continued eagerness to cooperate with him in the gospel.

Some commentators have found Paul's wording here very oddly chosen for an expression of thanks: Dibelius speaks of his "thankless thanks." But his words have to be read in the light of the deep mutual affection existing between him and the Philippian church and in the light of his well-attested financial policy.

The phrase **after so long a time** might imply, if it stood by itself, that the Philippians had let an inordinately long time elapse since last they sent Paul a gift; but the context shows that no such reflection is intended. It is conceivable, indeed, that in the covering note they sent with this gift they said, "After so long a time we are glad to send you a gift once more," and that Paul takes them up and says, "After so long a time, as you put it. . . . " But the long interval was probably due to Paul's own policy in the matter of accepting gifts from his churches. He makes it plain that, if only now they **once more had the chance of showing** that they cared for him, it was not that there was any intermission in their care for him but rather that they **just had no chance to show it**. And why not? Because Paul himself had deprived them of any such chance.

In Macedonia—especially in Thessalonica—and again in Corinth Paul had learned that, if he accepted material aid for himself from his converts, this was misrepresented by his detractors as evidence that he aimed to live at their expense. (These detractors in Thessalonica appear to have been outside the church; in Corinth they were inside.) Hence, perhaps, he had to request his converts not to send him money for his personal use. Moreover, when he got down in earnest to organizing the relief fund for the Jerusalem church, he was anxious that all available gifts from his churches should be channeled into that fund, and he knew that even so there were some people who would seize on any pretext to suggest that money intended for it was being diverted to his own pocket. The Macedonian churches, we know, had overstretched their resources in their generous giving to the relief fund (2 Cor. 8:1–5).

But now the relief fund had been completed and the money taken to Jerusalem. During his visit to Jerusalem with representatives of the contributing churches Paul was arrested and, having spent two years in custody in Caesarea, was now living under house arrest in Rome. His situation had changed: his friends in Philippi judged that now, **after so long a time**, it was opportune to send him a gift **once more**, and they sent one by the hand of Epaphroditus.

4:11 / Paul greatly appreciated the Philippians' kind thought, but he assures them that he had not felt **neglected**: he does not **need** support of this kind. His language may suggest the embarrassment felt by his independent and sensitive spirit at saying "Thank you" for a spontaneous gift even from such well-loved and loving friends as the Christians in Philippi.

Paul's policy was not to live at the expense of his converts. He agreed that, like other apostles and Christian leaders, he was entitled to be supported by them, but he chose not to avail himself of this right (1 Cor. 9:12; 2 Thess. 3:9). He traveled light; his possessions were restricted to the clothes he wore and perhaps some tools of his trade and the few papyrus and parchment scrolls mentioned in 2 Timothy 4:13. He could survive on very little; in fact, he had schooled himself to do so. **I have learned to be satisfied with what I have**, he says, supplying the words that John

Bunyan expanded in the shepherd boy's song:

> I am content with that I have,
>> Little be it or much,
> And, Lord, contentment still I crave,
>> Because thou savest such.
>
> Fullness to such a burden is
>> That go on pilgrimage:
> Here little, and hereafter bliss,
>> Is best from age to age.

"Be satisfied with what you have" (Heb. 13:5) seems to have been a general precept in the early church. This attitude is the opposite of covetousness, against which both Jesus (cf. Luke 12:15) and his disciples uttered solemn warnings, describing it as a deadly evil, "a form of idolatry" (Eph. 5:5).

The word rendered **satisfied** (Gk. *autarkēs*) was current in Stoicism to denote the ideal of the totally self-sufficient person. Paul uses it to express his independence of external circumstances. He was constantly conscious of his total dependence on God. He was not so much self-sufficient as "God-sufficient": "The capacity we have comes from God" (2 Cor. 3:5).

4:12 / Paul had had long experience of having less than sufficient at some times and more than sufficient at other times: it made little difference to him. **I have learned this secret**, he says, borrowing a term from the vocabulary of the mystery religions ("I have become adept" is F. W. Beare's rendering), of being **full or hungry**, having **too much or too little**. What Paul would have regarded as **too much** may be guessed at—anything above the minimum requirements of food and clothing, no doubt. For a man brought up in Paul's environment, his conversion meant an initiation into a new way of life. One could not be a citizen of Tarsus without possessing substantial means. But for the sake of Christ Paul had "thrown everything away" (3:8), including (we may be sure) his material heritage; he learned henceforth to live on what he could earn by his part-time "tentmaking" (cf. 1 Thess. 2:9; 2 Thess. 3:8; Acts 18:3; 20:34).

4:13 / He takes no credit to himself for having learned this lesson of contentment: it is thanks to his "enabler" that he has **the strength to face all conditions**. It was, indeed, when he was most conscious of personal weakness that he was most conscious of the power of Christ resting on him. "I am content," he says, "with weaknesses, insults, hardships, persecutions, and difficulties for Christ's sake. For when I am weak, then I am strong" (2 Cor. 12:9, 10).

Additional Notes

4:10 / **It is a . . . joy**: the aorist *echarēn* ("I rejoiced") refers back to the moment of Paul's receiving the gift, but his joy persists into the present.

After so long a time: Gk. *ēdē pote*. See J. H. Michael, "The First and Second Epistles to the Philippians," *ExpT* 34 (1922–23), pp. 106–9, for the view that Paul here quotes their words. See also p. xxvi above.

You once more had the chance of showing that you care for me: Gk. *anethalete to hyper emou phronein*, lit., "you flourished again (intransitive) with regard to your thought for me" or "you caused your thought for me to flourish again" (transitive). This is the only NT instance of *anathallein* (or indeed of *thallein* or any compound of it).

You . . . had no chance: Gk. *ēkaireisthe*, imperfect of *akaireisthai*, "to lack *kairos* (opportunity)"; this is the only occurrence of this rare verb in the Greek Bible.

4:11 / **To be satisfied with what I have**: Gk. *en hois eimiautarkēs einai*, "to be content (in the circumstances) in which I am." The Stoic emphasis on *autarkeia* in the sense of self-sufficiency goes back to Socrates who, when asked who was the wealthiest person, replied, "The one who is content with least, for contentment (*autarkeia*) is nature's wealth" (Stobaeus, *Florilegium* 5.43). On Paul's natural independence of spirit and outlook see C. H. Dodd, "The Mind of Paul, I" in *New Testament Studies*, pp. 71–73.

4:12 / A rhythmical pattern has been detected in vv. 12 and 13, but here at least it is not to be explained in terms of a quotation from some other source.

I have learned this secret: Gk. *memyēmai*, "I have been initiated" (from the root *my* in this verb *myein* is derived *mystērion*, "mystery").

4:13 / **By the power that Christ gives me**: lit., "in my strengthener (enabler)" (Gk. *en tō endynamounti me*), i.e., Christ. With this use of the present participle of *endynamoun* cf. the aorist participle in 1 Tim. 1:12, "I thank my strengthener (*tō endynamōsanti me*, 'him who empowered me'), Christ Jesus our Lord."

31

Appreciation of Earlier Gifts

But it was very good of you to help me in my troubles. [15]You Philippians know very well that when I left Macedonia in the early days of preaching the Good News, you were the only church to help me; you were the only ones who shared my profits and losses. [16]More than once when I needed help in Thessalonica, you sent it to me. [17]It is not that I just want to receive gifts; rather, I want to see profit added to your account.

Paul remembers with gratitude the Philippian Christians' kindness to him in the period immediately following their conversion.

4:14 / If the Philippian readers got the impression that some modern commentators get, that Paul is saying, "Thank you for your gift, but it really wasn't necessary," Paul removes any impression of ungraciousness on his part by assuring them again of his grateful appreciation. They had renewed their kindness both by helping him financially and by sharing his **troubles**. By his **troubles** he means primarily his current imprisonment; in showing him practical fellowship in that situation they were also showing him practical fellowship in the apostolic ministry that he continued to discharge in spite of his current restrictions.

4:15 / By sending him a gift now they were repeating earlier acts of kindness. They did not neet Paul's reminder of these: but it was encouraging for them to realize that Paul still recalled their kindness with gratitude.

In the early days of preaching the Good News (lit., "in the beginning of the gospel") does not refer to the beginning of Paul's apostleship but to the beginning of the Philippians' Christian experience and participation in the gospel enterprise. At that time, Paul says, **you were the only church to help me** "in the matter of giving and receiving"—which might be taken to mean their giving and his receiving. But the phrase may be drawn from the vocabulary of accountancy (cf. 3:7, 8); hence GNB renders **you were the only ones who shared my profits and losses**.

The time he has in mind was the difficult period after he **left Macedonia**, more particularly, probably, after he had settled in Corinth. In

2 Corinthians 11:8, 9 he says to the Corinthian Christians, "While I was working among you, I was paid by other churches. I was robbing them, so to speak, in order to help you. And during the time I was with you I did not bother you for help when I needed money: the brothers who came from Macedonia brought me everything I needed." There is probably a further reference to this help in Acts 18:5, where Silas (Silvanus) and Timothy return from Macedonia and join Paul in Corinth, enabling him to give "his whole time to preaching the message," instead of spending part of it in tentmaking as he had done for the first few weeks after his arrival in Corinth. Both in 2 Corinthians 11:8, 9 and in Acts 18:5 "Macedonia" implies pre-eminently Philippi. (The context of the former passage makes it plain that, even if help had not come from Macedonia, Paul would not have asked the Corinthian church for any.)

4:16 / Indeed, he adds, even before he left Macedonia, while he was **in Thessalonica** (to which he and his companions went immediately after their departure from Philippi), they sent him **help** to meet his needs. The question arises whether the phrase **more than once** refers to the period of his stay **in Thessalonica** (which is how GNB and most other versions understand it) or to the time after that. The sentence might be rendered: "Both (when I was) in Thessalonica and more than once (in other places) you sent me (something) for my need." This rendering would cover what he had received from them in Corinth as well as **in Thessalonica**.

In writing to the Thessalonian Christians, Paul and his associates remind them how they "worked day and night" while they were with them so as to earn their own livelihood and not be chargeable to their converts (1 Thess. 2:9), how they "did not accept anyone's support without paying for it" (2 Thess. 3:8). Why is no mention made there of support that Paul at least received from Philippi while he was still **in Thessalonica**? Perhaps the gift from Philippi was not enough to remove completely the need for manual labor **in Thessalonica**; it may be, too, that Paul and his friends did not wish to embarrass the Thessalonian Christians by mentioning gifts received from Christians elsewhere. In writing as he did in 2 Corinthians 11:8, 9, Paul felt it necessary to induce in the Corinthian Christians a salutary sense of shame; there was no such necessity with regard to the Thessalonian Christians—quite the contrary.

4:17 / Once more, Paul cannot remain content with thanking the Philippians for their gift. He emphasizes that he is grateful not simply because they sent it to him but also because their sending it is a token of heavenly grace in their lives and, so to speak, a deposit in the bank of heaven that will multiply at compound interest to their advantage. They meant Paul to be the gainer from their generosity, and so indeed he is; but on the spiritual plane the permanent gain will be theirs.

Additional Notes

4:14 / **It was very good of you**: Gk. *kalōs epoiēsate*, "you did well." Cf. Acts 10:33, *kalōs epoiēsas paragenomenos*, "you have been good enough to come" (GNB) or "thank you for coming." As in the past tense *kalōs poiein* conveys the sense of "thank you," so in the future it expresses a request: "please" (as in 3 John 6, "Please help them to continue their trip," lit., "you will do well, *kalōs poiēseis*, by sending them forth").

4:15 / **You Philippians**: the vocative *Philippēsioi* has a form based on Latin *Philippenses*, as was appropriate for citizens of a Roman colony. With this vocative compare "Galatians" in Gal. 3:1 and "Corinthians" in 2 Cor. 6:11, where bewilderment and exhortation are respectively intended; here nothing is intended but affectionate gratitude.

In the early days of preaching the Good News: M. J. Suggs, "Concerning the Date of Paul's Macedonian Ministry," *NovT* 4 (1960), pp. 60–68, dates the evangelization of Macedonia in the early 40s, which would have been a fairly early stage of Paul's apostolic ministry, but there are serious obstacles in the way of accepting this dating.

4:16 / **More than once**: Gk. *kai hapax kai dis*, lit., "both once and twice," an idiomatic expression for "more than once"; cf. L. Morris, "*Kai hapax kai dis*," *NovT* 1 (1956), pp. 203–8. It occurs also in 1 Thess. 2:18. For the view that the phrase does not have exclusive reference to Paul's visit to Thessalonica see the same article by L. Morris (p. 208) and R. P. Martin, ad loc.

4:17 / **Profit**: Gk. *karpos*, "fruit," perhaps meaning "interest" (if so, Paul continues to use the language of accountancy, and the accompanying participle, *pleonazonta*, "multiplying" rather than **added**, may suggest that the interest is compound).

32

Acknowledgment of Present Gift

Here, then, is my receipt for everything you have given me—and it has been more than enough! I have all I need now that Epaphroditus has brought me all your gifts. They are like a sweet-smelling offering to God, a sacrifice which is acceptable and pleasing to him. ¹⁹And with all his abundant wealth through Christ Jesus, my God will supply all your needs. ²⁰To our God and Father be the glory forever and ever! Amen.

Paul gives them his receipt for the gift and promises them every blessing.

4:18 / Continuing his "accounting" language, Paul says, "I am paid in full": **here . . . is my receipt for everything you have given me**. If he knows "what it is to be in need and what it is to have more than enough" (v. 12), they have given him occasion once more to have **more than enough!** With the **gifts** brought him on their behalf by **Epaphroditus** he is full to overflowing. He has mentioned Epaphroditus with appreciation already (2:25–30) as the one who (he says) "has served as your messenger in helping me"; the handing over of the Philippians' gift was one of the ways in which Epaphroditus helped him.

The gift was welcome to Paul. But Paul was engaged in the service of **God**; the gift was therefore a gift to God as well as to Paul, and it was at least as welcome to God as it was to Paul. Paul now abandons the vocabulary of accounting and takes up the language of worship. Their gift to Paul was an **offering to God . . . acceptable and pleasing to him**. The phrase **a sweet-smelling offering** is found repeatedly in the OT, from the description of Noah's sacrifice in Genesis 8:21 onward; it is specially common in the directions for the levitical sacrifices (cf. Exod. 29:18, etc.). In the NT it is used figuratively of the self-offering of Christ (Eph. 5:2) and similar language is used of the self-offering of his people to God (Rom. 12:1; 2 Cor. 2:14–16; Heb. 13:16).

4:19 / They may rest assured, says Paul, that what they have given to God will be amply repaid by him from the limitless resources of his **wealth**. Paul cannot even think of the divine **wealth** now without linking it with **Christ Jesus**: he is the mediator through whom all God's blessings are communicated to men and women. Paul speaks of **my God** (cf. 1:3) because he had long since experienced his power to **supply all** his personal **needs**, and to supply them through Christ. At a time when he was most painfully conscious of his own inadequacy he received the assurance from the risen Lord, "My grace is all you need" (2 Cor. 12:9), and in effect it is that assurance that he now imparts to his friends.

4:20 / Paul's expression of thanks is fittingly concluded with a doxology, which also fittingly concludes the letter as a whole. J. B. Lightfoot, commenting on the doxology in Galatians 1:5, points out that (like the present doxology) it contains no verb and argues that the verb supplied should be the indicative "is," not the imperative **be**. "It is an affirmation rather than a wish. Glory is the essential attribute of God." (He refers to the doxology of 1 Peter 4:11, where the verb "is" appears in the Greek text, as it does also in the later doxology appended to the Lord's Prayer in Matt. 6:13, KJV.)

Additional Notes

4:18 / **Here, then, is my receipt for everything**: this is the sense of Gk. *apechō de panta* (lit., "and I have everything"); there is abundant evidence that *apechō* was in contemporary use to mean "Paid in full." Similarly GNB renders *apechousin ton misthon autōn* (lit., "they have their reward") in Matt. 6:2, 5, 16 as "they have already been paid in full"; cf. G. A. Deissmann, *Bible Studies*, p. 227: *"they can sign the receipt of their reward*: their right to receive the reward is realised, precisely as if they had already given a receipt for it."

4:19 / **His abundant wealth**: **abundant** is a less than adequate equivalent for Paul's phrase *en doxē*, "in glory" (cf. RSV: "his riches in glory"). The phrase probably does not refer to the life to come; it might be rendered (with the adjoining words) "his glorious abundance" (F. W. Beare takes it as an adverbial phrase with the verb **supply**: "my God shall fully supply every need of yours gloriously").

Through Christ Jesus: Gk. *en Christō Iēsou*, which J. B. Lightfoot takes to be incorporative: "through your union with, incorporation in, Christ Jesus."

33

Final Greetings

Greetings to each one of God's people who belong to Christ Jesus. The brothers here with me send you their greetings. ²²All God's people here send greetings, especially those who belong to the Emperor's palace.

The letter closing was probably penned by Paul himself. It was no uncommon thing in antiquity for the sender of a letter, after dictating most of it, to write the last sentence or two in his own hand. It was not usual to append one's personal signature, although Paul does so—probably for special reasons—in 1 Corinthians 16:21; Colossians 4:18; 2 Thessalonians 3:17 (see also his signed I. O. U. in Philem. 19a). It was his autograph, not his signature, that was his authenticating mark in "every letter" (2 Thess. 3:17); thus he starts the last section of his letter to the Galatians with the words: "See what big letters I make as I write to you now with my own hand!" (Gal. 6:11).

4:21 / Paul sends final **greetings to each one of God's people who belong to Christ Jesus**—literally (and more succinctly) "to every saint in Christ Jesus" (for the designation cf. 1:1). Indeed, "in Christ Jesus" might well be construed with "greetings" ("greet them in Christ Jesus"—as fellow members of Christ) were it not for the analogy of 1:1, where "in Christ Jesus" undoubtedly goes with "all the saints." "Greet every saint," says Paul; since the greetings are extended to all the believers in Philippi, who are addressed in the verb "greet" (imperative plural)? Perhaps the "church leaders and helpers" who are specially mentioned in 1:1; it would be for them to see to it that the letter was read, and the greetings conveyed, to the whole church.

It is not only Paul who sends his **greetings**; **the brothers** who are with him do likewise. Since **the brothers here with me** are mentioned separately from **all God's people here**, who also **send greetings** (v. 22), they are probably Paul's co-workers.

4:22 / Among the "saints" in the place where Paul is, **all** of whom **send** their **greetings**, special mention is made of **those who belong to the Emperor's palace** or, more literally, "those who belong to Caesar's household." (The GNB rendering, by referring to the imperial **palace**, which stood in Rome, preempts the question of the place from which the letter was sent.)

Caesar's household included not only members of the imperial family in the narrower sense but also a great number of slaves and freedmen. From the ranks of the freedmen the imperial civil service was staffed. These were to be found far and wide throughout the provinces, but nowhere was there such a concentration of them as in Rome—a concentration large enough to include a significant proportion of converts to the Christian faith.

If this letter was sent *from* Rome, and the greetings in Romans 16:3–16 were sent *to* Rome (three or four years earlier), it might be asked if any of the saints in Caesar's household were included among the recipients of greetings in the earlier letter. Two groups in particular are mentioned that could well have belonged to the imperial household: "the family of Aristobulus" and "the family of Narcissus" (Rom. 16:10, 11). The family of Narcissus has been thought by many commentators from John Calvin onward to have comprised the slaves of Tiberius Claudius Narcissus, a wealthy freedman of the Emperor Tiberius who exercised great influence under Claudius but was executed soon after Nero's accession in A.D. 54, at the instance of Nero's mother Agrippina. His goods were confiscated, and his slaves would have become imperial property, being distinguished from others in the imperial household by the designation *Narcissiani*. More speculative is the position of the family of Aristobulus. J. B. Lightfoot and others have suggested that this Aristobulus was identical with a grandson of Herod the Great (Aristobulus by name) who is known to have lived in Rome as a private citizen and, like his elder brother Herod Agrippa I ("King Herod" of Acts 12:1), enjoyed the friendship of Claudius. If, on his death, he bequeathed his property to the emperor (we have no express evidence that he did so, although this was not an uncommon procedure), his slaves would have been distinguished in the imperial household as the *Aristobuliani*. Herodion, whom Paul mentions in Romans 16:11 between the *Aristobuliani* and the *Narcissiani*, may also have had some association with the Herod family. At an earlier date Herod Agrippa I himself is described by Philo, in exactly the same phrase as Paul uses here, as a member of "Caesar's household" (*Flaccus*, 35).

Additional Notes

4:21 / On Paul's letter closings see H. Gamble, *The Textual History of the Letter to the Romans*, pp. 56–95, 143, 144, and for remarks on Philippians, pp. 88, 94, 145, 146.

The brothers here with me: they are identified with Paul's companions or co-workers by J. B. Lightfoot (ad loc.) and E. E. Ellis, "Paul and his Co-Workers," *NTS* 17 (1970–71), p. 446.

4:22 / "Caesar's household" (*Kaisaros oikia*) is called *domus Caesaris* by Tacitus (*Histories* 2.92); an inscription of A.D. 55 refers to the *populus et familia Caesaria* at Kilia in the Thracian Chersonese. Guilds (*collegia*) of the "freedmen and slaves of our Lord Augustus" are recorded on a second-century inscription from Ephesus (J. T. Wood, *Discoveries at Ephesus* [London: Longmans, 1877], Inscriptions from Tombs, Sarcophagi, etc., No. 20).

For possible references in Rom. 16:3–16 to some of the "saints in Caesar's household" see J. B. Lightfoot, *Philippians*, pp. 171–78. For Narcissus see Tacitus, *Annals* 13.1.4; Dio Cassius, *History* 60.34; also Juvenal, *Satire* 14.329 (*Narcissiani* are mentioned in *CIL* 3.3973; 6.15640). For Aristobulus see Josephus, *War* 1.552; 2.221; *Ant.* 18.133, 135, etc.

34

Grace-Benediction

| May the grace of the Lord Jesus | Christ be with you all. |

The grace-benediction is the most regular feature of Paul's letter closings. There are variations of wording, but the sense is uniformly the same. Outside the Pauline corpus, the NT has grace-benedictions in Hebrews 13:25 and Revelation 22:21; the Letter of Clement of Rome also ends with one (1 Clem. 65:2). This form of words may have been imported into epistolary usage from the blessing pronounced at the end of Christian services of worship.

4:23 / **Be with you all**: literally, "be with your spirit"; here "your spirit" is simply a more emphatic way of saying "you" (equivalent to "yourselves"). Compare the liturgical versicle and response: "The Lord be with you / And with your spirit" (see also 2 Tim. 4:22).

The wording here is identical with that in Philemon 23, and similar to that in Galatians 6:18, where the pronoun "our" qualifies "Lord Jesus Christ" and the vocative "brothers" (with a concluding "Amen") is added at the end.

Postscript

It is not easy for us in the Western world today to imagine what it must have felt like to belong to a small community of "citizens of heaven" in one of the eastern provinces of the Roman Empire in the first century A.D. Gentile Christians found themselves transplanted into membership in a new society that enjoyed no high esteem in the neighborhood, and they discovered that membership in it involved, in some important respects, a breach with the society to which they had previously belonged. The many social and business functions that were related to one pagan cult or another were henceforth barred to them.

Their new society was organized on two or more levels. In the first instance they would find themselves members of a house-church, which met regularly in the home of one of their number; but in many cities there would be a number of house-churches, all of which were incorporated in the wider city-church. The consciousness of membership in the city-church might be stronger in some house-churches than in others, just as consciousness of membership in a worldwide fellowship would be stronger in some city-churches than in others.

In Philippi the sense of membership in a citywide church was probably quite strong. This is suggested by the fact that this letter is addressed "to all God's people in Philippi . . . including the church leaders and helpers" (1:1). In none of the other Pauline letters (apart from the Pastorals) do we find such special reference made to a definite body of people in the church exercising supervisory and administrative functions. The Corinthian Christians would probably have been impatient with any such exercise of authority over them; the church of Rome at this time appears to have been too decentralized to have one citywide college of leaders. Paul might conceivably have nominated the leaders at Philippi, but the Philippian church was doubtless well qualified to elect them itself.

One feature that strikes us about the Philippian church, both in Acts and in Paul's letter, is the active part played in it by women. In Luke's narrative Lydia, the purple-seller from Thyatira, and her companions, with the members of her household, are the foundation-members of the Philippian church. In the letter Paul makes special mention of Euodia and Syntyche as women who contended by his side in the gospel ministry (4:3); he describes their service in athletic language that implies no merely auxiliary role. This is not only consistent with what is known of the independence and initiative of Macedonian women (see p. xvi above, with n. 18), it is in line with Paul's affirmation in Galatians 3:28 that in Christ "there is no difference . . . between men and women"—an affirmation that does not deny the distinction between the two sexes but abolishes any inequality between them in respect to religious roles.

We know the principal features that distinguished the Jewish community in a Gentile city from its neighbors, but many of these (such as circumcision, Sabbath observance, food restrictions) did not obtain in a church of Paul's Gentile mission field. If Paul had been asked what marked off one of his churches from its environment, he might have replied that the cross of Christ "fenced off" believers from the world (there may be a hint at this idea in Gal. 6:14, where he says that through the cross "the world is dead to me, and I am dead to the world"). But the cross of Christ exercised a positive rather than a negative influence on their lives. The society in the midst of which the Philippian Christians lived might be described as "corrupt and sinful," but they were commended for shining there "like stars lighting up the sky" and offering them "the message of life" (2:15, 16).

Each local church might be compared to a garden planted in a wilderness, but the church's concern was not so much to prevent the wilderness from encroaching on the garden as to see to it that the garden took over more and more of the wilderness. The garden was not to be "walled around"; its boundaries were to be flexible and expandable. To change the figure, each colony of heaven was to extend its territory and incorporate more and more of its neighborhood. Every church was to be a missionary church, and the history of the expansion of early Christianity shows that many churches realized and fulfilled this mission. Among those that did so the church of Philippi, like the other Macedonian churches, holds an honored place.

Abbreviations

A	Codex Alexandrinus
ad loc.	at the place
Aleph	Codex Sinaiticus
ANF	*The Ante-Nicene Fathers* (series)
Ant.	Josephus, *Antiquities*
ASNU	Acta Seminarii Neotestamentici Upsaliensis
ASV	American Standard Version (1901)
B	Codex Vaticanus
BC	*The Beginnings of Christianity*
BDF	*Greek Grammar of the New Testament and Other Early Christian Literature*
BFCT	Beiträge zur Forschung christlicher Theologie
Bib.	*Biblica*
BJ	Bible de Jérusalem
BJRL	*Bulletin of the John Rylands Library*
BT	Bibliotheca Teubneriana
BZAW	Beihefte zur Zeitschrift für die alttestamentliche Wissenschaft
BZNW	Beihefte zur Zeitschrift für die neutestamentliche Wissenschaft
C	Codex Ephraemi
CB	Coniectanea Biblica
CBC	Cambridge Bible Commentary
CBQ	*Catholic Biblical Quarterly*
CBSC	Cambridge Bible for Schools and Colleges
cf.	compare
chap. (chaps.)	chapter (chapters)
CIJ	*Corpus Inscriptionum Judaicarum*
CIL	*Corpus Inscriptionum Latinarum*
1 Clem	Letter of Clement of Rome to the Corinthians
Clem Hom	*Clementine Homilies*
CNT	Commentaire du Nouveau Testament
D	Codex Claromontanus
D*	Firsthand in D
D^1	First corrector of D
D^2	Second corrector of D
EGT	Expositor's Greek Testament

EPC	Epworth Preacher's Commentaries
EQ	*Evangelical Quarterly*
ETL	*Ephemerides Theologicae Lovanienses*
ExpT	*Expository Times*
F	Codex Augiensis
f. (ff.)	and following verse or page (verses or pages)
FRLANT	Forschungen zur Religion und Literatur des Alten und Neuen Testaments
G	Codex Boernerianus
GNB	Good News Bible (Today's English Version)
HDB	*Hastings' Dictionary of the Bible*
HNT	Handbuch zum Neuen Testament
HNTC	Harper's New Testament Commentaries
HTR	*Harvard Theological Review*
IB	Interpreter's Bible
IBNTG	*Idiom-Book of New Testament Greek*
ICC	International Critical Commentary
JB	Jerusalem Bible
JBL	*Journal of Biblical Literature*
JRStatSoc	*Journal of the Royal Statistical Society*
JTC	*Journal for Theology and the Church*
JTS	*Journal of Theological Studies*
KEK	Kritisch-Exegetischer Kommentar
KJV	King James Version
L	Codex Angelicus
LXX	Septuagint (pre-Christian Greek translation of the OT)
MNTC	Moffatt New Testament Commentary
NASB	New American Standard Bible
NCB	New Century Bible
NClarB	New Clarendon Bible
NEB	New English Bible
NICNT	New International Commentary on the New Testament
NIGTC	New International Greek Testament Commentary
NIV	New International Version
NovT	*Novum Testamentum*
NovTSup	*Novum Testamentum Supplement*
NPNF	*Nicene and Post-Nicene Fathers* (series)
NT	New Testament

NTC	New Testament Commentary
NTD	Das Neue Testament Deutsch
NTF	Neutestamentliche Forschungen
NTS	*New Testament Studies*
NTTS	New Testament Tools and Studies
OT	Old Testament
P	Codex Porphyrianus
P[46]	Chester Beatty papyrus
par.	parallel
PNTC	Pelican New Testament Commentaries
Psi	Codex Athous Laurae
RB	*Revue Biblique*
RNT	Regensburger Neues Testament
RSPT	*Revue des sciences philosophiques et théologiques*
RSR	*Recherches de science religieuse*
RSV	Revised Standard Version
SBLDS	Society of Biblical Literature Dissertation Series
SBT	Studies in Biblical Theology
SD	Studies and Documents
SE	*Studia Evangelica*
SNT	Die Schriften des Neuen Testaments
SNTSMS	Society for New Testament Studies Monograph Series
TB	*Tyndale Bulletin*
TDNT	*Theological Dictionary of the New Testament*
Test Zeb	*Testament of Zebulun* (in *Testaments of the Twelve Patriarchs*)
THKNT	Theologischer Handkommentar zum Neuen Testament
TKNT	Theologischer Kommentar zum Neuen Testament
TU	*Texte und Untersuchungen*
TZ	*Theologische Zeitschrift*
v. (vv.)	verse (verses)
WBC	World Biblical Commentary
WC	Westminster Commentaries
WUNT	Wissenschaftliche Untersuchungen zum Neuen Testament
ZK	Zahn Kommentar
ZNW	*Zeitschrift für die Neuen Testament*

For Further Reading

Commentaries on Philippians (In English)

Barth, K. *The Epistle to the Philippians*. Translated by J. W. Leitch. London: SCM Press, 1962.

Beare, F. W. *A Commentary on the Epistle to the Philippians*. HNTC. New York: Harper, 1959.

Bengel, J. A. *Gnomon of the New Testament* (1742), "Epistle to the Philippians." Translated by J. Bryce, vol. 4, pp. 119–56. Edinburgh: T. & T. Clark, 1857.

Caird, G. B. *Paul's Letters from Prison*. NClarB, pp. 95–154. Oxford: Clarendon Press, 1976.

Calvin, John. *The Epistles of Paul the Apostle to the Galatians, Ephesians, Philippians and Colossians* (1548). Translated by T. H. L. Parker, pp. 225–95. Edinburgh: Oliver & Boyd, 1965. Grand Rapids: Eerdmans, 1979.

Chrysostom (Saint John Chrysostom). *Homilies on the Epistle of St. Paul the Apostle to the Philippians* (between A.D. 398 and 404). Translated by W. C. Cotton. NPNF, Series 1, vol. 13, pp. 181–255. Grand Rapids: Eerdmans, 1956.

Collange, J.-F. *The Epistle of St. Paul to the Philippians*. Translated by A. W. Heathcote. London: Epworth, 1979.

Grayston, K. *The Epistles to the Galatians and to the Philippians*. EPC, pp. 75–116. London: Epworth, 1957.

_____. *The Letters of Paul to the Philippians and to the Thessalonians*. CBC, pp. 3–48. Cambridge: Cambridge University Press, 1967.

Hendriksen, W. *Philippians*. NTC. Grand Rapids: Baker, 1962.

Houlden, J. L. *Paul's Letters from Prison*. PNTC, pp. 29–116. Harmondsworth: Penguin Books, 1970. WPCS. Philadelphia: Westminster, 1978.

Jones, M. *The Epistle to the Philippians*. WC. London: Methuen, 1918.

Kennedy, H. A. A. *The Epistle to the Philippians*. EGT, vol. 3, pp. 397–473. London: Hodder & Stoughton, 1903. (On the Greek text.)

Lightfoot, J. B. *St. Paul's Epistle to the Philippians*. 6th ed. London: Macmillan, 1881. (On the Greek text.)

Martin, Ralph P. *Philippians*. NCB. London: Oliphants, 1976. NCBCS. Grand Rapids: Eerdmans, 1980.

Meyer, H. A. W. *The Epistles to the Philippians and Colossians*. Translated by J. C. Moore and W. P. Dickson. Edinburgh: T. & T. Clark, 1885.

Michael, J. H. *The Epistle of Paul to the Philippians*. MNTC. London: Hodder & Stoughton, 1928.

Moule, H. C. G. *The Epistle of Paul the Apostle to the Philippians*. CBSC. Cambridge: Cambridge University Press, 1889.

Müller, J. J. *The Epistles of Paul to the Philippians and to Philemon*. NICNT. Grand Rapids: Eerdmans, 1955.

Plummer, Alfred. *A Commentary on St. Paul's Epistle to the Philippians*. London: Robert Scott, 1919. Old Tappan, N.J.: Revell, 1980.

Scott, E. F. *The Epistle to the Philippians*. IB, vol. 11. New York and Nashville: Abingdon, 1955.

Smith, R. R. *The Epistles of St. Paul's First Trial*. Cambridge: Macmillan & Bowes, 1899.

Vaughan, C. J. *St. Paul's Epistle to the Philippians*. London: Macmillan, 1885. (On the Greek text).

Vincent, M. R. *Critical and Exegetical Commentary on the Epistles to the Philippians and to Philemon*. 3d ed., ICC. Edinburgh: T. & T. Clark, 1922. (On the Greek text).

Commentaries on Philippians (In Other Languages)

Benoit, P. *Épître aux Philippiens*. 2d ed., BJ. Paris: Editions du Cerf, 1956.

Dibelius, M. *An die Thessalonicher I–II. An die Philipper*. HNT 11. Tübingen: Mohr, 1937.

Ewald, P. *Der Brief des Paulus an die Philipper*. Revised by Wohlenberg. ZK 11. Leipzig and Erlangen: Deichert-Scholl, 1923.

Friedrich, G. *Der Brief an die Philipper*. In *Die kleineren Briefe des Apostels Paulus*. 10th ed., NTD 8. Göttingen: Vandenhoeck & Ruprecht, 1965.

Gnilka, J. *Der Philipperbrief*. TKNT. Freiburg: Herder, 1968.

Haupt, E. *Der Brief an die Philipper*. In *Die Gefangenschaftsbriefe*. 7th ed., KEK 9. Göttingen: Vandenhoeck & Ruprecht, 1902.

Lipsius, R. A. *Der Brief an die Philipper*. 2d ed., HCNT II.2. Freiburg: Mohr, 1892.

Lohmeyer, E. *Der Brief an die Philipper*. Revised by W. Schmauch. 14th ed., Göttingen: Vandenhoeck & Ruprecht, 1974.

Lueken, W. *Der Brief an die Philipper*. 3d ed., SNT II. Göttingen: Vandenhoeck & Ruprecht, 1917.

Michaelis, W. *Der Brief des Paulus an die Philipper*. THKNT 11. Leipzig: Deichert, 1935.

Staab, K. *Die Thessalonicherbriefe. Die Gefangenschaftsbriefe*. 5th ed., RNT. Regensburg: Pustet, 1969.

Victorinus (C. Marius Victorinus Afer). *Commentarii in Epistulas Pauli* (between A.D. 360 and 370). Edited by A. Locher. BT, pp. 72–122. Leipzig: Teubner, 1972.

Bibliography on the Christ Hymn (Phil. 2:6–11) (In English)

Bornkamm, G. "On Understanding the Christ-Hymn, Phil. 2, 5–11" (1950). In *Early Christian Experience*, pp. 112–22. Translated by P. L. Hammer. London: SCM Press, 1969.

Dunn, J. D. G. *Christology in the Making*, pp. 114–21. London: SCM Press, 1980. Philadelphia: Westminster, 1980.

Ehrhardt, A. A. T. "Jesus Christ and Alexander the Great" (1948). In *The Framework of the New Testament Stories*, pp. 37–43. Manchester: Manchester University Press, 1964.

Fairweather, E. R. "The 'Kenotic' Christology." In F. W. Beare, *Philippians*, pp. 159–74.

Furness, J. M. "Behind the Philippian Hymn." *ExpT* 79 (1967–68), pp. 178–82.

Gifford, E. H. *The Incarnation: A Study of Philippians ii.5–11*. London: Longmans, 1911.

Glasson, T. F. "Two Notes on the Philippians Hymn (II.6–11)." *NTS* 21 (1974–75), pp. 133–39.

Hooker, M. D. "Philippians 2:6–11." In *Jesus und Paulus: Festschrift für W. G. Kümmel*. Edited by E. E. Ellis and E. Grässer, pp. 151–64. Göttingen: Vandenhoeck & Ruprecht, 1975.

Hoover, R. W. "The Harpagmos Enigma: A Philological Solution." *HTR* 64 (1971), pp. 95–119.

Käsemann, E. "A Critical Analysis of Philippians 2:5–11" (1950). Translated by A. F. Carse. *JTC* 5 (1968), pp. 45–88.

Knox, W. L. "The 'Divine Hero' Christology in the New Testament." *HTR* 41 (1948), pp. 229–49.

Marshall, I. H. "The Christ-Hymn in Philippians 2:5–11." *TB* 19 (1968), pp. 104–27.

Martin, R. P. *Carmen Christi: Philippians ii.5–11 in Recent Interpretation and in the Setting of Early Christian Worship*. SNTSMS 4. Cambridge: Cambridge University Press, 1967.

Moule, C. F. D. "Further Reflexions on Philippians 2:5–11." In *Apostolic History and the Gospel . . . Essays presented to F. F. Bruce*. Edited by W. W. Gasque and R. P. Martin. Exeter: Paternoster, 1970, pp. 264–76.

Murphy-O'Connor, J. "Christological Anthropology in Phil 2:6–11." *RB* 83 (1974), pp. 25–50.

Sanders, J. T. *The New Testament Christological Hymns*. SNTSMS 15. Cambridge: Cambridge University Press, 1971. Pp. 9–12, 58–74.

Schweizer, E. *Lordship and Discipleship*. SBT 28. London: SCM Press, 1960. Pp. 61–67.

Wallace, D. H. "A Note on *morphē*." *TZ* 22 (1966), pp. 19–25.

Warren, W. "On *heauton ekenōsen*." *JTS* 12 (1911), pp. 461–63.

Bibliography on the Christ Hymn (Phil. 2:6–11—) (In Other Languages)

Cerfaux, L. "L'hymne au Christ-Serviteur de Dieu." In *Recueil Lucien Cerfaux*, vol. 2, pp. 425–38. Gembloux: Duculot, 1954.

Grelot, P. "Deux notes critiques sur Philippiens 2, 6–11." *Bib.* 54 (1973), pp. 169–86.

Hofius, O. *Der Christushymnus Philipper 2, 6–11.* WUNT 17. Tübingen: Mohr, 1976.

Jeremias, J. "Zur Gedankenführung in den paulinischen Briefen." In *Studia Paulina in honorem J. de Zwaan.* Edited by J. N. Sevenster and W. C. van Unnik, pp. 152–55. Haarlem: Bohn, 1953.

––––––. "Zu Phil 2.7: *heauton ekenōsen,*" *NovT* 6 (1963), pp. 182–188.

Jervell, J., *Imago Dei: Gen. 1,26f. im Spätjudentum, in der Gnosis und in den paulinischen Briefen,* FRLANT 76 (Göttingen: Vandenhoeck & Ruprecht, 1960), pp. 227–31.

Larsson, E. *Christus als Vorbild.* ASNU 23, pp. 230–75. Uppsala: Almquist & Wiksells, 1962.

Lohmeyer, E. *Kyrios Jesus: Eine Untersuchung zu Phil 2, 5–11.* Heidelberg: Akademie der Wissenschaften, 1928, 2d ed., 1961.

Works Relevant to the Study of Philippians (In English)

Bandstra, A. J. *The Law and the Elements of the World.* Kampen: Kok, 1964.

Baur, F. C. *Paul: His Life and Works.* (First German edition, 1845). 2 vols. Translated by A. Menzies. London: Williams & Norgate, 1875.

Beker, J. Christian. *Paul the Apostle.* Edinburgh: T. & T. Clark, 1980. Philadelphia: Fortress, 1980.

Bruce, F. F. *Paul: Apostle of the Free Spirit.* Exeter: Paternoster, 1977.

––––––. *Paul: Apostle of the Heart Set Free.* Grand Rapids: Eerdmans, 1977.

––––––. *Tradition Old and New.* Exeter: Paternoster, 1970.

Carr, W. *Angels and Principalities.* SNTSMS 42. Cambridge: Cambridge University Press, 1981.

Clarke, W. K. L. *New Testament Problems.* London: SPCK, 1929.

Conybeare, W. J., and Howson, J. S. *The Life and Epistles of St. Paul.* London: Longmans, 1877.

Cullmann, Oscar. *The Christology of the New Testament.* Translated by S. C. Guthrie and C. A. M. Hall. London: SCM Press, 1959. Rev. ed. NTL. Philadelphia: Westminster, 1964.

––––––. *The Early Church.* Translated by A. J. B. Higgins and S. Godman. London: SCM Press, 1956.

Davies, W. D. *Paul and Rabbinic Judaism.* London: SPCK, 1948. Philadelphia: Fortress, 1980.

DeBoer, W. P. *The Imitation of Paul.* Kampen: Kok, 1962.

Deissmann, A. *Bible Studies.* 2d ed. Translated by A. Grieve. Edinburgh: T. & T. Clark, 1909.

––––––. *Light from the Ancient East.* 2d ed. Translated by L. R. M. Strachan. London: Hodder & Stoughton, 1927.

Dodd, C. H. *According to the Scriptures.* London: Nisbet, 1952.

_____. *New Testament Studies*. Manchester: Manchester University Press, 1953.

Duncan, G. S. *St. Paul's Ephesian Ministry*. London: Hodder & Stoughton, 1929.

Ehrhardt, A. A. T. *The Framework of the New Testament Stories*. Manchester: Manchester University Press, 1964. Cambridge: Harvard University Press, 1964.

Evans, O. E. *Saints in Christ Jesus: A Study of the Christian Life in the New Testament*. Swansea: John Penry Press, 1975.

Funk, R. W. *Language, Hermeneutic and Word of God*. New York: Harper & Row, 1966.

Gamble, H. *The Textual History of the Letter to the Romans*. SD 42. Grand Rapids: Eerdmans, 1977.

Goodspeed, E. J. *Problems of New Testament Translation*. Chicago: University of Chicago Press, 1945.

Gundry, R. H. *"Sōma" in Biblical Theology: With Emphasis on Pauline Anthropology*. SNTSMS 29. Cambridge and New York: Cambridge University Press, 1976.

Gunther, J. J. *Paul: Messenger and Exile*. Valley Forge, Pa. Judson, 1972.

Hanson, R. P. C. *Tradition in the Early Church*. London: SCM Press, 1962.

Hengel, M. *Acts and the History of Earliest Christianity*. Translated by J. Bowden. London: SCM Press, 1979. Philadelphia: Fortress, 1980.

_____. *Crucifixion*. Translated by J. Bowden. London: SCM Press, 1977. Philadelphia: Fortress, 1977.

Holmberg, B. *Paul and Power: The Structure of Authority in the Primitive Church as Reflected in the Pauline Epistles*. CB NT Series 11. Lund: Gleerup, 1978. Philadelphia: Fortress, 1980.

Hort, F. J. A. *The Christian Ecclesia*. London: Macmillan, 1897.

Hunter, A. M. *Paul and His Predecessor*. 2d ed. London: SCM Press, 1961.

Kim, S. *The Origin of Paul's Gospel*. WUNT 2.4. Tübingen: Mohr, 1981. Grand Rapids: Eerdmans, 1982.

Kümmel, W. G. *Introduction to the New Testament*. Translated by A. J. Mattill. London: SCM Press, 1966.

Larsen, J. A. O. *Greek Federal States*. Oxford: Clarendon Press, 1968.

Lincoln, A. T. *Paradise Now and Not Yet*. SNTSMS 43. Cambridge and New York: Cambridge University Press, 1981.

Manson, T. W. *Studies in the Gospels and Epistles*. Manchester: Manchester University Press, 1962.

Marxsen, Willi. *Introduction to the New Testament*. Translated by G. Buswell. Oxford: Blackwell, 1968. Philadelphia: Fortress, 1968.

Montefiore, H. W. *Paul the Apostle*. London: Collins, 1981.

Moore, A. L. *The Parousia in the New Testament*. NovTSup 13. Leiden: Brill, 1966.

Moule, C. F. D. *An Idiom-Book of New Testament Greek*. Cambridge and New York: Cambridge University Press, 1953.

———. *The Origin of Christology*. Cambridge and New York: Cambridge University Press, 1977.

Moule, H. C. G. *Philippian Studies*. London: Hodder & Stoughton, 1897. Grand Rapids: Kregel, 1977.

O'Brien, P. T. *Introductory Thanksgivings in the Letters of Paul. NovTSup* 49. Leiden: Brill, 1977.

O'Sullivan, F. *The Egnatian Way*. Newton Abbot: David & Charles, 1972.

Pfitzner, V. C. *Paul and the Agon Motif: Traditional Athletic Imagery in the Pauline Literature*. NovTSup 16. Leiden: Brill, 1967.

Ramsay, W. M. *St. Paul the Traveller and the Roman Citizen*. 14th ed. London: Hodder & Stoughton, 1920.

Renan, E. *Saint Paul*. Translated by W. M. Thomson. London: Mathieson, 1889.

Rigaux, B. *The Letters of Paul*. Translated by S. Yonick. Chicago: Franciscan Herald, 1968.

Rivkin, E. *A Hidden Revolution*. Nashville: Abingdon, 1978.

Robinson, H. W. *The Cross of the Servant*. London: SCM Press, 1926.

Robinson, J. A. T. *Redating the New Testament*. London: SCM Press, 1976.

Sanders, E. P. *Paul and Palestinian Judaism*. London: SCM Press, 1977. Philadelphia: Fortress, 1977.

Schmithals, W. *Paul and the Gnostics*. Translated by J. E. Steely. Nashville and New York: Abingdon, 1972.

Schubert, P. *Form and Function of the Pauline Thanksgivings*. BZNW 20. Berlin: Töpelmann, 1939.

Schweitzer, A. *The Mysticism of Paul the Apostle*. Translated by W. Montgomery. London: A. & C. Black, 1931.

Sherwin-White, A. N. *Roman Society and Roman Law in the New Testament*. Oxford: Clarendon Press, 1963.

———. *The Roman Citizenship*. 2d ed. Oxford: Clarendon Press, 1973.

Stauffer, E. *New Testament Theology*. Translated by J. Marsh. London: SCM Press, 1955.

Stendahl, K., ed. *The Scrolls and the New Testament*. London: SCM Press, 1958.

Tarn, W. W., and Griffith, G. T. *Hellenistic Civilisation*. 3d ed. London: Arnold, 1952. Rev. ed. New York: New American Library, 1961.

Thornton, L. S. *Christ and the Church*. London: Dacre Press, 1956.

Thrall, M. E. *Greek Particles in the New Testament*. NTTS 3. Leiden: Brill, 1962.

Weiss, J. *Earliest Christianity*. 2 vols. Edited by F. C. Grant. New York: Harper Torchbooks, 1959.

White, J. L. *The Form and Function of the Body of the Greek Letter*. SBLDS

2. Missoula, Mont.: Scholars Press, 1972.

Wiles, G. P. *Paul's Intercessory Prayers*. SNTSMS 24. Cambridge: Cambridge University Press, 1974.

Zahn, T. *Introduction to the New Testament*. 3 vols. Edited by M. W. Jacobus. Edinburgh: T. & T. Clark, 1909.

Ziesler, J. A. *The Meaning of Righteousness in Paul*. SNTSMS 20. Cambridge and New York: Cambridge University Press, 1972.

Works Relevant to the Study of Philippians (In Other Languages)

Appel, H. *Einleitung in das Neue Testament*. Leipzig: Deichert, 1922.

Bouttier, M. *En Christ*. Paris: Presses Universitaires de France, 1962.

De Wette, W. M. L. *Lehrbuch der historisch-kritischen Einleitung in die kanonischen Bücher des Neuen Testaments*. 4th ed. Berlin: G. Reimer, 1842.

Dupont, J. *Gnosis: La connaissance religieuse dans les épîtres de saint Paul*. Louvain: Nauwelaerts and Paris: Gabalda, 1949.

Feine, P. *Die Abfassung des Philipperbriefes in Ephesus*. BFCT 20.4. Gütersloh: Bertelsmann, 1916.

Güttgemanns, E. *Der leidende Apostel und sein Herr*. FRLANT 90. Göttingen: Vandenhoeck & Ruprecht, 1966.

Holtzmann, H. J. *Einleitung in das Neue Testament*. Freiburg: Mohr, 1886.

Lütgert, W. *Die Vollkommenen im Philipperbrief und die Enthusiasten in Thessalonich*. BFCT 13. Gütersloh: Bertelsmann, 1909.

Michaelis, W. *Die Gefangenschaft des Paulus in Ephesus und das Itinerar des Timotheus*. NTF 1.3. Gütersloh: Bertelsmann, 1925.

Seesemann, H. *Der Begriff KOINŌNIA im Neuen Testament*. BZNW 14. Giessen: Töpelmann, 1933.

Collected Essays

Bammel, E.; Barrett, C. K.; and Davies, W. D., eds. *Donum Gentilicium: New Testament Studies in Honour of David Daube*. Oxford: Clarendon Press, 1978.

Banks, R., ed. *Reconciliation and Hope: New Testament Essays on Atonement and Eschatology presented to L. L. Morris*. Exeter: Paternoster, 1974.

Barclay, W., and Anderson, H., eds. *The New Testament in Historical and Contemporary Perspective: Essays in Memory of G. H. C. Macgregor*. Oxford: Blackwell, 1965.

Black, M., and Fohrer, G., eds. *In Memoriam Paul Kahle*. BZAW 103. Berlin: Töpelmann, 1968.

Buckler, W. H., and Calder, W. M., eds. *Anatolian Studies presented to S⸍ William Mitchell Ramsay*. Manchester: Manchester University P 1923.

Farmer, W. R.; Moule, C. F. D.; and Niebuhr, R. R., eds. *Christian History and Interpretation: Studies presented to John Knox*. Cambridge and New York: Cambridge University Press, 1967.

Gasque, W. W., and Martin, R. P., eds. *Apostolic History and the Gospel: Biblical and Historical Essays presented to F. F. Bruce*. Grand Rapids: Eerdmans, 1970.

Newman, J. H. *Parochial and Plain Sermons*, vol. 6. London: Longmans, 1896.

Sevenster, J. N., and van Unnik, W. C., eds. *Studia Paulina in honorem Johannis de Zwaan*. Haarlem: Bohn, 1953.

van Unnik, W. C., ed. *Neotestamentica et Patristica: Eine Freundesgabe O. Cullmann zu seinem 60. Geburtstag überreicht*. *NovTSup* 6. Leiden: Brill, 1962.

Commentaries on Other NT Books

Bruce, F. F. *The Epistle to the Galatians*. NIGTC. Grand Rapids: Eerdmans, 1982.

_____. *1 & 2 Thessalonians*. WBC. Waco, Tex.: Word, 1982.

Burton, Ernest D. *A Critical and Exegetical Commentary on the Epistle to the Galatians*. ICC. Edinburgh: T. & T. Clark, 1921.

Haenchen, Ernst. *The Acts of the Apostles*. Translated by B. Noble and G. Shinn. Oxford: Blackwell, 1971. Philadelphia: Westminster, 1971.

Swete, Henry B. *The Gospel according to St. Mark*. 3rd ed. London: Macmillan, 1909. Grand Rapids: Kregel, 1978.

Subject Index

Accountancy, language of, use, 92, 127, 129, 130, 131
Adam, contrasted with Christ, 45, 52
Afraid, use of word, 35–36
Agrippa, 84
Agrippina, 133
Alexander I, xiv
Alexander III (the Great), xiv, 52
Ambition, Paul's, 95–98
Ambrosiaster, 14, 97
Ananias of Damascus, 34
Andriscus, xv
Annas, 24
Antiochus Epiphanes, 84
Antony, xiii
Aphrodite, 74
Apodosis, 29, 40
Apostle, as messenger, 57
Apostolic *parousia*, 66, 68–69, 73
Appel, H., 106
Apprehend, use of word, 98
Aquila, 74
Archippus of Colossae, 74
Aristobulus, family of, as "Caesar's household," 133, 134
Aristotle, 119, 122
Arnold, Matthew, 117
Artaxerxes, 1
Athletic imagery and language, use, 35, 36, 61, 62, 70, 95–98, 114, 136–137
Augustus, xv
Authorship of letter, xx–xxi

Bacchae, xviii
Bandstra, A. J., 54
Barnabas, 2, 68
Barth, K., 115
Baruch, 4
Bauernfeind, O., 62
Baur, F. C., xx–xxi
Beare, F. W., 4, 26, 51, 54, 58, 77, 92, 119, 120, 125, 131
Be joyful, as common form, 76
Bengel, J. A., 11, 13, 107
Benjamin, tribe of, 83, 85
Benoit, P., 115
Best, E., 4
Bodily desires, choice of phrase, 105
Bookkeeping language, use. *See* Accountancy, language of, use
Book of the living, 114
Bornkamm, Günther, xxvi
Bouttier, M., 18
Bowels, as heart, seat of emotions, 11, 41
Brutus, xiii
Bunyan, John, 124–125

Caesarea, as site of Paul's writing, xxii–xxiii
"Caesar's household," identity of, 133, 134
Caird, G. B., 36, 69, 71, 77
Callistratus, xiii
Calvin, John, 13, 133
Carr, W., 55
Cassius, xiii
Celsus, xviii
Cerfaux, L., 51
Chiasmus, 20, 21
Christ: contrasted with Adam, 45, 52; exaltation of, 47–51; as example, 39–40; humanity of, 46, 53–54; importance of in Paul's thought, 4, 29; nature of, 44–47; power of name, 49–50; pre-existence of, 45; resurrection of, power of, 90, 91, 109, 111; tradition of, in New Testament, 122
Christ hymn, 44–55
Christianity, coming of to Macedonia, xv–xviii
Chrysostom, 3, 101
Church, organization of, 136–137
Church leaders and helpers, use of phrase, 3–4
Cicero, xiii, 54
Circumcision, 105, 107; as collective noun, 78; as sacral term, 78–80; of Timothy, 2, 4
"Citizens of heaven": life-style of, 136; Philippians to live as, 32, 35, 110; responsibility of, 108–111
Claudius, xv, 133
Clemens, Titus Flavius, xxi
Clement, xxi, 114
Clement of Alexandria, 115
Clement of Rome, 135
Closing, as written by Paul himself, 132
Code of values, Paul's: former, 82–86; present, 87–94
Collange, J.-F., 15, 21, 27, 30, 33, 41, 65, 106, 110, 115
Colony, Roman, Philippi as, xiii–xiv
Compassion, importance of, 37–38, 41
"Concerning the Date of Paul's Macedonian Ministry," 129
Consideration, call for, 37–43
Courage, choice of word, 29
Crucifixion, degradation of, 47, 54
Cullman, O., 30, 52
Cyclops (Euripides), 106

Daniel, 3, 46, 48
David, 2
Day of Christ [Jesus], 8, 13, 15, 25, 56, 61, 89, 93, 99, 102
Day of the Lord, 8
Death, as preferable to Paul, 23, 25–26
Deep desire, choice of phrase, 25
Deep feeling, choice of phrase, 11
Delling, G., 115
Destruction, choice of word, 105, 106

Diakonoi, episkopoi, 3, 5
Dibelius, M., 19, 35, 51, 123
Dionysus, xviii
Diotrephes, 38
Disclosure formula, 18
The Divinely Inspired Woman, xvii
Docetism, 46
Dodd, C. H., xxv, xxviii
Dogs, as unclean animals, 79, 80–81
Domitian, xxi
Doxology, 131
Dreissmann, A., xxii
Duncan, G. S., xxii

Egnatian Way, xv, 71
Elijah, 84
Ellis, E. E., 134
"Enemies of the cross," warning against , 104–107
Epaphras of Colossae, 74
Epaphroditus, xxii, 4, 7, 11, 35, 37, 75, 76, 77, 103, 112, 124, 130; commendation of, 70–71, 72–73; as "faithful partner," 115; illness of, xxv, xxvi–xxvii, 71–72, 74; meaning of name, 74; to return to Philippi, xx, xxix, 70, 72
Ephesus, as site of Paul's writing, xxii, xxv–xxvi
Epictetus, xviii
Episkopoi, diakonoi, 3, 5
Epithymia, meaning of word, 30
Erasmus, 69, 115
Erastus, 67
Euodia, 113–115, 136
Euripides, xviii, 30, 106
"The Everlasting Mercy," 89
Every and all, repetition of, 7
Ewald, P., 76, 77, 115
Excursus, 19
Ezra, 1

"Faithful partner," identity of, 113–114, 115
Farmer, W. R., 24, 68
Fear and trembling, meaning of, 57, 58
Felix, xxiii
Festus, xxiii
The Form and Function of the Body of the Greek Letter, 18
Friedrich, G., 115
Fruit, harvest, in ethical sense, 13, 14
Funk, R. W., 24, 68, 73
Furness, J. M., 51
Furnish, V. P., 77

Galba, Emperor, 41–42
Gamaliel, 84
Gasque, W. W., 52
Gentle attitude, Philippians to have, 117, 119
Gnilka, J., 42, 115
Gnostics, Gnosticism, xx, 19, 74, 81, 85, 88, 93, 101, 106, 115
Goal, use of word, 98
God's people, choice of phrase, 3, 5

"God-sufficient," Paul as, 125
Go forward, use of phrase, 101
Gould, S. Baring, 115
Grace, 36
Grace and peace, wish for, 4
Grace-benediction, 135
Grayston, K., 42
Grelot, P., 51

Hájek, M., 115
Hannibal, xiv
Harmony, importance of, 32, 59
Harpagmos, meaning of, 52
Hasidaeans, 83
Haupt, E., 77, 106, 115
Hawthorn, T., 21
Hebrew, Paul as, 83
Hell, use of word, 105
Hendiadys, 74
Herod Agrippa I, 24, 133
Herodion, 133
Herod the Great, xxii, 133
Hezekiah, King, 50
Hippolytus of Rome, 106
Hofius, O., 51
Holtzmann, H. J., 80
Homer, xvi
Honorable things, set minds on, 121, 122
Hooker, M. D., 110
Humility: of Christ, 44, 47, 54; importance of, 38–39, 41–42

Ignatius, xix, 55, 64, 97
Intercessory prayer, 12–15
Introduction to the New Testament, 33
Irenaeus, 97
It does not matter!, choice of phrase, 28

Jacob, 62, 83, 85
Jesus. *See* Christ
Jewett, R., 21, 69
Job, 24, 29
John Mark, 68
John the Baptist, 85
Jonah, 2, 30
Josephus, 41, 74, 84
Joshua, 2
Joy: death as, to Paul, 64; in the Lord, 76–77, 116; in thinking of Philippians, 7, 31, 38, 112
Judah the Prince, Rabbi, 92
Judas, 24
Judas Maccabaeus, 84
Julius Caesar, xiii

Käsemann, E., 42
Kenotic theory, 53
Kindness, importance of, 37–38, 41
Knowledge, meaning of term, 88, 92–93
Kümmel, W. G., xxix
Kyrios, 51

Lee, G. M., 30
Levertoff, P. P., 51
Libanius, 30
Libation: in Old Testament, 64; Paul's life blood as, 63–65
Lightfoot, J. B., 18, 26, 30, 31, 35, 36, 41, 42, 46, 51, 52, 75, 80, 115, 122, 131, 133, 134
"Light for the whole world," Christians to be, 60, 62
Lipsius, R. A., 77
Location of writing of letter, xxi–xxvi, 133
Lohmeyer, Ernst, xxii, 28, 51, 106, 110
Lord, designation of, 4, 48–49, 50–51, 54–55
Lovely things, set minds on, 121
Lueken, W., 106
Luke, xiii, xviii, xxiii, xxiv, 17, 84; as "faithful partner," 113, 115; travels in Macedonia, xvi–xviii
Lütgert, W., 101
Luther, Martin, 24
Lydia, xvi, 115, 136

Macedonia: coming of Christianity to, xv–xviii; history of, xiv–xv
Macedonian War, Third, xiv
Manson, T. W., xxviii, 21, 115
Martin, R. P., 42, 51, 52, 110
Marxsen, Willi, 33
Masefield, John, 89
Mattathias, 84
Maturity, spiritual, 99–101
Mediator, Christ as, 131
Merchant of Venice, 117
Message of life, 60
Messengers of churches, status of, 70–71
Micah, 39
Michael, J. H., 77
Michaelis, W., 28, 51
Military imagery and language, use of, 35, 36, 70, 74
Montefiore, H. W., 45, 79, 100
Montgomery, James, 39
Moses, 2, 59, 86
Moule, C. F. D., 42, 52, 53, 54, 68
Müller, J. J., 115
Myers, F. W. H., 99
Mystery religions, 97

Narcissus, family of, as "Caesar's household," 133, 134
Narcissus, Tiberius Claudius, 133
Nero, xxiv, 133
Newman, J. H., 118
The New Testament: An American Translation, 77
Niebuhr, R. R., 68
Noah, 130
Noble things, set minds on, 120–121, 122
Note of thanks, as insertion into letter, xxvi–xxvii

Obedience, importance of, 56–57
O'Brien, P. T., 6, 9, 11
Occam's razor, 104

Octavian, xiii
Offering, gift as, 130
"One in soul," Paul and Timothy as, 67–68, 69
Opponents of church, in Philippi, 33
Origen, xviii
Oxymoron, 105

Parousia, apostolic, 66, 68–69, 73; use of word, 31
Participation, meaning of word, 9
Paul: ambition of, 95–98; as author of letter, xx–xxi, 1; as controversial figure, 20; early association with Timothy, 2; as example to be imitated, 102–103, 121; former code of values, 82–86; hardships of, 34; present code of values, 87–94; present situation of, xxi–xxvi, 16–18; "second conversion" of, xxviii; travels in Macedonia, xv–xviii
Paul and the Gnostics, 82
Paul the Apostle, 45, 100
Pay attention, choice of phrase, 103
Peace of God, 119, 121–122
Pentheus, xviii
Perfect, use of word, 97
Perfect judgment, choice of phrase, 12–13, 14
Perseus, xiv, xv
Peter, 24
Pharisee: described, 83–84, 86; meaning of term, 84, 86; Paul as, 83–84
Philemon, xxv, 74
Philip II, xiii, xiv
Philip V, xiv
Philippi: church at, xviii–xix; first missionary visit to, xvi–xviii; as Roman colony, xiii–xiv
Philo, 78, 133
Phinehas, 84
Phoebe, 72
Pilate, 24
Place of letter writing, xxi–xxvi, 133
Plutarch, 52
Polycarp, xix, xxvi, 4, 35, 106
Praetor, xiii–xiv
Praetorium, meaning of, xxii–xxiii, 17
Pray, choice of word, 14
Prayer, meanings of word, 118, 119
Preachers, motives for, 19–22
Preaching, importantance of content of, not preacher, 23–24
Prescript, contents, 1
Priscilla, 74
Privilege: suffering as, 34; use of word, 10, 11
Prize, use of word, 95, 96, 97
Protasis, 29
Punic War, Second, xiv
Pure things, set minds on, 121
Purpose of letter, xxix
Pythonic spirit, xvii

Recipients of letter, 2–3
Refutation of Heresies, 106
Relief fund, Jerusalem, xviii, xxiii, 7, 124
Renan, E., 115

Resurrection: of believing dead, 26–27, 91–92, 94, 108–109; Christ's, power of, 90, 91, 109, 111
Righteousness, in Christ, 90, 93
Right things, set minds on, 121
Roman colony, Philippi as, xiii–xiv
Rome, as site of Paul's writing, xxii, xxiii–xxvi, 133
Rules, place in Christian life, 100–101

Sacrifice, Christian's life as, 63
Sadducees, 84
"Saint Paul," 99
"Salt for all mankind," Christians to be, 60
Salvation, as near, 56–57
Satisfied, choice of word, 125, 126
Saul, 85. See also Paul
Savior, choice of word, 110
Schmithals, W., 21, 35, 58, 61, 74, 77, 81, 82, 85, 93, 101, 106, 115, 122
Scott, E. F., 51
Seesemann, H., 9
Selfish ambition, choice of phrase, 21
Servant, Christ as, 46
Servants of Christ Jesus, use of term, 2, 5
Servant song, fourth, of Isaiah, 53, 54
Shakespeare, William, 117
Silvanus (Silas), 128; as "faithful partner," 115; travels in Macedonia, xv–xviii
Simonians, 106
Simon the high priest, 64
Slave: choice of word, 53; Christ as, 46
Slaves of Christ Jesus, use of term, 2
"Snippers, the," 79
Socrates, xviii, 126
Spirit, 29, 35, 37, 41
Spiritual body, to replace natural body, 109, 110–111
Spiritually mature, use of phrase, 99, 101
Staab, K., 115
Stephanas, 72
Stephanos vs. diadēma, 112
Stoicism, 125, 126
Suffering, as privilege, 32, 34, 90–91, 93
Sufficiency of Paul, 124–126
Suggs, M. J., 129
Synechō, use of word, 30
Synergos, use of word, 74
Synstratiōtēs, use of word, 74
Syntyche, 113–115, 136

Tacitus, 134
Testament of Joseph, xvii–xviii

Testaments of the Twelve Patriarchs, xviii
Thanks, for gifts, 123–124, 127–131
Thanksgiving, introductory, as custom, 6, 8
Theos, 51
Thessalonica, beginnings of church in, xv
Tiberius, Emperor, xv, 133
Timothy, xviii, 73, 77, 80, 103, 128; biographical data, 1–2; circumcision of, 2, 4; as "faithful partner," 115; as "fellow worker," 74; "one in soul" with Paul, 67–68, 69; as sender of letter, xix, 1; travels in Macedonia, xv–xviii; to visit Philippi, xx, xxix, 66–69
Tithing, of Pharisees, 86
Titus, 74
To the Philippians, xxvi, 4
To the Trallians, 55
Tradition of Christ, in New Testament, 122
Travelogue. See Apostolic parousia
True knowledge, choice of phrase, 12–13, 14
True things, set minds on, 120

Unity of letter, question of, xxvi–xxix
Unity of mind, importance of, 37–43, 59, 113
Urbanus, 74

Victorinus, Marius, 115

Wallace, D. H., 52
War, 41
Warning against troublemakers, as insert into letter, xxvii–xxviii
Warren, W., 53
Watch out, use of phrase, 80
Wesley, Charles, 49, 64
Wette, W. M. L. de, xx
White, J. L., 18
Witness, God as, 11
Women, place in Macedonian churches, xvi, 136–137
"Workers of iniquity," warning against, 78–81
World below, meaning of, 50, 55
Worry, no need for, 118
Worship, language of, use, 130

Xerxes, xiv

Yahweh, 48, 51

Zahn, T., 106
Zeal, importance of, 84
Zealots, 84, 86

Scripture Index

OLD TESTAMENT

Genesis **1:14-19**, 60; **2:7**, 109; **3:5**, 52; **8:21**, 130; **17:12**, 83; **35:16-18**, 83; **49:27**, 85

Exodus **19:6**, 3; **29:18**, 130; **32:32**, 114

Leviticus **11:45**, 3; **19:2**, 86; **19:28**, 79; **21:5**, 79

Numbers **11:1-6**, 59; **14:1-4**, 59; **20:2**, 59; **21:4**, 59; **21:5**, 59; **25:7-13**, 84

Deuteronomy **10:16**, 78; **14:1**, 79; **21:23**, 47; **32:5**, 59, 60, 62; **32:20**, 59

Joshua **24:29**, 2

1 Kings **18:28**, 79; **19:10**, 84; **19:14**, 84

2 Kings **14:25**, 2; **16:13**, 64

Ezra **7:12**, 1

Nehemiah **10:29**, 2; **11:7-9**, 83; **11:31-36**, 83

Job **13:16**, 24, 28

Psalms **5:5**, 79; **6:8**, 79; **8:6**, 109, 111; **11:7**, 121; **16:4**, 64; **32:11**, 76; **33:1**, 76; **33:6**, 45; **34:18**, 118; **36:4**, 121; **43:4**, 76; **55:13**, 69; **69:28**, 114; **89:20**, 2; **106:30**, 84; **106:31**, 84; **110:1**, 48, 109, 111; **119**, 84; **119:151**, 118; **145:18**, 118; **148**, 50

Proverbs **3:19**, 45; **3:34**, 38; **8:22-31**, 45; **11:30**, 14

Isaiah **4:3**, 114; **14:14**, 52; **38:18**, 50; **42:8**, 48; **45:23**, 49; **52:13**, 48, 54; **52:13-53:12**, 53; **53:12**. 53

Jeremiah **4:4**, 78; **7:18**, 64; **9:24**, 80

Daniel **7:13**, 46, 48, 54; **7:14**, 46, 48; **7:18**, 3; **7:22**, 3; **7:27**, 3; **12:3**, 62

Hosea **6:6**, 88; **9:4**, 64

Amos **5:18-20**, 8; **5:20**, 8; **6:12**, 14; **8:4-6**, 121

Jonah **4:3**, 30; **4:8**, 30

Micah **6:8**, 39

Habakkuk **2:4**, 60

Malachi **3:16-4:3**, 84

NEW TESTAMENT

Matthew **5:13**, 60; **5:14-16**, 60; **5:45**, 60, 61; **5:48**, 60; **6:2**, 131; **6:5**, 131; **6:13**, 131; **6:16**, 131; **6:25-34**, 118; **6:26-32**, 118; **11:29**, 38; **15:26**, 81; **23:11**, 48; **23:23**, 86; **26:37**, 74; **27:27**, 17; **28:18**, 54

Mark **4:24**, 80; **8:15**, 80; **10:20**, 85; **10:42-45**, 73; **10:45**, 39; **12:38**, 80; **13:5**, 80; **14:33**, 74; **15:16**, 17

Luke **1:6**, 85; **2:14**, 58; **6:15**, 86; **8:31**, 50; **11:42**, 86; **12:15**, 125; **12:24-30**, 118; **12:46**, 117; **16:8**, 62; **22:42**, 47

John **1:1-3**, 45; **1:9**, 60; **3:19**, 60; **4:6**, 62; **4:24**, 80; **5:21**, 109; **5:22**, 49; **5:23**, 49; **5:25-29**, 109; **8:12**, 60; **8:58**, 53; **9:5**, 60; **12:36**, 62; **12:46**, 60; **13:3**, 54; **13:3-5**, 46; **13:13-15**, 73; **14:27**, 119; **18:28** ff., 17

Acts **1:13**, 86; **2:33**, 48; **5:20**, 60; **5:34**, 84; **6:1**, 83; **7:58**, 83; **9:4**, 91; **9:5**, 91; **10:33**, 129; **10:36**, 55; **12:1**, 133; **13:9**, 83; **13:13**, 68; **13:50**, 60; **14:8-20**, 2; **15:38**, 68; **16:1-3**, 2; **16:6-18:5**, xv; **16:9**, xvi; **16:10**, xvi; **16:11-40**, 1; **16:12**, xiii; **16:14**, 115; **16:16**, xvii; **16:17**, xviii, 113; **16:20**, xvii; **16:21**, xvii; **16:22**, xiii; **16:25-34**, xvii; **16:35**, xiii, xiv; **16:36**, xiii; **16:38,**

xiii, xiv; **16:40**, 115; **18:3**, 125; **18:5**, 128; **19:22**, 67; **20:4**, xviii; **20:5**, xviii, 113; **20:6**, xviii; **20:25**, xxiv; **20:28**, 3; **20:34**, 125; **21:20**, 86; **21:40**, 83; **22:2**, 83; **22:3**, 84, 86; **22:7-10**, 89; **23:1**, 85; **23:6**, 84; **23:8**, 84; **23:35**, xxii, 17; **24:5**, xxiv; **24:16**, 14, 85; **25:26**, 77; **26:5**, 84; **26:14**, 83; **27:12**, 94; **28:16**, 17; **28:21**, 17

Romans **1:1**, 2; **1:3**, 53; **1:5**, 10; **1:7**, 2,3; **1:8**, 6, 8; **1:9**, 6, 9, 11; **1:10**, 94; **1:11**, 11; **1:13**, 18; **1:16**, 25; **1:17**, 60; **2:18**, 13; **2:29**, 80; **3:1**, 88; **3:2**, 88; **3:21**, 93; **3:22**, 93; **3:25**, 36; **3:26**, 93; **5:1**, 97, 119; **5:5**, 12, 24, 37; **5:8**, 90; **5:11**, 76; **5:15**, 4; **5:41**, 34; **6:1**, 104; **6:2-11**, 91; **6:5**, 111; **6:7**, 104; **6:23**, 60; **8:3**, 57; **8:4**, 57; **8:15**, 57; **8:17**, 91; **8:19**, 25, 109; **8:21**, 25; **8:34**, 48; **9:4**, 83; **9:5**, 83; **9:16**, 34; **10:2**, 85; **11:1**, 83; **11:14**, 94; **12:1**, 41, 63, 130; **12:4** f., 3; **12:8**, 5; **13:1-7**, 21; **13:6**, 74; **13:11**, 56; **14:9**, 50; **15:1**, 99; **15:1-3**, 39; **15:16**, 74; **15:19-24**, 96; **15:23**, 11; **15:24**, xxiv, 28; **15:27**, 75; **15:29**, xxiv, 28; **15:33**, 122; **16:2**, 72; **16:3**, 74; **16:3-16**, 133, 134; **16:6**, 62; **16:9**, 74; **16:10**, 133; **16:11**, 133; **16:12**, 62; **16:17**, 103; **16:18**, 105; **16:20**, 122; **16:21**, 74; **16:22-23**, 34

1 Corinthians **1:2**, 2, 3; **1:4**, 6, 8; **1:9**, 41; **1:11**, 35; **1:12**, 20; **1:17**, 106; **1:18**, 106; **1:31**, 80; **2:3**, 58; **3:13**, 8; **4:3**, 61; **4:4**, 61; **4:5**, 8, 15; **4:8**, 91; **4:8-13**, 95; **4:12**, 62; **4:17**, 67, 68, 69, 100; **4:19**, 69; **5:2**, 105; **5:6**, 106; **5:8**, 14; **5:25**, 109; **6:2**, 3; **6:7**, 40; **6:12**, 104; **6:13**, 105; **6:20**, 29; **7:1**, 104; **8:1**, 13, 88; **8:3**, 89; **8:6**, 45, 51; **8:9**, 80; **9:1**, 56; **9:2**, 56; **9:7**, 74; **9:12**, 124; **9:15-18**, xxi; **9:24**, 97; **9:24-27**, 61; **9:27**, 102; **10:10**, 59; **10:32**, 14; **10:32-11:1**, 102; **11:18**, 35; **12:3**, 50; **12:12** f., 3; **12:13**, 35, 41; **13:6**, 121; **14:3**, 41; **14:15**, 12; **14:25**, 57; Chapter **15**, 94; **15:1**, 122; **15:9**, 84; **15:10**, 11, 62; **15:12**, 91; **15:20**, 92; **15:23**, 31; **15:24-28**, 111; **15:31**, 91; **15:42-50**, 110; **15:42-53**, 109; **15:44**, 110; **15:45**, 110; **15:45-49**, 4; **15:51**, 27; **15:52**, 27; **15:58**, 75; **16:10**, 67, 75; **16:11**, 67; **16:15-18**, 3, 73; **16:16**, 62; **16:17**, 31; **16:21**, 132

2 Corinthians, 113; **1:1**, 2, 3; **1:3**, 6, 8, 41; **1:3-7**, 34; **1:5**, 90; **1:8**, xxviii, 128; **1:8-10**, 27; **1:12**, 14; **1:14**, 28; **1:15-2:1**, xxiv; **2:14-16**, 130; **2:15**, 106; **2:17**, 14; **3:1-3**, 56; **3:4-6**, 57; **3:5**, 125; **4:2**, 106; **4:3**, 106, **4:10**, 91; **4:14**, 27, 92; **5:1**, 28, 92; **5:1-10**, 27, 30; **5:2**, 11; **5:14**, 30; **5:18-21**, 104-105; **6:11**, 129; **7:4**, 28; **7:6**, 31; **7:7**, 11, 31; **7:11**, 11, 121; **7:15**, 58; **8:1-5**, 7, 124; **8:9**, 45; **8:23**, 70-71, 74; **8:24**, 36; **9:2**, 28; **9:3**, 28; **9:14**, 11; **10-13**, xxvii, xxviii, 82; **10:1**, 24, 117, 119; **10:3**, 31, 72; **10:4**, 74; **10:6**, 56; **10:10**, 31; **10:17**, 80; **11:2**, 121; **11:4**, 24; **11:4-6**, 79; **11:9**, xxi, 128; **11:11**, 11; **11:12-15**, 79, 82; **11:13**, 79; **11:13-15**, xxi; **11:20**, 79; **11:21**, xxvii; **11:21** ff., 82; **11:22**, 83, 85; **11:23-27**, 34; **11:25**, 34; **11:31**, 11; **12:1**, 100; **12:9**, 126, 131; **12:10**, 126; **12:15**, 11; **13:11**, 76, 122; **13:13**, 41

Galatians **1:2**, 3; **1:5**, 131; **1:9**, 122; **1:13**, 84; **1:14**, 84, 86; **2:2**, 61, 62; **2:7-9**, 78; **2:9**, 11; **2:16**, 90, 93; **2:19,**

91; **2:20**, 26, 89, 91; **2:21**, 104; **3:1**, 129; **3:5**, 29; **3:11**, 60; **3:13**, 47, 89; **3:28**, 137; **4:3**, 54; **4:4**, 46, 53, 54; **4:9**, 54; **4:11**, 61, 62; **4:19**, 11; **4:25**, 110; **5:15**, 80; **5:20**, 122; **5:22**, 12, 13; **5:23**, 13; **6:2**, 39, 101; **6:11**, 132; **6:14**, 28, 47, 137; **6:16**, 100, 101; **6:18**, 135

Ephesians **1:1**, 2, 3; **1:3**, 6, 8; **1:4**, 61; **1:16**, 6, 9; **1:19**, 90; **1:20**, 90; **3:7**, 11; **3:8**, 11; **3:9**, 11; **4:1**, 35; **4:3**, 41; **4:4**, 35; **5:2**, 130; **5:3**, 121; **5:5**, 125; **5:8**, 62; **5:9**, 14; **5:23**, 110; **5:27**, 61; **6:5**, 58; **6:6**, 57; **6:12**, 34; **6:19**, 25

Philippians **1:1**, 17, 68, 73, 132, 136; **1:3**, 7, 131; **1:3-6**, 10; **1:4**, 7, 12, 14, 31, 38; **1:5**, 9, 41, 73; **1:6**, 9, 13, 61, 69; **1:7**, 11, 20; **1:8**, 41, 112; **1:9-11**, 10; **1:10**, 8, 61; **1:11**, 14, 30; **1:13**, xxii; **1:14**, 66, 69; **1:15**, 20, 58; **1:15-17**, 21; **1:15-18**, xxiii, xxviii; **1:16**, xxii, 10, 20, 21, 67; **1:16-17**, 21; **1:17**, 20, 69; **1:18**, 7, 31; **1:19**, 7, 28; **1:20**, 24, 64; **1:20-24**, 109; **1:21**, 91; **1:22**, 31; **1:23**, xxviii, 26, 97, 109; **1:25**, 7, 64, 69, 77; **1:25-27**, xxiv; **1:26**, 58, 61, 62, 66; **1:27**, 108, 112, 114; **1:28**, 106; **1:29**, 33, 90; **1:30**, 33; **2:1**, 11; **2:1-4**, 77; **2:2a**, 114; **2:2**, 7, 12, 31, 40, 67, 69; **2:3**, 21; **2:4**, 28; **2:5**, 32, 42, 73; **2:6**, 53; **2:6-8**, 110; **2:6-11**, xx, 42, 51, 110; **2:7**, 47, 52, 54, 93; **2:8**, 52, 53; **2:9**, 4, 36; **2:9-11**, 46, 110; **2:11**, 8, 55; **2:12**, 31; **2:13**, 7; **2:15**, 59, 137; **2:16**, 8, 14, 28, 95, 137; **2:17**, 7, 74; **2:18**, 7, 77; **2:19**, 1, 6, 8; **2:19-23**, xxv; **2:19-24**, 68, 73; **2:19-30**, 66, 68, 103; **2:20**, 115; **2:20-22**, 2; **2:21**, 21; **2:23**, 66; **2:24**, xxiv, xxv, 66; **2:25**, xxii, xxv, 74; **2:25-30**, xxvi, 7, 73, 130; **2:26**, xxv, 11, 112; **2:26-28**, xxvii; **2:28**, xxv, 7, 31, 74, 77; **2:29**, 7, 31, 77; **2:30**, 65, 74; 3, 13; **3:1**, xx, xxvii, xxix, 7, 31, 77, 116, 120, 122; **3:2**, xxvi, xxviii, 76, 77, 81, 104, 106; **3:2 ff.**, xxvii, xxviii, 33; **3:2-19**, xxi; **3:2-4:1**, 77; **3:2-4:3**, 77; **3:3**, 28; **3:4-16**, xxvii; **3:7**, 127; **3:7-14**, 78; **3:8**, 92, 93, 125, 127; **3:8-11**, 93, 97; **3:9**, 13, 54, 93, 97; **3:10**, 17, 34, 93, 94, 109, 111; **3:11**, 97, 109; **3:12-14**, 58; **3:13**, 99; **3:13-16**, xxviii; **3:17**, 122; **3:18**, xxviii, 78, 93, 103, 104; **3:19**, xxviii, 78, 93, 103, 104; **3:20**, xxviii, 8, 26, 32, 35, 92, 110, 117; **3:21**, xxviii, 26, 30, 58, 92, 110; **4:1**, xxviii, 7, 31, 35; **4:1-3**, 61; **4:1-9**, xx; **4:2**, 37, 77; **4:3**, xxi, xxviii, 7, 35, 74, 136; **4:4**, 7, 31, 76; **4:6**, 14; **4:7**, 4, 122; **4:8**, xxvii, xxix, 77, 121; **4:8-9**, 61; **4:9**, xxviii, 77, 102; **4:10**, xxvi, 7, 31; **4:10-20**, xx, xxvi, xxix, 7, 75, 123; **4:12**, 97, 126, 130; **4:13**, 126; **4:15**, xxviii, xxi; **4:16**, xviii, xxi; **4:18**, xxv, xxvi, 63, 70; **4:21-23**, xxix; **4:22**, xxi, xxiv, 132; **4:23**, 4; **4:25**, 75

Colossians **1:2**, 2, 3; **1:3**, 1, 6, 8; **1:7**, 74; **1:10**, 35; **1:15**, 51; **1:16**, 45; **1:16-20**, 50; **1:17**, 45; **1:22**, 61; **1:24**, 34, 91; **1:29**, 62; **2:3**, 88; **2:6**, 122; **2:8**, 80; **2:11**, 80; **2:15**, 54; **3:1**, 48, 107; **3:2**, 107; **3:4**, 29, 109; **3:12**, 41; **3:15**, 4, 119; **4:12**, 74; **4:18**, 132

1 Thessalonians **1:1**, 3; **1:2**, 6, 8, 9; **1:10**, 8, 108; **2:2**, xv, 36; **2:5**, 11; **2:8**, 11; **2:9**, 125, 128; **2:12**, 35, 41; **2:17**, 30; **2:18**, 129; **2:19**, 28, 31, 61, 112; **3:1-5**, 67; **3:2**, 74; **3:6**, 9, 11; **3:13**, 31; **4:1**, 122; **4:15**, 27, 31; **5:5**, 62; **5:8**, 8; **5:9**, 8; **5:12**, 3, 5, 62; **5:16**, 116; **5:23**, 13, 31, 122; **5:24**, 7

2 Thessalonians **1:1**, 3; **1:3**, 6, 8; **1:5**, 36; **1:5-10**, 33; **2:1**, 31; **2:8**, 31; **3:1**, 21; **3:8**, 125, 128; **3:9**, 124; **3:17**, 132

1 Timothy **1:2**, 69; **1:12**, 126; **1:13**, 84; **1:14**, 84; **2:5**, 49; **3:2**, 5; **3:8-13**, 3; **3:16**, 51; **5:17**, 5

2 Timothy **1:3**, 6, 8, 9; **1:4**, 11; **2:9**, 16; **4:6**, 64; **4:7**, 34; **4:8**, 24, 96, 97; **4:13**, 124; **4:22**, 135

Titus **1:5**, 5; **1:7**, 5

Philemon **1:1**, 74; **1:2**, 74; **1:4**, 6, 8, 9; **1:19a**, 132; **1:22**, xxv; **1:23**, 74, 135

Hebrews **1:2**, 45; **1:3**, 48; **2:5-9**, 111; **5:14**, 13, 14; **7:26**, 54; **11:5**, 54; **12:11**, 14; **13:5**, 125; **13:16**, 130; **13:20**, 122; **13:25**, 135

James **3:18**, 14; **4:6**, 38

1 Peter **1:3**, 6; **1:11**, 44; **3:22**, 54; **4:11**, 131; **5:5**, 38

2 Peter **3:1**, 14

1 John **4:2**, 46; **4:3**, 46

2 John **1:7**, 46

3 John **1:6**, 129; **1:9**, 38

Jude **1:6**, 50; **1:13**, 106

Revelation **3:5**, 114; **3:14**, 45; **5:6-14**, 49; **5:12**, 54; **13:8**, 114; **17:8**, 114; **20:11-15**, 114; **22:15**, 80; **22:21**, 135

APOCRYPHA

The Wisdom of Solomon **2:19**, 117; **7:1-6**, 53

2 Baruch **78:2**, 4

1 Maccabees **2:24-28**, 84; **2:42**, 84; **7:14**, 84

2 Maccabees **14:6**, 84

NONCANONICAL BOOKS

Testament of Zebulon **9:8**, 54

Sira **50:15**, 64

1 Clement **65:2**, 135